Medieval Meteorology

The practice of weather forecasting underwent a crucial transformation in the Middle Ages. Exploring how scientifically based meteorology spread and flourished from ca. 700 to ca. 1600, this study reveals the dramatic changes in forecasting and how the new science of 'astrometeorology' developed. Both narrower and more practical in its approach than earlier forms of meteorology, this new science claimed to deliver weather forecasts for months and even years ahead, on the premise that weather is caused by the atmospheric effects of the planets and stars, and mediated by local and seasonal climatic conditions. Anne Lawrence-Mathers explores how these forecasts were made and explains the growing practice of recording actual weather. These records were used to support forecasting practices, and their popularity grew from the fourteenth century onwards. Essential reading for anyone interested in medieval science, *Medieval Meteorology* demonstrates that the roots of scientific forecasting are much deeper than is usually recognized.

ANNE LAWRENCE-MATHERS is Professor of Medieval History at the University of Reading, and a Fellow of the Royal Historical Society and of the Society of Antiquaries. Specialising in the history of medieval magic, she is the author of *The True History of Merlin the Magician* (2012) and co-author of *Magic and Medieval Society* (2014) with Carolina Escobar-Vargas.

Medieval Meteorology

Forecasting the Weather from Aristotle to the Almanac

Anne Lawrence-Mathers

University of Reading

CAMBRIDGE
UNIVERSITY PRESS

CAMBRIDGE
UNIVERSITY PRESS

University Printing House, Cambridge CB2 8BS, United Kingdom

One Liberty Plaza, 20th Floor, New York, NY 10006, USA

477 Williamstown Road, Port Melbourne, VIC 3207, Australia

314–321, 3rd Floor, Plot 3, Splendor Forum, Jasola District Centre,
New Delhi – 110025, India

79 Anson Road, #06–04/06, Singapore 079906

Cambridge University Press is part of the University of Cambridge.

It furthers the University's mission by disseminating knowledge in the pursuit of
education, learning, and research at the highest international levels of excellence.

www.cambridge.org
Information on this title: www.cambridge.org/9781108418393
DOI: 10.1017/9781108289948

First published 2020

Printed in the United Kingdom by TJ International Ltd, Padstow Cornwal

A catalogue record for this publication is available from the British Library.

ISBN 978-1-108-41839-3 Hardback
ISBN 978-1-108-40600-0 Paperback

Contents

Preface

This book is the history of how it was that a key question came to be formulated and answered in western, Christian Europe in the medieval period. The question was one that classical meteorology had failed to answer fully. It was: how, if the seasons are caused by regular and repeating patterns based on the shape of the Earth and its position in relation to the Sun, can seasonal weather vary so much from one year to the next?

Leading philosophers and astronomers of Greek antiquity had made fundamental discoveries concerning the shape and size of the Earth, the distances and movements of the visible planets, and the role of the Sun in bringing seasonal change to differing locations on the surface of the Earth. However, these could not explain the complexity of actual weather patterns, as analysis of Aristotle's work on meteorology will show. It was this limitation that led medieval scholars to ask troubling questions. An example is found in the work of the twelfth-century philosopher, William of Conches, who wrote an exposition of classical science for his patron, Geoffrey of Anjou, then duke of Normandy. The duke, in William's account, is made to ask the very question set out above.

Further breakthroughs had in fact been made through the geometrical and mathematical models of planetary movements introduced by Hellenistic scientists, and by Ptolemy of Alexandria in particular. These made it possible to calculate with considerable accuracy and detail the celestial coordinates of any planet on any chosen day, as observed from a given location on Earth. This work, together with the knowledge that the positions of the Sun and Moon in relation to one another and to the Earth brought about not only the recurring seasons but also the cyclical patterns of day and night and the ebb and flow of the tides, led to important conclusions across the medieval period. Since the positions of the Sun and Moon had such fundamental effects, but could not alone account for the complex nature of weather, scholars and scientists across the medieval world argued that the other planets must also be influencing factors such as temperature, wind flows and rainfall. Equipped with newly detailed knowledge of planetary movements and positions, it was possible for astronomers and natural philosophers to study the constantly changing interrelationships between them. This was undertaken in the Islamicate world from the eighth century onwards.

A further element of complexity was introduced by the belief that the zones of the universe through which the planets moved had characteristics of their own, and that these could inflect the influences produced by the planets as they passed through successive zones. Central to this was the theory that the stars as well as the planets had both power and varying sets of characteristics. The concept that gave the most important expression of this theory was that of the belt of the zodiac. This mapped out the zone of the heavens within which all the planets could be seen to stay as they (apparently) moved around the Earth, and then divided that zone into sections based on the presence of major star-groupings. These constellations gave both names and distinctive characteristics to 'their' sections of the zone of planetary movement. The bringing together of all these factors, with their very complex patterns of variation and interaction, provided a highly sophisticated model with which to explain the complex variations in actual seasonal weather patterns on Earth (amongst other things). However, they did more than that. Because they were based on geometrical and mathematical calculations which, if correctly carried out, would produce an accurate model of the universe for any chosen day and location, they also introduced the possibility of accurate forecasting of the weather. This is the revolutionary breakthrough that this book seeks to chart.

Acknowledgements

I should like to express my sincere thanks to the Arts and Humanities Research Council for the award of a Research Leadership Fellowship in 2013–2014 (in the Science in Culture theme), which made possible the main research for this book. I am also very grateful to the University of Reading, for the award of a 2020 Research Fellowship in 2017–2018, which enabled me to undertake further research and writing. In addition I thank all the librarians and archivists who have given me access to items in their holdings.

On a more personal note I thank my family for all their support, patience, and interest; and give special thanks to my husband, Pete Mathers, and my sister, Helen Savigar.

Introduction
Ancient Meteorology and the Transition to the Middle Ages

It is a truth universally acknowledged (at least among non-medievalists) that classical scientific knowledge died with the Roman Empire, and had to be disinterred once the Middle Ages were over. However, the history of meteorology provides an immediate challenge to this view – so much so that it was possible for an historian of ancient meteorology to write that the tradition of meteorological scholarship 'survived through late antiquity and was developed further in the medieval period, in both the Arabic and Latin traditions'.[1] This book is an attempt to fill in the missing history of meteorological discoveries and practices during the long period from the eighth century to the sixteenth. Within that, special emphasis will be placed upon the central period of the twelfth and thirteenth centuries, which saw the crystallisation of a distinctively medieval form of meteorology. This medieval meteorology was built upon foundations provided by the classical past; but it was also the beneficiary of radical and extensive advances made in the Arab Empire, and in the Islamicate world more broadly.[2] The importance of these discoveries is so great that four chapters of the book, from Chapters 3 to 6 inclusive, are dedicated to tracing their nature and impact up to ca. 1300. However, if the scale of the breakthrough represented by the new, scientific models for understanding and forecasting weather is to be understood, the state of meteorological knowledge in the early Middle Ages must also be examined; this is the task of Chapters 1 and 2. Equally, a major argument of this book will be that the demand for weather forecasts

---

[1] L. Taub, *Ancient Meteorology*, London & New York, Routledge, 2003, at p. 8.
[2] The term 'Islamicate' performs the valuable function of designating the diverse cultural heritage and products of the Arab Empire. As the editors of the journal *Intellectual History of the Islamicate World* (Leiden and Boston: Brill, ISSN: 2212-943X), state: 'In the medieval, late medieval and pre-modern world of Islam, Muslims, Jews and Christians constituted a unique cultural and intellectual commonality. They shared a language, Arabic (and at times Persian) ... . Moreover, they often read the same books, so that a continuous, multi-dimensional exchange of ideas, texts, and forms of discourse was the norm'. https://brill.com/view/journals/ihiw/ihiw-overview.xml (accessed 1 November 2018).

and meteorological expertise remained high in the early modern period, even as the scientific basis on which medieval meteorology rested was falling from favour. Thus, the concluding chapters will show that no new method for producing trusted forecasts was found until the nineteenth century, and that 'medieval' meteorology had an extremely long afterlife.

As is clear from this outline, the book will necessarily take a chronological approach, tracing both the key discoveries and the scientists, astronomers, mathematicians and astrologers who made and built upon those discoveries. At first this is a story, at least in western and northern, Christian Europe, of isolated individuals who often conformed to the heroic stereotype of the lonely, marginalised or even persecuted, seeker after scientific truth. Most crossed boundaries, either political or cultural (or both) in their search for new, accurate knowledge of how the universe worked. Some undertook long travels, lasting for years, in order to gain access to texts, teachers and knowledge not available in their homelands. Others, usually Jewish scholars, were already expert in both medicine and the science of the stars, and offered this knowledge to new audiences. In many cases, however, key texts are either anonymous or clearly pseudonymous, and focusing the discussion on supposed authors would be misleading and unhelpful. Partly for that reason it is important to look also at how the new ideas and techniques were received, modified and further spread into northern Europe. Thus this book, whilst attempting to tell a clear and coherent story, will necessarily shift its focus from individuals to groups and institutions, according to the nature of the evidence and the numbers of important players involved. The discoveries of any individual, no matter how heroic, are of little long-term significance if they remain locked in isolated, unread manuscripts. Readers, users, followers and teachers are also needed if discoveries are to be accepted and put into practice; and for this to happen in medieval Europe, patrons were needed. In this regard, meteorology in the sense of scientific modelling and predicting of the weather occupied a privileged position, since access to specialist weather forecasts was highly desired by the elite – and was much less open to criticism than the desire for access to knowledge of future human actions.

Central to this new and compound, medieval meteorology, was the role played by the planets and stars in transmitting rays and influences from the higher levels of the universe down to the surface of the Earth. The effects of these celestial forces upon the actions of individual human beings was a matter of often-heated debate; but it was accepted as scientific fact that they could and did affect the material world. This material world included not only the Earth but the atmosphere surrounding it, up to the sphere occupied by the Moon. In other words, the region within which the interplay of these celestial forces produced the constantly modulating phenomena experienced on Earth as weather. It was an important part of the theory that these crucial rays and influences were conceived of as susceptible to mutual interaction and modification, depending upon the ever-changing spatial and geometrical relationships between the bodies emitting them. The complexity of the resulting model had the satisfying effect of providing a convincing explanation for the changeable and complex patterns of weather on the surface of the Earth. It followed from this that accurate knowledge of the courses of the planets and the positions of the stars would make true understanding of weather a real possibility. In this way, medieval meteorologists appeared to have made a highly significant, scientific advance upon classical meteorologists. The work of the latter could produce three-dimensional models of the zones of the Earth, in relation to the perceived path of the Sun around it, and could thus define concepts such as the Equator and the Tropics of Cancer and Capricorn, as well as the climatic conditions and the seasonal variations to be experienced in each zone. However, it could not produce a satisfactory means of producing detailed weather forecasts for specific dates and places. For these, only the time-honoured method of observing and interpreting weather signs, could be called upon. The importance of this breakthrough, illusory as it may have turned out to be, is hard to exaggerate.

However, the patrons of this new, medieval meteorology, were not necessarily interested in scientific knowledge for its own sake. One obvious reason for the ongoing interest of the rich and powerful was that knowledge of coming weather was especially important in what were essentially agrarian societies. As was frequently stated, for instance by Virgil in his widely copied *Georgics,* the fundamental activity of farming and food-production benefits greatly from knowledge about the weather, as also does fishing. Other areas exposed to meteorological phenomena, and of considerable political importance, were naval and military actions. The ability of societies to feed their citizens, to manage resources, and to be successful in relations with neighbours was crucially dependent upon the weather. This gave knowledge of coming weather a strong, and complex, relationship to power; and this was especially the case since the weather was held to be sometimes determined by, and always open to, divine intervention. There was inevitably a complex debate as to when extreme weather was to be understood as the result of purely natural factors, and when it should be accepted as a direct result of divine intervention. However, these two possible causes of weather events were not mutually exclusive. It was part of the theory of planetary influence upon the weather that certain combinations of planetary positions, and consequent influences, could directly produce devastating meteorological effects. What was crucial was the issue of predictability. If tempests and floods could be predicted from coming planetary interactions, then it would be a sign of ignorance, and even of superstition, to attribute them to a wrathful God. On the other hand, there was no attempt to deny that God certainly could, and sometimes did, cause meteorological events.

For Christian society, the Bible provided both clear evidence of God's role in meteorological events, and examples of ways in which knowledge of future weather could be obtained through naturally occurring signs. Extreme weather events were sometimes stated to be caused by divine anger or favour, with the punitive rains that produced Noah's Flood being a well-known example. However, God was always just, and therefore gave fair warnings. Thus, both the possibility of foreknowledge through such warnings, and the value of the accurate interpretation of signs and warnings, were equally stressed. This had the effect of making foreknowledge of unusual weather a matter of religious, as well as economic and political, significance. An example is provided by the story of Pharaoh's dreams in Genesis, chapter 41. In this sequence of dreams, visions of well-fed and then starved cattle were followed by visions of good grain followed by grain blasted by the east wind. Pharaoh and his courtiers were unable to interpret this, but Joseph understood that God was sending warning of a coming sequence of seven good years for agriculture, to be followed by seven disastrous years. The warning was heeded, preparations were made, and the land of Egypt was saved from a potentially disastrous famine. Joseph's status as intermediary between earthly and divine rulers was also confirmed.

Of course, not everyone could expect such warnings; but more ordinary knowledge and use of weather signs was confirmed in the Gospels by no less a figure than Christ.[3] Such signs gave information only for the short term, and for a restricted area; but they attested to two fundamental ideas. The first was that there is a close link between the appearance of the sky, in terms of the level and colour of light and the patterns of clouds, and weather for the coming day. The second, which follows from the first, was that the weather is governed by a system that links conditions on Earth to phenomena in the atmosphere in observable and comprehensible ways. A great, poetic statement of the extent to which God's Creation constituted a vast and interactive system was delivered in

[3] See, for instance, Matthew, 16, 2–3.

God's message to Job and his interlocutors, recounted in the Book of Job, chapters 38 and 39. This emphasised that the universe is ordered by measure, and that it operates according to divinely established rules, which keep the heavens, the stars, the Earth and the seas in their places, as well as maintaining regular units of time. Rain, snow, hail, thunder and wind are all parts of this system, and operate entirely independently of humanity. Complex but divinely governed connections between the heavens and the Earth are touched upon. Warm rains bring growth and green grass while frost brings ice, and all these phenomena are associated with the risings of the stars of the Pleiades, the movements of Arcturus, the regular appearances of the day star and evening star, and the whole order of heaven (*ordinem caeli*). This is further emphasised a little later, when questions about clouds, waters and lightning are followed by emphasis on the wisdom needed in order to know the order and harmony of heaven.

Meteorology thus had scriptural authority, even if the triumph of Christianity entailed the rejection of those classical theories that contradicted the concepts of a divine creation and a coming end of time. A sequence of patristic writers, including almost all the great founding figures, wrote exegeses of Genesis' account of the Creation, drawing upon established information from meteorology and natural philosophy in their commentaries. St Augustine wrote no fewer than five commentaries on the Creation story. Some were simply intended to disprove specific heretical arguments; but others effectively established that pagan knowledge of cosmology and meteorology, when based upon rational study of the universe, had value. Indeed, it could clearly be brought into the new, philosophical arena of biblical exposition. Meteorological knowledge is brought into play, for instance, in Book Three of Augustine's work *On the Literal Meaning of Genesis*, where information about the spheres and courses of the planets and the phases of the moon is brought together with discussion of the origins of clouds and earthly waters.[4]

This reuse and reinterpretation of classical theories and models entailed some technical problems. An important example was the much-disputed issue of how to distinguish between legitimate enquiry into celestial phenomena and their effects on Earth, on the one hand, and illegitimate claims to knowledge of future human actions, on the other. A usefully encyclopaedic, and much-consulted, source of information on the observable workings of the natural world was provided by the *Natural History* of Pliny the Elder. Pliny himself was a highly experienced veteran

---

[4] See *St Augustine; On Genesis*, Ed. J.E. Rotelle, Trans. E. Hill, New York, New City Press, 2002, pp. 215–250.

officer, scholar, and member of the upper echelons of Roman government and provincial administration, who had travelled widely. He died whilst attempting to observe the eruption of Vesuvius in 79 CE, and to bring some rescue to those fleeing the destruction. His survey was able to cover much of the Roman Empire, and to combine personal observations with information from witnesses and learned sources; he was still working on it at his death. It was very much wider in its range than works on theoretical meteorology. Nevertheless, it offered a store of useful quotations, from both Greek and Roman works, together with authoritative accounts of natural phenomena. In accordance with the established approach, given high status by the influential works of Aristotle and his successors, Pliny separated discussion of the celestial phenomena themselves from description of their practical effects and applications on Earth. It was also established that the celestial phenomena, being higher both literally and in their essential nature, should be dealt with first. Thus, astronomy and associated questions on the air, the winds, and the atmosphere are dealt with in Book Two of Pliny's work.[5] Significantly, more earthbound, and more localised, experiences of actual weather are dealt with together with agriculture, in Book Eighteen. Pliny is also aware of, and accepts, the Aristotelian concept of 'exhalations' as causes of mutability in material phenomena. These were held by Aristotle to play a major role in bringing about physical processes, and also had a role in causing developments in the weather.[6]

In accordance with their lower position in this hierarchical model of the workings of the universe, Pliny deals with the earthbound topics of agriculture and the farming year in the later part of his work. It is thus a section of Book Eighteen, which provides a long (and very influential) list of weather signs.[7] These are arranged in calendrical sequence and linked, as was customary in Greek as well as Roman works on the topic, to the risings and settings of named stars. Pliny is also informative as to the variations and disagreements amongst his sources of knowledge on the timings of these occurrences, in a way that both confirmed the complexity of the topic and passed on a range of ancient views to later readers.

---

[5] For discussion see L. Taub, *Science Writing in Greco-Roman Antiquity*, Cambridge, Cambridge University Press, 2017, and the analysis there of Pliny's work as an 'Encyclopaedia' (especially pp. 77–80).

[6] Ibid., p. 80. See also M. Wilson, *Structure and Method in Aristotle's* Meteorologica; *A More Disorderly Nature*, Cambridge, Cambridge University Press, 2013 (esp. Part 1, chapter 3, 'The exhalations' pp. 51–72).

[7] See: Pliny, *Natural History, Volume V: Books 17-19*, Trans. H. Rackham, Loeb Classical Library 371, Cambridge, Harvard University Press, 1950. Helpful context is provided by J. Healy, *Pliny the Elder on Science and Technology*, Oxford, Oxford University Press, 1999.

Once again the Pleiades and their phases are important, something that was noted by later readers of the work, as will be seen in Chapter 1. Pliny also points out that, whilst Hesiod is clear that crops should be sown at the time of the setting of the Pleiades, and it is well-known that this is close to the autumn equinox, dates given by different authorities vary by twenty-three days.[8] Pliny theorises that the dates preferred by different writers relate to their geographical locations, but it is left to the reader to interpret the information provided. Related to this is his assertion in chapter 56 that food production, as much as navigation, depends upon knowledge of the interrelationship between the heavens and the weather. As often, Virgil is cited as authority for this.

It is also in Book Eighteen, and for the same reasons, that Pliny moves on to another complex phenomenon with a fundamental relationship to weather – that of the winds. He gives detailed discussion of the names, locations, and effects of identifiable winds, together with practical instructions for constructing a wind rose in order to make use of all this information.[9] A key topic linking the various meteorological discussions is that of the solar solstices and equinoxes.[10] As Pliny sets out in chapter 59 of Book Eighteen, these are dated both by the Roman calendar and by the Sun's position in the zodiac. Pliny gives irregular intervals between them, ranging from eighty-eight days and three hours between the autumn equinox and the winter solstice to ninety-four days and twelve hours between the spring equinox and the summer solstice. Nevertheless, he says that the seasons that they initiate each begin when the sun reaches the eighth degree of the relevant zodiac sign. These are Libra, Capricorn, Aries and Cancer. Pliny is slightly vague as to the actual dates of the solstices and equinoxes, though he provides the information that the winter solstice is 'usually' eight days before the kalends of January. He is naturally aware of the dominant Roman system of time measurement, which regarded every period from sunrise to sunset as containing twelve hours, and thus produced hours of frequently changing actual duration. However, for scientific accuracy, Pliny gives his time measurements in equal, equinoctial hours. Pliny's complete assemblage of meteorological knowledge exceeds the scope of this book, whose main subject is medieval meteorology; nevertheless, his work requires discussion here since it played a crucial role in the transition from classical to medieval meteorology. It was well known in the early centuries of the Middle Ages, at least in partial versions, and was held in high regard.

---

[8] Pliny, pp. 316–317 and 324–325. [9] Chapters 76–77; ibid., pp. 394–403.
[10] Pliny's bringing together in his work of both philosophical meteorology and practical weather signs is emphasised by Taub in *Science Writing in Greco-Roman Antiquity*, p. 79.

Ironically, it was in turn to be treated rather as Pliny had treated his own early sources. In other words it became a repository and quarry of information, both practical and theoretical, to be applied within new parameters.

Pliny's own attitudes in relation to meteorological study may be demonstrated by a few examples. Most striking, perhaps, is that whilst he shows knowledge of Aristotle's fundamental *Meteorology* he displays no desire to follow it in detail. Indeed, as others have noted, Pliny tends to emphasise Roman experience over Greek 'writings'.[11] Pliny's tendency to point out disagreements between his authorities also works to undermine any idea of there being a clearly authoritative reference work on these matters. Thus, practical experience and recorded observations (adapted to varying conditions across diverse territories of the Roman Empire) emerge as the fundamental factors in the creation of meteorological knowledge. It has further been suggested that Pliny's attitude to Greek authors in general reflected a Roman sense of superiority and distinctiveness, and this does emerge at least at certain points.[12] Whether this also helps to explain the relative lack of interest in Aristotle's *Meteorology* displayed by the Fathers of the western Christian Church is unclear. However, it does seem to have been predominantly in centres such as Alexandrea and Caesarea that knowledge and study of the work continued in the Christian period.[13]

What can be observed is that Pliny's emphasis on practical expertise and direct observation fitted well with the emerging early medieval, Christian understanding of weather. Both gave attention to techniques for forecasting the weather in a way that Aristotle did not. Aristotle's work was calculated to deliver a rigorously logical, internally consistent model of the workings of the universe and its component parts. Ephemeral phenomena such as local variations in weather were not integral to this. Thus Pliny's attention to methods of weather prediction provided an important basis for taking meteorological study in a new direction. Even so, the type of meteorological knowledge that was transmitted in this transitional period took for granted the assumption that forecasts, as opposed to theoretical modelling of climatic norms, could only be very local and very short term. This was because, as both the Bible and the information amassed by Pliny illustrate, forecasting was seen as being

---

[11] Ibid., p. 79.

[12] This argument is made in particular by T. Morgan Murphy, *Pliny the Elder's Natural History: The Empire in the Encyclopedia*, Oxford, Oxford University Press, 2004.

[13] For discussion see G. Karamanolis, 'Early Christian Philosophers on Aristotle' in A. Falcon, Ed., *Brill's Companion to the Reception of Aristotle in Antiquity*, Leiden, Brill, 2016, at pp. 460–461.

necessarily based on the observation of 'signs' in the changing appearances of the sky or the current behaviour of birds and animals. It was only in the central medieval period that a new model of meteorology took shape, which combined theoretical models with practical techniques for weather forecasting. This is the medieval meteorology with which this book is concerned.

Nevertheless, it is important to consider the question of whether any significant quantity of meteorological knowledge was rejected or mislaid when direct access to Aristotle's work dwindled in the western part of the Roman Empire. This is also necessary if the argument that medieval meteorology was an essentially new, hybrid creation is to be evaluated. Therefore, both to prepare for later chapters and to illustrate the difference between Aristotle's approach and Pliny's, a brief account of the former's central arguments will be given here. Aristotle's theories on the skies, the movements of the heavens and the planetary bodies, and the effects of all this upon the Earth below, were spread across several of his works. This in itself led to complications, since the terms in which Aristotle discussed key concepts were not necessarily identical across these works themselves, and they were subject to further variation in the processes of translation. The treatises concerned are *On the Heavens*; *On Generation and Corruption*; *On the Soul*; and *Meteorology*. Aristotle offered a wide-ranging coverage of the nature of the Earth and its waters (both fresh and salt), as well as hypothesising that the Sun evaporates water, and causes the vapour to be carried up to the upper part of the sky, where it is affected by cold and so falls to Earth again. This fits into the more general model of the processes of 'change and becoming and decay', which the heat and motion of the Sun set in train on Earth. Both earthquakes, as the result of pressures caused by underground winds, and aerial phenomena such as thunder, lightning and rainbows, are covered by the model. Rather less satisfyingly, it is necessary for meteors, comets and even the Milky Way to be atmospheric phenomena, since they are parts of the processes of change rather than purely external causes. A further step in the argument is that all change is perceived as cyclical, although many of the processes posited take place over very long periods of time, far exceeding any human life.[14] Thus 'these changes are

---

[14] See M. Scharle, '"And these things follow": teleology, necessity and explanation in Aristotle's *Meteorologica*' in D. Ebrey, Ed., *Theory and Practice in Aristotle's Natural Science*, Cambridge, Cambridge University Press, 2015, pp. 79–99.

not observed, and before their course can be recorded from beginning to end whole nations perish'.[15]

The topics to be covered in the *Meteorology* are set out in the introduction to Book 1, where Aristotle says that the 'natural changes', which come under the heading of meteorology 'take place in the region nearest to the motion of the stars. Such are the Milky Way, and comets, and the movements of meteors'. Meteorology in this sense also covers 'all the affections we may call common to air and water, and the kinds and parts of the Earth and the affections of its parts. These throw light on the causes of winds and earthquakes and all the consequences the motions of these kinds and parts involve'. Affection is being used here as a technical term to cover the processes of interactive change under discussion, and Aristotle states clearly that he does not have a full explanation for all the phenomena that come under his definitions. Indeed, the more extreme elements of meteorology, including thunderbolts, whirlwinds and fire winds, are handled separately, since by definition they are not regular or cyclical in their patterns and occurrence. Book 1 itself goes on to outline the elements and bodies that are the component and dynamic parts of meteorology, conceived as a complex set of systems and processes of change taking place across the zones from the spheres of the stars down to the Earth. The emphasis here is on clarifying the processes involved, and the range of phenomena for which they can account. Reports of geological, geographical and climatic data and observations are considered carefully for the data they contribute to the model, which is intended to be fully comprehensive as well as internally coherent. There is no attempt to deal with the possibility of, or methods for, prediction of local weather events.

In Book 2 attention turns first to the sea, its origins and its relationship to the various bodies of fresh water. This is where the theory of the drawing up of water from the sea, and its return to Earth as fresh water, is set out. However, the emphasis is again on setting out a theory that will account for all known phenomena (and do so more effectively than previous ones) rather than on discussing the practical prediction of rain. A long discussion of the winds, conducted in a similar manner, follows and this leads in turn to the subject of earthquakes. The connection is, as mentioned above, that wind is argued to have a causative relationship to earthquakes, although the full model set out is considerably more complex in the phenomena included. The theory is summed up thus: 'Water

---

[15] *Meteorologica*, Book I, chapter 14, Trans. E. Webster, in *The Works of Aristotle Translated Into English*, Oxford, Clarendon Press, 1923, sections 351a and 351b. All quotations are from this translation.

has been known to burst out during an earthquake. But that does not make water the cause of the earthquake. The wind is the efficient cause whether it drives the water along the surface or up from below: just as winds are the causes of waves and not waves of winds. Else we might as well say that earth was the cause; for it is upset in an earthquake, just like water (for effusion is a form of upsetting). No, earth and water are material causes (being patients, not agents): the true cause is the wind'.

The final part of Book 2 turns to thunder, lightning, fire winds and thunderbolts, which are all argued to be causally and substantially related to wind. Once again, Aristotle first relates these phenomena, extreme as they are, to the arguments he has already set out, showing how they also relate to reports of observed experience. He then deals with the theories of others, each of which is found wanting either logically or in relation to the data. The resounding conclusion on this subject is: 'We say that the same stuff is wind on the earth, and earthquake under it, and in the clouds thunder. The essential constituent of all these phenomena is the same: namely, the dry exhalation. If it flows in one direction it is wind, in another it causes earthquakes; in the clouds, when they are in a process of change and contract and condense into water, it is ejected and causes thunder'. The opening of Book 3 continues with this theme: 'We have now explained thunder and lightning and hurricane, and further firewinds, whirlwinds, and thunderbolts, and shown that they are all of them forms of the same thing and wherein they all differ'. Further discussion as to what determines which phenomenon is now given, again related to direct observations, and again a causal explanation of deliberately pared-down simplicity is produced. The same approach is taken to the further topics of 'the nature and cause of halo, rainbow, mock suns, and rods, since the same account applies to them all'.

The broad conclusion on this topic is that the atmospheric conditions prevailing on a given day will determine which meteorological outcomes will actually prevail. The integration of empirical data into the model has two important consequences here. Firstly, it is accepted that actual atmospheric conditions will vary according to geographical location and to season. Secondly, the fact that weather is thus by definition highly localised and highly variable means that knowledge of it is heavily dependent upon human observation. For this reason, careful attention has to be paid to the role of the observer and to the specifics of human vision. This is especially the case in the discussion of rainbows and solar phenomena, where perceptions of colour and size may vary in ways that potentially challenge the production of a conclusive model. However, whilst human variability is thus accepted and integrated into the argument, atmospheric variability is given less attention. Indeed, it is noticeable that there is no attempt to set out any means of judging in advance what specific atmospheric conditions will apply in a given place on a given day. This means that Aristotle's impressive analysis is capable of delivering very clear and well-substantiated explanations for both normal and extreme weather conditions after they have happened – but its value for weather forecasting is extremely limited. Book 4 provides further evidence that discussion of atmospheric phenomena such as weather is now considered to be complete, since it turns to changes within and below the Earth rather than those above. It deals with what Aristotle argued to be the outcomes of the same 'exhalation' when it took place below ground. Thus stones and metals were also brought into the overall system, and handled as part of the subject matter of meteorology, since they were the result of this process.

This information on precious stones and metals was to be sought out later, as was the main body of Aristotle's handling of theoretical meteorology. Nevertheless, it appears that it was not until the twelfth century that the *Meteorology* was translated into Latin.[16] By contrast, the text was studied, annotated and added to in the Islamicate world, as is shown by the complexity of the medieval Arabic versions. These not only draw upon Syriac intermediaries but also incorporate ideas and terminology based upon new study on the topics involved.[17] It is important to note that it was this new, updated version of Aristotle's work that played an important role in the formation of the new, medieval meteorology in the Latin world in the twelfth century, as will be discussed in Chapter 4.

Meanwhile, an unexpected but important route for transmission of classical meteorological ideas into Christian Europe was provided by one of Pliny's preferred sources. This, somewhat unexpectedly, was none other than the work of perhaps the greatest and most celebrated of the Roman poets, Virgil. It was fundamental for this that Virgil was accepted by Christian authorities, from the Emperor Constantine on, as having foretold the coming of Christ, and was therefore perceived as something very close to a prophet.[18] This reputation was further enhanced by St

---

[16] See P. Schoonheim, *Aristotle's* Meteorology *in the Arabico-Latin Tradition*, Leiden/Boston/Köln, Brill, 2000, pp. xiii–xx.

[17] Ibid.; and P. Lettinck, 'Aristotle's *Meteorology* in the Arabic World', in S.M. Razaullah Ansari, Ed., *Science and Technology in the Islamic World: Proceedings of the XXth International Congress of History of Science*, Brepols, Turnhout, 2002, pp. 189–194.

[18] See Eusebius, *Life of Constantine*, IV. 32, Trans. T. Cushing, in P. Schaff and H. Wace, Eds., *Nicene and Post-Nicene Fathers*, 2nd series, 1, New York, Christian Literature Publishing Company, 1890.

Augustine, thus guaranteeing Virgil's status as an authoritative source of knowledge on a range of subjects (although in fact a pagan).[19]

It was in one of his *Eclogues* that Virgil secured his reputation as a prophet; but he gave considerable space to weather signs in the *Georgics* and especially in the first poem in that sequence.[20] Lines 204 to 350 here list broader, annual weather signs, before the poem turns to more specific and local signs in lines 351 to 463. Virgil's main source for these has been identified as a Latin translation of the work of Aratus of Soli, a scholar and poet of the third century BCE, who seems to have written for the Macedonian court at Athens and whose work was appreciated in Rome also.[21] Aratus' long poem, the *Phaenomena,* dealt with the stars and planets in its first section before turning to a detailed compilation of information on weather signs in its second section. Largely thanks to its popularity in Rome, it had a direct influence in early medieval Europe, which will be discussed in Chapter 2. However, it should be noted here that Aratus' material on weather signs drew in turn upon Aristotle. Thus, knowingly or unknowingly, Virgil was effectively transmitting a version of some of Aristotle's information.[22] In this way, some of Aristotle's statements on weather, and the signs of coming weather, reached early medieval readers thanks to Virgil, without their being aware of the fact. However, it is also clear that Virgil, like western Christian scholars in the early Middle Ages, was more interested in the practical side of Aristotle's work than in his physical and cosmological theories.

This can also be said about the works of Posidonius and Priscian, which transmitted small amounts of Greek (though not exclusively Aristotelian) meteorological knowledge to the early medieval, Latin world. The latter, Priscian of Lydia, was one of a group of philosophers who left Athens in 531 CE, when the Christian emperor, Justinian, put an end to pagan teaching. They found new employment at the court of King Chosroes I of Persia, who requested information from them on a range of subjects within natural philosophy. Priscian wrote an account of the replies he himself gave to problems put to him by the king, which included astronomical and meteorological topics. This only survives in

---

[19] Particularly in *The City of God,* Book 10, chapter 27; for discussion see E. Bourne, 'The Messianic Prophecy in Vergil's Fourth Eclogue', *The Classical Journal,* 11, 7, 1916, pp. 390–400.

[20] See L. Jermyn, 'Weather-Signs in Virgil', *Greece and Rome,* 20, 59, 1951, pp. 49–59.

[21] D. Sider and C. Brunschön, 'Survey of ancient weather literature', in Sider and Brunschön, Eds., *Theophrastus of Eresus; On Weather Signs,* Leiden, Brill, 2007, p. 21. For a detailed analysis of Aratus' achievement see R. Hunter, 'Written in the stars: Poetry and philosophy in the *Phaenomena* of Aratus', *Arachnion,* 2, 1995, pp. 1–34.

[22] For a translation see Aratus, *Phaenomena,* Trans. A. Poochigian, Baltimore, Johns Hopkins University Press, 2010, pp. 27–38.

a poor Latin translation, in which Priscian does not name Aristotle as a source for his information on meteorology. Instead, he cites the more recent work of Posidonius, a Stoic philosopher who had died in Rome or Rhodes in ca. 51 BCE. Posidonius appears to have been influential in transmitting a version of Aristotle's natural philosophy to the elite of Rome, including Pompey and Cicero, whilst he was ambassador from Rhodes. This is not straightforward, since only fragments of Posidonius' work survive, and he may only have had direct access to Aristotle's works when newly discovered copies were brought to Rome.[23] However that may be, the fact that Priscian names him is perhaps evidence that Posidonius' reputation remained strong, at least in Athens, into the sixth century. Neither author was widely read in western Europe in the early Middle Ages. Nevertheless, even if Priscian was modest as to his knowledge of Aristotle, he makes reference to the latter's *On the Heavens* and *On Generation and Corruption*. Moreover, Posidonius seems to have known the *Meteorology* well, and his work will have provided Priscian with important parts of it. Thus Virgil was not entirely alone in providing a route along which a small amount of Aristotelian teaching on cosmology and meteorology was transmitted.[24]

It is important to note that this sketch of the complex and fragmentary routes along which ideas from Aristotle's natural philosophy, and the *Meteorology* in particular, were transmitted into early medieval, western Europe is not intended to imply that the emergence of medieval meteorology was heavily dependent upon the 'rediscovery' of Aristotle's work. As has been seen, Aristotle was not much concerned with the theory or practice of weather forecasting. His work was consequently of limited value to those who desired such practical knowledge. It was in the Islamicate world that study of Aristotle's theories was brought together with more recent work on the application of geometrical and mathematical calculation to astronomy. This brings the argument to something of a paradox. On the one hand it was a moment of great potential significance when Aristotle's long-missing *Meteorology* was translated into Latin in the twelfth century. But on the other hand its actual impact on medieval

---

[23] See I. Leyra, 'The *Aristotelian Corpus* and the Rhodian Tradition: New Light from Posidonius on the Transmission of Aristotle's Works', *The Classical Quarterly*, 63.2, 2013, pp. 723–733.

[24] For the text, edited by I. Bywater, see *Prisciani Lydi quae extant; Metaphrasis in Theophrastum et Solutionum ad Chosroem liber*, Berlin, Reimeri, 1886. See also: Priscian, *Answers to King Khosroes of Persia*, Trans. P. Huby et al., London, Bloomsbury, 2016. For the influence of the work in the early middle ages see M.-T. d'Alverny, '"Les solutions ad Chosroem" de Priscianus Lydus et Jean Scot', in *Jean Scot Erigène et l'Histoire de la Philosophie*, Paris, Colloques internationaux du C.N.R.S., 561, 1977, pp. 145–160.

understanding and prediction of the weather was very limited. This was not only because of the nature of the work itself, but also because a much greater scientific revelation accompanied it, which was that of Islamicate work in the fields of astronomy and astrology. When these latter were newly translated into Latin by excited pioneers, cosmology and meteorology in western Europe broke out of their rather narrow, Roman and patristic moulds. This is the story told in the central chapters of this book, and it is an important one.

From the twelfth century on, as the works which made up the 'new science of the stars' were translated, studied and absorbed, it becomes possible to trace a new part of the history of scientific forecasting of the weather. The demand for this knowledge, and the means by which forecasts were produced and disseminated, grew consistently from the twelfth century onwards. As the later chapters of this book show, it became a duty of astronomers and astrologers to produce annual prognostications, providing detailed weather forecasts for a whole coming year, together with overviews of factors affecting politics and economic production, and judgements on their likely outcomes. Demand for these was so great that they became a staple of the early printing presses, and helped to make the fortunes of the pioneering printers. And thus, arguably, was born the lasting and ongoing place of weather forecasting as a central element of news bulletins as well as of the annual ritual of prognostication by experts that still accompanies the arrival of each New Year. Of course, modern weather forecasts are made on an entirely different basis from those produced in the medieval period; it is no longer accepted as scientific fact that the movements of the stars and planets cause complex changes in the atmosphere that in turn bring about the weather. Nevertheless, the break away from traditional lists of localised, short-term weather signs and the creation of a complex and dynamic model of how weather patterns and changes were believed to be caused, constitutes one of the great turning points in the history of meteorology.

With all that said, it is necessary to turn first to the period that laid the basis for this new, highly compound and yet characteristically medieval, science. There is no denying that the early medieval period in western Europe saw a radical reduction in the number and range of texts on overtly scientific subjects in circulation. However, it must also be remembered that this was not the perception of scholars living in that society. For them, the fundamental works of their religion provided an exciting and satisfying key to the true understanding of the universe, through insights into the powers of the God who had created it, and vice versa. The highest form of knowledge was that which provided the best access to the divine. However, whilst this was most directly produced through the study of scripture, there was a growing belief that knowledge of the created world could provide clues about that world's creator. A further important factor came into play here. Such knowledge was also valued by those who wished to achieve or to maintain wealth and power; and they therefore provided patronage for scholars who could deliver it. This produced a considerable drive towards the creation of meteorological knowledge that could satisfy both types of demand, and do so whilst drawing upon the known works of recognised authorities. For these reasons, scientific study in Christian, western Europe was much more intellectually demanding than it has sometimes appeared. Part of the problem is one of a failure of modern perception. Whereas classical meteorology had produced long treatises composed in highly abstract language, calculated to deliver integrated theories of impressive explanatory power, the products of early medieval meteorology look very different. The most characteristic are simple-looking tables, consisting of grids of letters and numbers, with only very sparse accompanying notes and instructions. Even less helpfully, they most often appear together with treatises on the monastic calendar and the calculation of Easter. Both their unpromising appearance and the overall nature of the surviving manuscripts in which they are found have tended to reduce their apparent value for the history of science. Yet it is with these texts, and the contexts that produced them, that the history of the new, applied science of medieval meteorology must begin.

1   Recreating Meteorology in the Early Middle Ages
Isidore and Bede

Ancient meteorology was, as has been seen, diverse in both content and theoretical approach. Nevertheless, it has convincingly been argued to have a founding figure in Aristotle, since his *Meteorology* set out its distinctive subject matter and core questions.[1] Many of these core questions needed urgently to be rethought once Christianity was established as the main source of philosophical and scientific explanation and exploration in Western Europe. Partly at least for this reason, the scholarly tendency in the early centuries of the Christian Middle Ages was for polymaths and theologians (often one and the same) to assemble collections of classical materials for reference and scrutiny, but not to continue directly with ancient traditions and genres of writing. Meanwhile, basic versions of major classical ideas and their associated methodologies, revised for use by Christians, satisfied the needs of the schools. The results of this for meteorology, astronomy, and natural philosophy more broadly, were somewhat less severe than in the areas of religious philosophy and ethics. Nevertheless, the all-encompassing change in beliefs concerning the causes and meanings of earthly and aerial events inevitably had major effects.

Crucially, the accumulated knowledge on these subjects was neither condemned nor merely 'lost'. Rather, since key questions as to the origin and motive force of natural phenomena now had an apparently straightforward and unshakeable answer, two new and distinct approaches to works of ancient meteorology and natural philosophy were adopted. On the one hand, such works could be of use to scholars engaged in studying the word of God as transmitted by the Bible. The wide-ranging empirical observations that had been recorded and used by pagan philosophers could now be quarried for factual information relevant to the analysis of texts such as the biblical account of Creation. On the other hand, those working to establish a unified framework for Christian worship, which

---

[1] Seneca, *Natural Questions*, Trans. H. Hine, Chicago, University of Chicago Press, 2010, Introduction, p. xx.

included a universally accepted calendar, with agreed units of time, also had recourse to works of ancient science. Drawing upon both, and in urgent need of works providing compelling answers to practical problems and vexatious questions, were missionaries and founders of new churches. These movements in many ways set the context for the story to be traced in this chapter.

As in other areas of scholarly work in this transitional period, it was the monasteries that produced and preserved the best record of these developments. What is more surprising is that it should be the remote territory of Anglo-Saxon Northumbria that saw the emergence of one of the great figures of early medieval natural philosophy, in the form of the Venerable Bede (ca. 673–735). The explanation, as comments provided by Bede in his historical and hagiographical works demonstrate, lies in the fact that even this relatively new addition to Christian Europe was in contact with scholars and religious leaders from a number of areas. Theodore of Tarsus, archbishop of Canterbury (668–690) and his assistant, Hadrian, are known to have taught at least parts of the Roman curriculum in their cathedral school. Indeed, study of commentaries and glosses produced in the Canterbury school has shown that Theodore, who had studied in Antioch, Byzantium and Rome, could teach on astronomy and even the calculation of astrological charts as well as on the ecclesiastical calendar and medicine.[2] There is also evidence that their syllabus included at least basic cosmology within its treatment of astronomy/astrology. Aldhelm, a pupil at their school, later wrote of having studied both astrology and astronomy at Canterbury, though he did not explain the distinction between them.[3] Sadly, too little remains of the curriculum taught at Canterbury and the texts that it produced for conclusions on meteorology to be drawn.

Fortunately, the contribution made by the scholarly bishop of Seville, Isidore (ca. 560–636) is much better recorded. His encyclopaedic work of reference, the *Etymologies*, was one of the main routes for the transmission of reinterpreted classical knowledge to Christian, western Europe. This ambitious collection of material is organised in twenty sections or 'books', with Book Thirteen covering 'The cosmos and its parts'.[4] This book, like all of Isidore's handling of natural philosophy and

---

[2] M. Lapidge, 'The Career of Archbishop Theodore', in Lapidge, ed., *Archbishop Theodore: Commemorative Studies in His Life and Work*, Cambridge, Cambridge University Press, 1995, pp. 1–29.

[3] On Aldhelm's education at Canterbury, and the subjects taught there, see M. Lapidge, 'The Career of Aldhelm', *Anglo-Saxon England*, 36, 2007, pp. 15–70.

[4] For a complete translation see *The Etymologies of Isidore of Seville*, Trans. S. Barney, W. Lewis, J. Beach and O. Berghof, Cambridge, Cambridge University Press, 2006.

the material world, made heavy use of Pliny's *Natural History*. However, since Isidore did not always name his sources, and early medieval readers were content to accept the judgement of this famous scholar, that fact was not much noticed, even though the *Etymologies* came to be a required work of reference for any serious library.[5] Isidore also wrote a short work of natural philosophy, *On the Nature of Things*, which was taught and glossed in the Canterbury school, and that certainly included outlines of meteorological topics.[6] This work was known to and used by Bede, and is of crucial importance in the transition from ancient to medieval meteorology, as will be seen.[7]

Besides the knowledge disseminated via Anglo-Saxon Canterbury, the contacts between the emerging Northumbrian church and the scholarship of monks and missionaries from Ireland and Iona are also clear.[8] Bede's attitude towards even Iona was complex, but the expertise of the Celtic Church in the technical skills required to calculate lunar and solar calendars is reflected even in his hostile account of their calculations.[9] Bede also recounts with pride the journeys made to Rome by his own abbot, and the books and other treasures brought back to Northumbria.[10] Such contacts made it possible for Bede's own monastery to put together an impressive library from wide-ranging sources. Moreover, Bede himself was very aware both of the geographical remoteness of Northumbria and of the fragility of human institutions. He appears to have been, as a child, one of the very few survivors of a devastating plague that nearly eliminated his monastery and the surrounding population. The preservation of both records and practical guides was an essential

---

[5] For brief discussion of Isidore's sources, and his use of them, see ibid., pp. 10–17.

[6] Lapidge, 'The Career of Archbishop Theodore'.

[7] For Bede's use of Isidore see: *Bede; The Reckoning of Time*, Trans. F. Wallis, Liverpool, Liverpool University Press, 1988, pp. lxiv–lxv. For discussion see W. McCready, 'Bede, Isidore and the *Epistola Cuthberti*', *Traditio*, 50, 1995, pp. 75–94.

[8] The education received earlier in his career by Aldhelm, at Malmesbury, appears to have been 'Irish-inspired'; see A. Orchard, 'Aldhelm's Library', in R. Gameson, ed., *The Cambridge History of the Book in Britain*, Vol. 1, Cambridge, Cambridge University Press, 2012, at p. 593. For more on Irish computus and its reception see I. Warntjes, *The Munich Computus: Text and Translation. Irish Computistics between Isidore of Seville and Bede, and Its Reception in Carolingian Times*, Stuttgart, Franz Steiner Verlag, 2010.

[9] This is a well-known topic in Bede's *Ecclesiastical History of the English People*. For discussion see for instance: C. Corning, *The Celtic and Roman Traditions: Conflict and Consensus in the early Medieval Church*, New York, Palgrave Macmillan, 2006, especially chapter 7; and the discussion of 'Iona and the English', in T. Charles-Edwards, *Early Christian Ireland*, Cambridge, Cambridge University Press, 2004, pp. 308–326. For some of the manuscripts brought to Wearmouth-Jarrow by Abbot Ceolfrith see P. Meyvaert, 'Bede, Cassiodorus and the Codex Amiatinus', *Speculum*, 71, 4, 1996, pp. 827–883.

[10] On this see Bede's *Historia abbatum*, Ed. and Trans. C. Grocock and I. Wood, in his *The Abbots of Wearmouth and Jarrow*, Oxford, Oxford University Press, 2013.

work in such circumstances, if carefully accumulated knowledge was to be made safe for the future, and some of Bede's earliest writings addressed this need. However, even short and apparently introductory works, such as *On the Nature of Things* (a title that deliberately placed his treatise in a classical tradition) demonstrate the way in which Bede united classical science and Christian pedagogy.

The title of this work clearly does not relate only to meteorology, even in its expansive, ancient definition. Nevertheless, books given such titles were conscious contributions to a well-established genre. They thus promised, at least implicitly, to deliver wide-ranging analyses and explanations of natural phenomena. Bede's most important model was Isidore who, as noted above, wrote perhaps a century earlier. Isidore's own *On the Nature of Things* was addressed to the Visigothic King Sisebut (612–621).[11] Its aim was practical, since king and bishop wished to challenge superstitious reactions to phenomena such as earthquakes and eclipses. There was no attempt to deny that such events could be intended by God to punish or warn humans. However, the 'traditional' understandings were no longer acceptable, and the approach of Isidore's book is twofold. Firstly, it demonstrates the superiority of classically informed, Christian understandings of the world, by showing that rational, scientific explanations can be provided by those with the training to understand such things. Secondly, it places the phenomena and their explanations squarely within the context of Christian theology. In combination, the two lines of argument show that the clergy (and their patrons) are those who are able to determine whether or not a particular event is 'natural' – and then to interpret it if it fits into the category of sign or portent.

Isidore's rational structuring of the natural world begins with the exposition of time, via the Christian calendar, the units of time that make it up, and the ways in which they are calculated. Time and its cycles lead into an outline of the seasons, and then of the elements that make up the whole Earth. Going further, the courses of the Sun, Moon and certain stars in relation to the Earth are set out, before the text moves on to the subjects of weather signs and ocean tides. Thus aspects of ancient meteorology are set out in some detail in chapters 29–48 of Isidore's book. The approach to understanding the weather is the traditional one; that is, seasonal norms are established, together with a logical explanation of how phenomena such as rain, hail, and snow accord both with the theory of the four elements and with the model of the universe as a

---

[11] See *Isidore of Seville, On the Nature of Things*, Trans. C. Kendall and F. Wallis, Liverpool, Liverpool University Press, 2016.

dynamic and ordered system. Classical authorities such as Aratus are cited as sources of information on subjects such as the regular movements of the Sun.[12] Moreover, as was standard in ancient meteorology, the regular times for seasonal weather events are related to the cycles of the planets and the stars. Authority for the reading of weather signs from observation of the sky and clouds, in particular, is provided by quoting Christ's words on the custom of interpreting red skies at morning or evening in this way.[13] As might be expected given the stated aim of the work, Isidore gives considerable space to listing reliable means by which short-term variations in weather may be predicted, with citations from classical authorities. In addition, chapter 38, which is devoted to 'Signs of storms or calm', assembles information that pays particular attention to the appearance of the Moon at certain points in each lunar month. Numerous authors are cited, including both Aratus and Virgil on the interpretation of the Moon in relation to rain and winds. This further demonstrates the range of classical knowledge on the subject and links the discussion back to the topic of the construction of the Christian lunisolar calendar.

Bede's reuse of Isidore's work has been discussed in detail by Wallis and Kendall.[14] Perhaps most significant, and long-lasting in its effects, was Bede's decision to deal with time, the calendar and their calculation separately and more expansively in other works. His own treatise *On the Nature of Things* is based on extensive passages from Isidore, but revises these by adding quotations and material from portions of Pliny the Elder's multivolume work on *Natural History* (of which Bede may only have known part). It is the information from Pliny, which enables Bede's discussion of meteorological phenomena to be longer and more detailed than Isidore's. The fact that Bede had access to at least part of Pliny's book, which was rare at the time, is impressive; but what is perhaps more surprising is that Bede removes much of Isidore's explicitly Christian, allegorising, comments and devotes himself to the construction of a logical, carefully worked-out model of the world and its workings. In so doing he produced one of the most widely read 'textbooks' on natural philosophy of the early Middle Ages, as is demonstrated by the evidence of surviving manuscripts.[15] No fewer than ninety-six copies of this work

---

[12] For Aratus see 'Introduction', above, at p. 20.
[13] Matthew 16:2–3; see also Luke 12:54–55 on the reading of clouds and winds.
[14] Bede, *On the Nature of Things* and *On Times*, Trans. C. Kendall and F. Wallis, Liverpool, Liverpool University Press, 2010.
[15] J. Westgard, 'Bede and the Continent in the Carolingian Age and Beyond', in S. DeGregorio, ed., *The Cambridge Companion to Bede*, Cambridge, Cambridge University Press, 2010, pp. 201–215.

can be dated to before the end of the twelfth century, a period from which surviving manuscripts are scarce. It was perhaps given still further authority and scope by the fact that Bede incorporated into it material from treatises (including Irish ones) on the ecclesiastical calendar-science of *computus*.

It is important to give a preliminary outline of *computus* here, as it is central to the arguments set out in the rest of this chapter. Briefly, by Bede's time the word (which originally had a more general meaning) had come to be applied almost exclusively to the battery of calculations and tables required both to make accurate forecasts for the date of Easter in any given year, and to understand the issues and techniques involved. The problem rested to some extent on the fact that the information provided by the synoptic gospels as to the date of the original Easter (the Crucifixion and Resurrection of Christ) was both slender and in some ways contradictory. More important for the history of science and meteorology, however, was the solution finally adopted to this problem. This specified that Easter should be celebrated each year, and that the day on which the Resurrection was commemorated should always be a Sunday, which must fall at, or shortly after, the full Moon that itself followed the Spring equinox.[16] It followed that it was necessary to keep track of both lunar and solar calendars and, much more problematically, to find an authoritative and widely accepted way to keep them in correlation with one another. This latter requirement was what produced the most complexities of all, since the lengths of the mean solar and lunar years could not be assimilated to one another in an exact fashion. It was this mathematical fact that helped to prolong the doctrinal and political debates as to the preferred solution during the early centuries of Christianity; and it is noteworthy that one product of these debates was the concept (and dating) of the Christian era itself.[17]

A key aspect of the problem, and of the techniques evolved to deal with it, is that neither the solar nor the lunar year is arithmetically simple. The Roman solar year (or Julian year) contains 365 complete days, plus approximately a quarter of a day. A lunar month is approximately twenty-nine and a half days long. It follows that a Julian year is

---

[16] This subject has been very helpfully discussed by Faith Wallis. For a brief introductory outline see '*Computus* as Problem-Based Science and *Doctrina Christiana*' in her 'Introduction' to *Bede: The Reckoning of Time*, at pp. xviii–xxxiv. A useful 'Brief Glossary of Computistical Terms' is given on pp. 427–429 of the same volume. Another valuable discussion is given in chapter 5 of McCluskey, *Astronomies and Cultures of Early Medieval Europe*, pp. 77–92.

[17] For a survey of this question see G. Declercq, *Anno Domini: The Origins of the Christian Era*, Brepols, Turnhout, 2000.

approximately eleven days longer than a year made up of twelve lunar months. For the purposes of calculating the Christian Easter it is necessary to keep the two synchronised with one another, if full Moons and solar equinoxes are to be correctly correlated. The requirement for Easter Day to fall on a Sunday added the further issue of calculating weekdays, given that the Julian year contains fifty-two weeks plus one day, and also of allowing for leap years. The calculations involved are not in themselves complex, but since no one method produced a completely satisfactory outcome, it was possible for different groups of Christians to adopt different solutions.

Tracing the history of these rival systems is not necessary for a history of the development of a new, medieval meteorology in western Europe. The important fact is that, from the sixth century on, a system that tracked and balanced the solar and lunar years across cycles of nineteen Julian years gradually prevailed in western Europe. This nineteen-year cycle had the advantage of producing an error of only 0.33 days in a century. However, its disadvantage was that a total of twenty-eight such cycles (532 years) is required to balance it completely against the weekday and leap year cycles. For this reason, tables that displayed all the variables needed to trace the calculation of Easter across this long, compound cycle, were challenging for scribes to copy – especially when using Roman numerals.[18] The rival eighty-four-year cycle, used by the Irish Church and adopted in seventh-century Northumbria, had the practical advantage of repeating fully after only eighty-four years. Unfortunately this came at the cost of producing an error of 1.52 days per century. However, its ultimate abandonment had rather more to do with politics than astronomical accuracy, as Bede's account of the Synod of Whitby illustrates. It was the king who made the final decision as to which practice should be followed in his kingdom, and his preference was to support Rome and St Peter.[19]

Nevertheless, the contribution made by the ecclesiastical science of *computus* to the emergence of the new meteorology was crucial in the long term. Even when the debates as to the correct means of calculating Easter, and the timing of the cycle of feasts and observances centred on it, were over, treatises produced during the controversy continued to be read. Still more importantly, it continued to be the case that monasteries were expected to train their members (or at least those judged suitable for

---

[18] A valuably clear discussion is given in McCluskey, *Astronomies and Cultures in Early Medieval Europe*, pp. 80–84.

[19] Bede, *Ecclesiastical History*, Ed. and Trans. B. Colgrave and R. Mynors, Oxford, Clarendon, 1969, at Book III, chapter 25.

the purpose) in the theories as well as the practices involved. This, together with the need to keep careful track of the hours during both daytime and night, in order for the daily cycle of liturgical services to be correctly timed, made basic study of matters such as astronomy, mathematics, and seasonal variations in daylight and climate, a part of the monastic curriculum. It was for this reason that scholars trained in early medieval monastic schools read not only the biblical and theological works prescribed by St Benedict but also Christian works of reference such as those by Isidore and even volumes preserving pagan, Roman knowledge of the heavens and the natural world, such as the work of Pliny. It is this which brings Bede once again to the forefront, as someone able to synthesise and apply knowledge on matters relating to weather from across this range of sources. Equally to the point, his own works rapidly became fundamental textbooks on the subjects of time, the seasons, and the astronomical cycles to which they relate.

The established views on the significance of celestial bodies in signalling coming weather are carefully covered by Bede, who adds considerably to what Isidore had provided, demonstrating the range of knowledge upon which he could draw. In chapter 11 of his own *On the Nature of Things*, Bede follows Isidore on stars, planets and the impossibility of falling stars; but he adds from Pliny that the appearance of windblown aerial fires (which produce the mistaken belief in falling stars) forecasts 'the imminent rise of violent winds'. He is unhesitating in accepting that powerful stars can produce water, frost, snow or hail, while others affect the temperature on Earth and still others produce gentle breezes in the air close to Earth. However he gives no details, leaving this as a matter for experts. More surprising is his use of the technical vocabulary shared by ancient astronomers and astrologers. For instance, still in chapter 11, Bede says that Saturn is one of the planets whose 'transits' bring rain, without offering an explanation of what this means.[20] In the following chapters he informs the reader as to the orbit of Saturn, including that it takes thirty years to complete its passage around the zodiac. Like Isidore, Bede accepts the view that when the planets appear to stand still in the sky or to go backwards this is because of the impact of the rays of the Sun; but he offers no details. Also following Isidore, Bede states that each planet has its own, circular path, and that these are not concentric with the Earth or one another. This disagrees with Aristotelian views of the universe, but has the merit of explaining how the perceived distance between any planet and the Earth (conceived as the centre of the

---

[20] For this information, and the same terminology, see Pliny, *Natural History*, Book 18, chapter 57.

universe) can vary. Saturn is said to be highest above the Earth when it is in Scorpio, and lowest when in the opposite sign (Taurus). The reader is thus left to infer that a transit of Saturn may be when Saturn is closest to Earth, but Bede, like his sources, does not expound.

A further point is that stars (here including the major planets in this category) each have a different makeup, with differing elements and qualities dominating, and it seems to be this that explains the variation in their effects on earthly weather. Some bring forth moisture, either in liquid form or, if they are cold as well as well as wet, frost, snow or hail. Others affect the air and, if warm, produce warm winds. Still others simply send out heat or cold. More complex is the fact that planets and stars can also exert influence upon one another, in such a way that their effect upon the Earth is modified. Both proximity between the stars themselves and the fact that rays from powerful stars can temporarily modify weaker planets can bring about these compound effects. In this way 'certain stars' can also cause rain, if they are affected by the closeness or rays of relevant planets. The example given is the star called 'Little Pig', located in the forehead of Taurus (in other words, in a prominent position in the constellation known as Taurus and customarily depicted as a bull). In other cases the situation is simpler, since stars like the pair known as the Haedi (in the constellation of Auriga) cause moistness and rain in a regular pattern at the time of their rising. The 'rising' referred to here is the point in the solar year at which particular stars become visible above the horizon at night. In the case of the star Arcturus the actual date is given in Bede's text, namely 13 September. It is presumably a star both cold and powerful, since its rising brings wind and hail. Also powerful is the constellation of Orion, which brings storms at its rising. The date of this is not given, but the time meant is presumably January, when Orion first becomes visible at evening in the northern hemisphere. In a parallel manner, Canicula (the 'dog star') rises on 18 July, and sends excessive heat.

Bede is clearly familiar with the sidereal 'calendar' and with the dates of risings of major stars. This is hardly surprising since stars and their times of rising and setting were crucial elements in the system of telling the time at night used in most early medieval monasteries.[21] The necessity for accurate timekeeping, if the specifications of the Benedictine rule as to the timing of the night and dawn services were to be observed, meant that monks were expert observers of the stars. Thus Bede would be in no doubt that this was simply an application of the statement in

---

[21] Information as to the teaching of Theodore and Hadrian would be immensely valuable, but is sadly lacking.

Genesis that God had given the heavenly bodies to provide both light and the means of measuring time for humanity. There was no need to connect it with the activities of the astrologers condemned by Augustine.[22] This point is emphasised again in the following chapters, which provide more details on the planets specifically. By contrast to the freezing cold of Saturn, Jupiter is temperate (and thus by implication benign), whilst Mars, which lies between Jupiter and the Sun, is 'blazing hot', a descriptor that implies negative climatic effects. The Sun, Venus and the Moon are not commented upon in terms of weather here. What is emphasised is that no planet affects the Earth on its own. Their interactions are expounded through reference to colour. Each planet has its own colour; but these colours, like the rays discussed earlier, are affected by the colour of any other planet that moves into close enough proximity.[23]

Indicative of the care with which Bede read his classical sources is that he includes information related to the rather technical theory of planetary 'stimulation' of certain fixed stars, as the planets move towards them.[24] This appears to come close to the astrological concept of 'application'; something that was not to be current in western European astronomy until the twelfth century. Bede is in fact quoting Pliny, as noted above, and his main example is that of the 'Little Pig' star, found in the constellation of Taurus. However, chapters 13–15 provide further information on the characteristics and natures of the planets. The effect of all this is to suggest that the scholar equipped with a detailed calendar of the risings and transits of planets, stars and constellations will have expert knowledge of likely weather events on those dates. This offers helpful, technical detail as to how weather forecasts might actually be made – whilst remaining silent as to practical procedure. Less unusual is the information that, as each zodiac sign in turn dominates the sky, seasonal weather conditions will apply. Bede's information, both on stars and on eclipses, is superior to that available to Isidore, since Bede's source is Pliny, who used the work of the Greek astronomer and mathematician, Hipparchus. This great astronomer of the third century BCE had calculated the paths of the Moon and Sun, established an astronomical calendar, and used observations of a solar eclipse recorded from different

---

[22] On knowledge of these 'calendars' see S. McCluskey, *Astronomies and Cultures in Early Medieval Europe*, Cambridge, Cambridge University Press, 1998, especially chapter 6. Augustine's views are well known, and were expressed in several of his works; a representative example is provided in *On Christian Doctrine*, Book II, chapters 21–23. See R. Green, Ed. and Trans., *Augustine, De Doctrina Christiana*, Oxford, Clarendon, 1995, pp. 92–99.

[23] Chapter 15.   [24] Chapter 11.

points on Earth to calculate the distance between the Earth and the Moon by applying a geometrical method. Much of his work is lost, and it was certainly not known directly to Bede. What is impressive is Bede's confidence with the mathematical and geometrical calculations necessary to follow Pliny's comments.

As noted above, Isidore had gone into some detail as to the relationship between the Moon and weather events on Earth. Bede omits almost all of this (and in another work is critical of some of it, as will be shown below). Nevertheless, his chapter 21 sets out what appears to be his own method for calculating mathematically the zodiac sign of the Moon on any given day. The calculation is based upon the fact that at new Moon (or conjunction) the Moon will be very close to the Sun, whose own position can be easily worked out from a Church calendar. This is because the Sun covers approximately one degree per day, and the days on which it transits from one sign to another are marked in such calendars. The Moon's speed is stated by Bede to be such that it takes two days, six hours and two-thirds of an hour to travel through each sign. Thus, calculating the days since new Moon, and making the allowances that Bede sets out, enables the reader to establish the sign of the Moon on the chosen day. Why this would be worthwhile is not here stated. However, subsequent chapters further emphasise the importance of the Moon in various aspects of life on Earth. The discussions of eclipses make it clear that these are perfectly ordinary and predictable events, which can be calculated on the basis of knowledge of the movements of the Sun and Moon (the issue of zodiac signs is not mentioned here). The fact that the Moon's path divides the upper, purer part of the universe from the coarser, sublunary air and that it is in the latter that clouds, tempests, winds, hail and snow, and other such phenomena, occur is set out in detail in chapter 25. While this may suggest a special connection between the Moon and the weather, this is nowhere directly stated in Bede's book. Indeed, he goes on to attribute the geographical and seasonal patterns of the winds directly to 'the ordinance of God' thus giving them a separate identity whilst also placing them within the ordered system of the created universe. It is perhaps this special status that explains why, as stated in chapter 27, the chief winds have causal effects on the seasons, weather, and living things.

The winds, thus, are stressed to be air stirred up and forced, by 'the ordinance of God' to flow down from high mountains. It is presumably also by divine decree that they follow a more regular pattern than other meteorological phenomena, to the extent that four major ones can be confidently identified, within an overall set of twelve significant winds.

These, Bede explains, are named after the parts of the sky from which they come, and each brings about a specific effect upon the Earth and its weather. The North wind brings cold and cloud, strengthened by the NNE wind, and stirred into snow and hail by the NNW wind. The East wind is more temperate, although it can cause thunder (especially in the East). Slightly confusingly, the ENE wind dries up the Earth, while the ESE generates clouds. The South wind is hot, moist and a bringer of lightning. Indeed, all the South winds bring greater storms than do the North ones, as well as destructive earthquakes. More specifically, the SSE wind is very hot; and the SSW is warm and temperate. Most desirable is the West wind, which dispels winter and brings the arrival of flowers. The WNW wind is more mixed in its effects, bringing rain clouds in the East but fair weather in India, while the WSW is bad news meteorologically, bringing storms, thunder and lightning. This information about which winds cause or affect clouds is important, and leads to an explanation of how both thunder and lightning are generated from clouds rubbing together. A more detailed point is introduced with the phrase 'some say', and this is that the air absorbs into itself both moisture from below and heat from above, which produces 'collisions' in the form of thunder. Either the water or the fire can prove stronger. If the fire wins, then the thunder will damage crops; but if the water wins, the storm will have beneficial effects.

As is common in works in this genre, thunder and lightning are treated both as natural parts of the 'nature of things' and as puzzling phenomena that require special explanations. Chapters 28 and 29 deal with thunder and lightning respectively, and focus in particular on their causes, while chapter 30 covers seasonal and geographical patterns in the occurrence of lightning. Thus once again the reader is equipped to discriminate between natural thunderstorms, and even natural lightning strikes, and those that are not natural. By inference, it is only the latter that should be understood to have any significance in terms of God's ongoing relationship with humanity, even though the former may be terrifying and destructive. It is the extreme heat or cold of the local climate, Bede says, that protects both Egypt and Scandinavia from lightning, while the mildness of the Italian climate has the unfortunate effect of making it particularly prone to the phenomenon. It would necessarily follow that the behaviour of human beings has nothing to do with this – but that a prudent reader would take note before travelling to those regions. In a similar vein, the short chapters 32–35 cover the natural causes and interactions of clouds, rain, hail and snow, together with some information on the patterns of their occurrence.

Bede's chapter 36 deals with 'Signs of Storms or Fair Weather' and, whilst mostly taken from Isidore, omits portions of the source. Bede is also silent on the sources from which Isidore quoted, even when he includes the biblically attested weather sign about red skies at evening or morning. The first group of signs given is based on observation of the sky and the sun. The second gives brief coverage of the timing and compass direction of thunder and lightning. More attention is given to the Moon. Its appearance on the fourth day of a lunar month, and when full, is significant, emphasising again the importance of a good calendar. It is chapter 37, which deals with pestilence, which brings the issue of divine punishment into the discussion. Human behaviour can merit 'excessive dryness or rain' and these in turn corrupt the air causing 'pestilence and death'. This is also the cause of prolonged and unseasonal tempests and cold winds in summer that, occurring out of their proper times, are to be understood as signs and portents. These questions of identifying the natural and the unnatural, and understanding the effects of the Moon, continue through the following discussions of water, tides and the seas, which conclude the meteorological part of the book. It is thus possible to suggest that making authoritative decisions as to when weather events were the direct result of a divine response to human behaviour, or a divine warning of events yet to come, was a very serious matter. Amateur, emotional responses to thunderstorms and other such events are almost certain to lead to error. In relation to weather forecasting, the established and recurrent weather signs are of value precisely because the weather is predominantly seasonal and cyclical, as are the movements of the celestial bodies. However the concept of celestial influence, or celestial causation, of certain weather patterns is explicitly accepted, and in a way that is astronomically and mathematically sophisticated by the standards of the eighth century.

It should not be assumed that Bede covered meteorological topics only in *On the Nature of Things*. He set out a clear and detailed exposition of natural history, across several key works. This makes it possible to put together an overview of his understanding of what determined the weather in any given place and time. Moreover, this can be distinguished from his views on those who looked for portents of future weather. The specific points made naturally varied with context. For example, it is hardly surprising that the material covered in the exposition of Genesis was somewhat different from that set out in *The Reckoning of Time*. An attempt will be made here to set out a full picture of the range of Bede's writings on the subject, whilst keeping material drawn from different texts clearly identifiable. Bede's fullest account of the weather and how it worked is perhaps that set out in several sections of his long work on computus and its component parts, *The Reckoning of Time*, which will be considered next.[25]

In this work as elsewhere Bede emphasises that he is guided by his understanding of both the needs of those whom he is seeking to inform and the material provided by scripture and the Church Fathers. It becomes clear that Bede was no slave to the authority of the authors whom he used. Despite the almost universal acceptance of Isidore's *Etymologies* as a source of knowledge on almost everything, Bede shows a marked tendency to use Pliny's account of the natural world, even though Pliny was by no definition a Father of the Church. Overall, Bede's account of the world and its phenomena is unique for its time. It brings complex and wide-ranging material together, and then melds these components into a logical and clearly visualised account of a working system. It is within this system that meteorological phenomena are seen to be produced, in patterns whose rules can be straightforwardly deduced. As in the classical sources the Earth is pictured as roughly spherical, with water both on its surface and in complex, interconnecting, subterranean networks. Light enough to stay above both, yet interacting with water in particular, is air, which is capable of holding moisture in the forms of mists and clouds. Between the Earth and the Moon the air is relatively thick, and even smoky, something that diminishes the amount of light that can reach the surface of the Earth. Above the Moon the air becomes much thinner and clearer; but the stars and planets that it contains, due to unchangeable divine dispensation, stay in their allocated positions and courses. This clearer, super-lunary zone is the ether. Bede is not entirely clear about it, since he also suggests that some distinction may exist between its lower layers and the ether itself. As the boundary of the firmament is approached the light of the stars will no longer be impeded by thick air, and so that zone is constantly filled with bright starlight. It is the effect of distance and the intervening air that makes the light of the stars very much weaker as seen from Earth, so that they appear only as small lights.[26]

Beyond the Moon, but still relatively close, is the Sun, whose vast size is proved by the fact that it is visible from enormous areas of the Earth simultaneously, and whose light, falling upon the surface of the Earth, is the light of day. Moreover, the shadow of the Earth extends out (following the rules applying to all shadows) towards the stars, and even to the 'frontier beyond air and ether'. When the Earth, the Sun and the

---

[25] For this work see Bede, *The Reckoning of Time*, Trans. F. Wallis, Liverpool, Liverpool University Press, 2nd edition, 2004.

[26] On the structure of the universe see particularly chapter 34.

Moon are in the correct positions it therefore follows that the shadow of the Earth will fall upon the Moon. Thus lunar eclipses have an entirely natural cause, and are predictable for anyone with the necessary information on the courses of the Sun and the Moon.[27] The stars are not affected by the Earth's shadow, since they are too far away. Bede is applying the theory that God put in place at the Creation immutable rules governing the operations of all parts of this multipartite universe. Not explicitly stated, but clear from the whole project of the book, is that humans have the intellect and the knowledge to deduce and comprehend these rules. What is explicitly stated is that solar eclipses, like lunar ones, are also governed by these rules, and are the result of recurring alignments between Earth, Sun and Moon.

The irregularity in the shape of the Earth is also important, as is the angle of the Sun's path, since these factors affect the distance between any part of the Earth's surface and the Sun, and produce irregularities in conditions on Earth. Because the Sun gives both light and heat, the regions furthest from its path at any given time will be colder and will experience longer nights. To an extent this phenomenon will be constant, because of the fixed position of the Earth and the regular path of the Sun around it. But it is added to by the angle between the Sun's path and the celestial equator, which affects the seasons and the varying lengths of night and day. That this was planned by God is demonstrated by the fact that work is to be done by daylight, and that God has given longer periods of dark and rest to those whose work is necessarily carried out in difficult conditions and extreme cold for most of the year. Thus weather patterns, and meteorological conditions more broadly, are placed within parameters created by the regular motions of the planets around the Earth. One meteorological pattern, related to this view, which Bede supports is the belief that the atmosphere is calmer and less troubled during the six months during which the days grow shorter than in the six months during which they lengthen.[28]

With impressive assurance Bede also argues that some established lore, even if passed on by authorities, cannot be accurate. A specific example is discussed at some length, in connection with an account of the ways in which the Sun and the Moon relate to one another as they follow their paths. This exposition challenges the belief that if a new Moon appears to be lying flat (that is, with its horns facing up or down) then the month following will be stormy.[29] Bede tactfully says nothing as to the source of the belief, though he states that it comes from those who 'have attempted

---

[27] On the positions of the Sun and Moon, and their eclipses, see chapters 26 and 27.
[28] See chapter 25.   [29] See chapter 25.

to investigate the upper air'. His approach is to demonstrate that it is impossible, on grounds of 'natural reason'. His first point is that since the Moon is placed high in the ether, well above the zone of air that experiences phenomena such as winds and clouds, it cannot be affected by earthly weather. The second point is more complex, and begins with a lengthy quotation from Augustine's commentary on Psalm 10, which points out that the Moon has no light of its own but rather is lit by the Sun. This is why, when the Moon is in conjunction with the Sun, the lit portion will be turned wholly away from the Earth, producing the dark of the Moon. As the Moon moves away from the Sun a crescent of light will grow at a regular pace until the fifteenth day of the lunar cycle, when the Moon will be opposite the Sun and thus full. This established, Bede next considers the varying speeds at which the Sun and Moon move and the angle between their paths. In Spring, he notes, the Sun's path is climbing from South to North in such a way that it will light up the Moon from below. This means that the crescent of the new Moon, seen at sunset at the equinox, will appear like a ship, and its horns will point upwards. Something that follows logically is that, since new Moons do not always exactly coincide with the equinox, this will be variable. This would give the mistaken view greater credibility, since the Moon would not always behave in this way on a given date. Bede goes on to point out that after the summer solstice the Sun's path turns south again, as does the position in which the new Moon will appear. Thus at the autumn equinox just after sunset a crescent Moon will appear to be standing upright, and with its horns pointing away from the Sun. For this reason, Bede says, new Moons appearing as the days are lengthening will appear high in the sky and lying flat, and will do so at a season when strong winds often occur. The erroneous view is thus apparently logical, but can only be believed by the 'untutored', who do not know the true paths of the Sun and Moon.

That weather prediction by the Moon was well established and hard to eradicate is suggested by the further points made at the end of this long discussion. People clearly wished to 'pronounce on atmospheric conditions'; and phenomena such as the colour of the Moon or Sun, the appearance of the heavens, the stars, or the shapes of clouds, were all apparently used in this way. But all these are dismissed by Bede as 'omens', even though they are found in authorities such as Isidore (though Bede refrains from saying so). A final specific piece of pseudo-forecasting to be dismissed with scorn is that fair weather for a month is predicted by the Moon appearing on its fourth day as an unblemished crescent, with its horns 'unblunted'. What is to be noted here is that Bede does not assert that all attempts to forecast the weather must be superstitious or magical. Meteorological phenomena are part of the ordered workings of the world. They are therefore predictable within certain parameters, but to believe in omens is to misunderstand how changes in the weather come about.

A case in point is provided by the discussion of the powers of the Moon.[30] An important authority here is Basil's *Hexameron* (especially book 6). The different phases of the Moon are stated to have different effects on the levels of moisture in all living things, as well as on the moisture in the air between the Earth and the Moon. This has the further effect that the Moon can cause changes and disturbances in the mixture of water and air that makes up the 'atmosphere' between the Earth and the Moon itself. The pull of the Moon on water is strongest when the Moon is new, and remains powerful whilst the Moon is waxing. Thus a new Moon can stir up large amounts of cloud and disturb the air containing those clouds. It should be noted that the Moon is not foretelling the impending arrival of clouds and wind but is instead their direct cause. In a similar way, as Bede (again drawing on Basil) says, the Moon's pull on water can affect the movements and thus the currents of the ocean, which in turn can affect sandbanks and coasts. In chapter 29 Bede again shows independent research into natural phenomena by setting out, with mathematical precision, the way in which the Moon's cycle is mirrored by the pattern of the tides. The Moon rises and sets each day four-fifths of an hour later than the previous day, with the result that in two lunar months, or 59 days, it will complete only 57 circuits around the Earth. The conclusion is that in twelve lunar months (354 days) the Moon will have circuited the earth only 342 times, and there will have been 684 tides. Again, all this is entirely regular and predictable.

An explanation of tides also touches upon the weather, since Bede demonstrates that there is a regular pattern in the increase and decrease of the tides but accepts that this pattern can be affected and even overthrown by strong winds and other 'natural forces'. The standard pattern is that if an evening tide occurs at full or new Moon it will be an increasing (or 'spring' tide) and for seven days the evening tide will be higher than the morning tide, and vice versa. Other patterns can also occur, but Bede is clear, despite authoritative statements to the contrary, that high tides reach different parts of the coast at different times according to a regular pattern. He goes further and suggests that a particularly high tide on one coast will be matched by a particularly low one on another. This is because the Moon's power to attract and repel

---

[30] See chapter 28.

water depends upon its position in relation to the Earth as well as upon its phase. This leads into further discussion, in chapter 30, of how equinoxes and solstices are produced by recurring patterns in the positions of the Sun and Moon in relation to the Earth, with the result that their dates are predictable (even if debated). This pattern also determines the recurring cycle of the seasons, with the turning points, as Pliny wrote and as all liturgical calendars would confirm, when the sun was in the signs of Aries, Cancer, Libra and Capricorn. However, no detailed comment is given on the patterns of weather for each season.

Of more meteorological interest is chapter 31, where Bede moves on to expound the fact that theoretical 'circles' or 'parallel lines' can be conceived around the Earth's surface, defining zones linked by their position in relation to the path of the Sun around the Earth. This is supported by reference to the observations of both 'gentiles' and Christians. The *Hexaemeron* of St Ambrose is an important source here, for the argument that these zones can be identified by the length of the shadow cast at noon on the day of the equinox by a gnomon of specified length. An extended quotation from Pliny expounds the fact that the seasons will vary in duration and strength in these different zones, which thus have different climates as well as different patterns of day and night. Bede stresses that these patterns are fixed, and that the light of the stars, just like that of the Sun, remains as strong as it was at the time of creation. Thus the fact that the star Canopus, which was important to the Egyptians, cannot be seen from Britain is not because the light of the stars fades (or because Canopus' light is too weak to reach the regions of Earth most distant from it) but because the 'mass of the Earth' is in the way.

Also relevant is the outline of how the climatic zones on Earth relate to the circles designated by the path of the Sun. A mosaic of quotations from Virgil and Pliny is used to expound and describe these, and the conclusion is clear. The equatorial zone of the Earth is so fiercely heated by the Sun that it is hostile to human life, whilst the extreme northern and southern zones are permanently frozen and wracked by storms, to such an extent that even the sea is frozen beyond the island of Thule. Thus it is the two solstitial circles that mark out the zones suitable for human habitation. On this subject Bede clearly prefers St Augustine's view that only the northern of these circles is actually inhabited, and supports this by pointing out that no one has ever discovered any account of an actual journey into the southern zone. As Bede says, even Pliny (who states that the Earth is inhabited all over) accepts that the two habitable zones are entirely cut off from each other by the impassable heat of the equatorial zone.

The exposition of the cycles of time through the calendar year is also relevant, since the pattern of the seasons relates to the Sun's visible course. Even in the temperate zones already described such seasonal variation will necessarily occur. As Bede (using Isidore) explains, this maintains their temperate climate whilst making possible the annual cycle of growth and harvest. It is the Sun's varying distance that necessarily brings about this cycle. The Sun's greatest distance is the cause of winter, with its predominance of cold and wet weather. In spring the wet lingers, but the increasing nearness of the Sun brings equally increasing warmth. In summer the heat increases and wet gives way to dry weather. Finally, in autumn, the dryness remains whilst the heat gives way once again to cold as the Sun sinks towards the south. These pairs of qualities also link the four elements that make up the world, and the four humours found in the human body. Bede gives the necessary basics of the medical theory related to all this, but it is not his main concern. Instead, he moves on to a detailed outline of something much less well known and much more closely related to scientific discussion of time, namely the views of learned cosmographers as to how the precise dates of the seasons should be fixed. Here, Bede acknowledges the views of both Isidore of Seville and Pliny, but effectively supports what he has found in 'the finest and most authoritative books of the cosmographers' as to the crucial role of the rising and setting of the Pleiades.[31]

What emerges from all this is a model of weather as the result of a complex but intelligible interplay between definite causal factors. These can be summarised as the behaviour of the elements upon and within the Earth itself; the impact of the light and heat given out by the Sun; the changing patterns produced by the movements of the Sun, Moon and stars around the Earth; and the still more complex patterns of interaction between the stars, which lead to modulated rays reaching and affecting the Earth. Overriding all of these is the possibility of divine intervention, which can itself be foreshadowed by warning portents, allowing time for humans to change their behaviour and thus potentially avert catastrophe. The regularity of the most important parts of this system makes general weather conditions predictable at a broad level. It also means that careful observation can produce lists of signals of impending winds, rain, storms, and other temporary changes in the weather. More striking is Bede's acceptance of the complex effects of stellar rays upon the Earth's atmosphere, and the ways in which these can in turn affect such things as wind and vapours. Bede had no access to Ptolemy's calculations and tables of

[31] Ibid., p. 101.

the paths of the stars around the Earth, but his comments on the stars and their rays, set out above, suggest that he would have accepted them as a valuable addition to knowledge of 'the nature of things'. It also appears that Bede's interest in meteorology grew along with his knowledge of the Earth, the universe and their workings. His short, early work *On Times*, whilst offering an outline account of many of the topics covered in more detail in *The Reckoning of Time*, had no meteorological content. This is logical for a study of time, but also makes the level of Bede's analysis of the systems governing weather and climate, set out in the later work, all the more remarkable.

The next step is to turn to those works in which Bede gave his interpretations of scripture, to see whether these add to, or indeed contradict, the material offered in his accounts of the workings of the world. Most relevant is his commentary *On Genesis*, since here scriptural exegesis and comment upon the nature of creation come together.[32] Not all of the original version of this work survives, but what is most relevant for the current enquiry is Bede's commentary upon the Creation itself, and that section is well attested. The range of authorities most used in this context are listed by Bede himself as Basil, Ambrose and Augustine; however, Pliny is again cited, especially for information on distant regions of the Earth. The information on the Earth, its makeup and its position within creation is highly consonant with that in the more technically 'philosophical' works. Bede did not offer one truth in one work and a different one in another. Moreover, the Church Fathers whose works he used drew upon a larger pool of the same classical knowledge used by Bede. Here once again the Earth is stated to be a sphere, with its 'upper parts' (roughly, the northern hemisphere) inhabited and also receiving more of the Sun's light. The latter claim is rather surprising, but this may only have been the case at the time of Creation rather than thereafter. More clearly stated is that the path of the Sun around the Earth was established by the 'first light', which preceded the creation of the Sun.

Bede is definite that the Sun's path encircles the Earth, and that night in the 'upper' part of the Earth is simply caused by the fact that the Sun is on the far side of the Earth's sphere. He goes out of his way to refute the idea that 'the light gradually disappeared and then gradually reappeared again in the morning'. No source is given for this erroneous idea, but it is likely that it came to Bede from classical works. It had been mentioned (and accepted as possible) by Lucretius in his long, didactic poem,

---

[32] Bede, *On Genesis*, Trans. C. Kendall, Liverpool, Liverpool University Press, 2008.

De rerum natura, which included both metaphysical and meteorological topics. Lucretius wrote in the first century BCE, and his work was studied by Cicero. The poem was possibly known to St Jerome and to Isidore, though not to Bede. The oldest surviving copy is from the ninth century.[33] Isidore does not mention this idea and so cannot have been Bede's source. Such a notion is clearly wrong as far as Bede is concerned, since it is in direct opposition to the regular system of the world that God established. The limitations to the effects that component parts of this system can have upon the Earth are also stressed, especially in the assertion that the stars and the planets do not cause seasons or times, but rather provide signs of them, which can be rationally analysed and interpreted. Bede follows Augustine in supporting the use of the stars for navigational purposes by sailors and those crossing vast deserts. Nevertheless, he takes the definition of signs further, by stating that the stars are also signs of 'what the state of the weather is going to be' since observation of the stars can make it possible for humans to make forecasts about impending weather.[34]

This discussion is followed by further comments on the role of the Sun in relation to the Earth, including the assertion that it gives not only light but also heat, since the Earth has no heat of its own. This is in accord with the view that celestial bodies interact with, and have effects upon, one another within regular patterns. In the comments on Genesis 1:20 Bede repeats the idea that air and water interact with one another, since air forms clouds from the water vapours it holds, and these in turn can be affected by air turbulence in the form of winds. Similarly, dew drops out of the air on clear nights and thus lands on the earth. Bede here supports his own comments by reference to Augustine's commentaries on both Genesis and the Book of Job. Moreover, guarded support for the idea that this regular system makes possible at least general forecasting of the weather is expressed once more in the same section. Here, Bede cites Christ's comments on the practice of making weather forecasts from clouds and winds. The reference is to Luke 12:54–56, where Christ says that a cloud arising from the west is said to foretell a shower, and that a south wind is said to presage a stronger wind. These observations are presented as based on experience, and as being reliable, a fact that strengthens still further the view that the world system is reliable and knowable, and capable of supporting deductions and thus predictions.

---

[33] On this see D. Butterfield, *The Early Textual History of Lucretius' De rerum natura.* Cambridge, Cambridge University Press, 2013, pp. 5–12.

[34] Bede, *On Genesis,* p. 81.

This belief emerges again when Bede stresses that the Earth still follows the patterns created during the six days of creation.[35] The idea of an established, and even fixed, system is so strong that it reappears in the discussion of a spring that flowed out of the earth.[36] Such a phenomenon clearly raised questions as to the source of this water, since any idea that earth could actually generate water would be troubling. Equally, if God had created a given quantity of water at the time of creation, it followed that no new water could be spontaneously generated. Bede approaches this tricky issue first by once again quoting Augustine, this time on the view that all earthly waters, both the sea visible on the earth's surface and the waters 'in hidden cavities' below the surface of the earth, in fact make up one body of water. Thus, the sources of springs and rivers can be explained as points at which water that had been held in subterranean spaces has made its way to the surface. That water could seep into the earth, both as rain and from the sea, is something that Bede observes at several points and that provides sufficient explanation for the origin of this water. The idea is not expanded upon here, but elsewhere Bede also expresses confidence that sweet water that ends up in the sea will become salty, and that the salt water of the sea, once taken up as vapour, can lose its salt before falling as rain.

This chapter has argued that Isidore made available a short and somewhat simplistic version of ancient meteorology within his outline of a Christian natural philosophy. Bede built upon this in turn, but also went further. His works contain strong arguments for considering the world as both a system that can be deduced from biblical and classical texts and one that can be explored and tested in empirical ways. However, it is also important not to take this too far; the evidence of biblical texts would always override every other source of knowledge. The belief that all of scripture could and should be brought into play, in the decoding of the system of the world, produced results that went far beyond what could be empirically tested, but which were in no way held to be weakened by this. In this Bede was fully in accord with his contemporaries, even if he was bolder in his use of 'pagan' sources of scientific knowledge. As Isidore had done before, his intent was to expound the workings of God's creation to the best of his ability and to make use of the best sources of knowledge for the purpose. What makes his work so important for the history of the transition from classical meteorology to medieval weather-forecasting is his demonstration that natural philosophy and the Christian model of time were not only compatible but dependent upon a

---

[35] Ibid., p. 107.   [36] Ibid., p. 108.

unified and intelligible model of the workings of the universe. Arguably this, together with his brief mentions of how the celestial bodies interacted with one another and with the Earth's atmosphere, did much to pave the way for the reception of Arabic astronomical and astrological science.

2   Meteorology, Weather Forecasting and the Early Medieval Renaissance of Astronomy

Telling the story of meteorology more broadly, and weather forecasting in particular, in the Carolingian and Ottonian periods is not a simple matter. This is because these topics did not exist independently, but rather were embedded within the complex histories of astronomy, computus and ongoing efforts to deliver religious education to societies in the process of cultural transition. Given the acceptance of the doctrine that what is above affects that which is below, it is hardly surprising that rulers were especially strongly interested in understanding celestial phenomena. Indeed, this was an important factor driving forward the study of astronomy. Links between secular and ecclesiastical courts remained as strong as in the seventh century despite power struggles between the two. There was a clear need for cooperation when it came to the dissemination and interpretation of knowledge about the heavens, the sublunary world and meteorological matters. Such knowledge had clear implications for ideas concerning the sources and distribution of power, as well as being fundamental to policymaking. However, it was not customary for confidential discussions between rulers and advisers to be recorded, and thus no details of such exchanges are available.

A further factor that causes problems for historians is that acceptable knowledge concerning the factors affecting earthly life continued to be embedded within the computus rather than being communicated separately. However, computus was not a monolithic or unchanging body of knowledge, and it was revised when Roman astronomical texts became available in the Carolingian Empire. This change affected understandings of the positions and movements of the stars and the planets, which were in turn important for weather forecasting. The second key factor is that the Church was working to eliminate 'superstitious' ideas on weather events, their causes, meanings and future occurrences. This raises questions concerning the widely copied, short texts now known as 'prognostics', some of which provided weather forecasts. These worked by interpreting various types of accepted signs, but have been seen as a form of divination by some historians. They appear in collections of valued materials, usually with computistical or liturgical texts, and are thus distinguished from divination, a term applied to techniques that were open to demonic deception. One of the most popular produced predictions of weather, crops, health and disasters for each season of a coming year. This and other weather-related prognostics occur most frequently together with texts on computus, and thus this enquiry will consider them within that context. However, there was also revived interest in classical astronomy itself, and this needs to be taken into account, since it affected the overall body of knowledge within which the new meteorology took shape.

The earliest evidence of active research into astronomical knowledge is provided by Carolingian enthusiasm for Pliny. The perception of Pliny as a leading authority on natural philosophy is found already in Bede, as noted in Chapter 1. Bede's work was influential in its own right, but it was also important that Alcuin, the Anglo-Saxon scholar recruited as an adviser by Charlemagne, held related views. This is demonstrated by a poem written by Alcuin, both celebrating and mourning the knowledge that had been available at York in the late eighth century. For Alcuin, the science of natural history was represented by the name of Pliny.[1] Alcuin's views are important, as he played a major role in formulating Charlemagne's policies on matters relating to religion and education. Moreover, Charlemagne's biographer recorded that the emperor sought instruction on astronomy from Alcuin with special enthusiasm, and that 'the art of calculation' was strongly linked to 'the investigation of the movement of the stars'.[2] The association of astronomy, mathematics and the calculation of time and the calendar is clear. Significantly, the emperor's educational programme, as represented by his encyclical known as the *Admonitio generalis*, represents scientific knowledge simply by the term 'computus'.[3] The context shows that this would have focused on study of the calendar and all the factors involved in its accurate calculation.

Moreover, the persistence of pre-Christian beliefs about weather could be a major source of concern. The writings of Agobard, bishop of Lyons under Charlemagne's son, Louis the Pious, make it clear that

[1] M. Garrison, 'The Library of Alcuin's York', in R. Gameson, Ed., *Cambridge History of the Book in Britain*, Volume 1, Cambridge, Cambridge University Press, 2012, pp. 633–664, at p. 649.
[2] See R. McKitterick, 'The Carolingian Renaissance of Culture and Learning', in J. Story, Ed., *Charlemagne: Empire and Society*, Manchester, Manchester University Press, 2005, pp. 151–166, at p. 158.
[3] A. Boretius, Ed., *Capitularia regum Francorum*, Vol. 1, *Monumenta Germaniae Historica, Leges*, sect. 2, Vol. 1, Hanover, MGH Institute, 1883, p. 60.

long-established, pagan beliefs about weather could be socially divisive, as well as fundamentally mistaken.[4] Agobard had become concerned after intervening to save the lives of three men and one woman about to be executed for ruining crops by calling up hail and thunderstorms. He investigated the accusations against them and took the trouble to write a condemnation of such beliefs, which he found to be widespread.[5] Agobard quoted from numerous books of the Bible to prove beyond doubt that not only storms but all weather are the province of divine power alone. No human in all of the Bible is stated to have been able to change the weather except by calling upon divine aid, whilst God is frequently stated to have used storms and weather events to punish humans, both directly and through the acts of evil angels. Agobard's overarching view is represented by the statement that 'everything that occurs in the skies is to be attributed to the command of God ... together with anything that descends from the skies to the earth'. The latter includes winds as well as hail, snow, rain and the rainbow.[6] Meteorological knowledge, and its place within the world of scholarship, were thus matters of importance within the overall cultural transformation being driven forward.

As would be expected, given Charlemagne's order that computus should be accurately taught, Bede's scientific works were widespread in the schools of the Carolingian Empire. However, there is also evidence that study of the subject was taken well beyond simple use of Bede's textbooks. Special attention was given to adding new information on both astronomy and meteorology, with Pliny's *Natural History* emerging once again as an authoritative source. Complete copies were now available, as is demonstrated both by surviving manuscripts and by references in works by Carolingian writers. Parts of a late eighth-century copy of the work survive in Rome, MS Vat lat. 3861 and Leiden, Voss lat. F 61.[7] Ongoing discussion of such matters at the highest level is reflected in the correspondence between Alcuin and Charlemagne. Several of Alcuin's letters include answers to questions concerning how celestial phenomena such as eclipses and comets relate to affairs on earth; and in these Alcuin cites Pliny as a key authority. Given all this, it is unsurprising that extracts

---

[4] On his career see J. Allen Cabaniss, 'Agobard of Lyons', *Speculum*, 26, 1, 1951, pp. 50–76.

[5] First edited as *Liber contra insulsam vulgi opinionem de grandine et tonitruis*, *Patrologia Latina*, vol. CIV, cols. 147–158.

[6] For the text see now L. Van Acker, Ed., *Agobardi Lugdunensis Opera Omnia*, (*C.C.C.M.*, Vol. 52) Brepols, Turnhout, 1981, pp. 3–15. See also P. Dutton, 'Thunder and Hail Over the Carolingian Countryside' in D. Sweeney, Ed., *Agriculture in the Middle Ages*, Philadelphia, Pennsylvania University Press, 1995, pp. 111–124.

[7] B. Eastwood, *Ordering the Heavens; Roman Astronomy and Cosmology in the Carolingian Renaissance*, Leiden, Brill, 2007, pp. 95–178.

from Pliny's Books Two and Eighteen, specifically on astronomy and meteorology, were compiled into a dossier; and this circulated amongst the monastic houses of the Carolingian Empire.[8]

One compilation based on this information was produced at St Gall early in the ninth century, and brings together extracts on the planets, their courses, eclipses, weather patterns, earthly waters and the regions of the earth.[9] The material was also copied, for instance, at Reichenau. However, other selections from the dossier were widely distributed in varying contexts, and became a part of the core knowledge of the Carolingian world. Thus, a scientific understanding of the structure of the universe, the regular movements of the heavens, and their interaction with cycles of human time and activity was actively constructed and taught. Moreover, aspects of meteorology were central within this area of scholarly work. True understanding of cosmology and meteorology was accepted as integral to the fight against error and superstition. An important stage in the production of a body of approved knowledge seems to have taken place in 809, with the calling together of a committee tasked with producing not just an updated and authoritative computistical treatise but also a wide range of supporting materials. Their work survives in numerous copies, divided across two main editions, and meteorological material is prominent in both of these editions.[10] Bede's *On the Nature of Things* was clearly still valued as a core textbook, since it is incorporated in its entirety into both editions. However, further meteorological material is added in both editions, primarily in the form of lengthy extracts from Pliny. The two editions are usually known as the *Three Book Computus* and the *Seven Book Computus*.[11]

The three-book version appears to have been produced first, but survives in only two copies, whereas the slightly later seven-book version was widely copied. The two together may be taken as constituting a sort of encyclopaedia of core knowledge in this field. The *Three Book*

---

[8] See V. King, 'An Investigation of Some Astronomical Excerpts from Pliny's *Natural History* found in Manuscripts of the Earlier Middle Ages', unpublished B. Litt. Thesis, Oxford, 1969.

[9] This collection survives as Leiden, Voss lat. Q 69, folios 3v to 46r.

[10] Eastwood, loc cit. This terminology will be followed here, for the sake of clarity. However, the text was edited under the general title of *Libri Computi* in A. Borst, Ed., *Die karolingische Kalendarreform; Schriften zur Komputistik im Frankenreich von 721 bis 818; MGH, Schriften zur Geistesgeschichte des Mittelalters, XXI*, 3 vols., Hannover, Monumenta Germaniae Historica, 2006, vol. 3.

[11] A slightly different terminology again is used by E. Ramirez-Weaver, *A Saving Science: Capturing the Heavens in Carolingian Manuscripts*, Philadelphia, University of Pennsylvania, 2017, where the seven-book compilation (the chief text discussed) is referred to as the 'Handbook of 809'.

Computus sets out in Book 1 material on the calendar and chronology, drawing heavily on Bede's *On the Reckoning of Time*. Like Bede, this section provides discussion of the four seasons alongside an exposition of the elements and the humours, following closely on coverage of the Moon and its powers over earthly phenomena. The twin themes of an ordered system and of the power of things above in relation to things below are thus once again present and correct. Book 2 moves on to more detailed coverage of the stars and planets, their places and cycles, and their effects. Chapter seven is titled 'Concerning Seasonal Changes' (*De temporum mutatione*) and is taken from Book 18 of Pliny. Chapter eight is headed 'Concerning Signs of Storms' and is a long extract from the same source.

The *Seven Book Computus* shows major interest in the planets and luminaries, and its Books 3 and 4 are devoted to the courses and cycles of the Sun and the Moon. Moreover, its handling of Pliny's astronomical data is usually accompanied by diagrams and images, frequently beautiful.[12] The authoritative status of this compilation is shown by the facts that it was widely distributed across the Empire and that, in the centres where it was received and copied, it became the repository for annals of key local and regional events.[13] A limitation in both of these editions of scientific and computistical material was that their teachings on the earthly effects of the cyclical movements of the stars and planets were hard to put into practical use in any detailed way. Their information on the courses of the planets other than the Sun and Moon was expressed in extremely broad terms, which did not make it possible to produce anything approaching accurate calculations of their positions on a given date and as seen from a specific location. On this matter, no real advance was made on the techniques expounded by Bede. The same applies to the specifically astronomical work known as the *Aratea*, which was usually Cicero's Latin translation of the *Phenomena* of Aratus.[14] This too was copied in luxury editions with beautiful and impressive illuminations and diagrams, but was of little use in actual astronomical calculations.[15] Thus, Pliny's detailed information on seasonal weather patterns and their

---

[12] Ramirez-Weaver, ibid., gives detailed discussion of a luxury copy produced for Drogo, bishop of Metz and illegitimate son of Charlemagne, now Madrid, Biblioteca Nacional, Ms 3307.

[13] For discussion of the full range of extracts from Pliny, and details on individual copies, see King, Investigation, and Eastwood, *Ordering the Heavens*.

[14] On this, see: E. Gee, *Aratus and the Astronomical Tradition*, Oxford, Oxford University Press, New York, 2013; and M. Dolan, *Astronomical Knowledge Transmission through Illustrated Aratea Manuscripts*, Cham, Switzerland, Springer, 2017.

[15] A well-known example is now Leiden, Ms Voss lat. 4° 79, produced at the court of Louis the Pious. For discussion of the text and the images it inspired see E. Dekker, *Illustrating*

predictive signs, remained the only basis for detailed weather forecasting. This helps to explain their acceptance, even though they are highly resistant to the type of patterned, structured and universalising teachings central to computus.

An expanded version of Pliny's meteorological information is found in the *Seven Book Computus*. Its first four books are devoted to the key, technical issues for computists, namely the units and calculation of time and the calendar, while book six deals with weights and measures, and book seven is based on Bede's *On the Nature of Things*. It is book five that deals with astronomy and the related meteorological issues of weather patterns and weather signs. This book has twelve chapters, and the last is 'On Signs of Storms' (*De praesagiis tempestatum*). The majority of these are based on observation of the Sun, the Moon, stars, atmospheric conditions, winds and terrestrial waters; but observation of animals and plants is also included, following Pliny.[16] This is a long chapter, testifying to the importance of its contents, and careful attention is given to the signs provided by the heavenly bodies as to the coming of unusual and threatening weather, as its title suggests. As usual, these are primarily short-term, mostly relating to the few days following a particular observation, or giving general characteristics for a coming season at most.

It should be noted that Pliny, in chapter 57 of Book 18, sets out a major problem that affected weather forecasting throughout the early Middle Ages in western Europe. This is that, on the one hand, a detailed knowledge of astronomy is needed for weather prediction, because 'although all these things depend on stars that are stationary and fixed in the sky, there intervene movements of planets and hailstorms and rain, these also having a considerable effect ... This is why Virgil teaches the necessity of acquiring a thorough knowledge of the system of the planets also, warning us to watch the transit of the cold star Saturn'.[17] On the other hand, the level of knowledge required raises formidable technical problems: 'Above all there is the variation due to the convexity of the world and the terrestrial globe, the same star revealing itself to different nations at a different time, with the consequence that its influence is not operative everywhere on the same days.' Local knowledge could provide information as to when particular stars were visible from a given location, but the courses of the planets were a far more complex matter. This is the

---

the *Phaenomena; Celestial Cartography in Antiquity and the Middle Ages*, Oxford, Oxford University Press, 2012.

[16] For this chapter see King, Investigation, pp. 156–169. Eastwood, *Ordering the Heavens*, argues that the best text is found in Madrid, Biblioteca Nacional, Ms 3307, ff. 69r–71v.

[17] This statement was noted by Bede, together with the information concerning the orbits and speeds of the planets, as discussed in Chapter 1.

central obstacle to making weather predictions involving planets other than the Sun and the Moon, despite Pliny's comments; and Pliny does not even attempt such predictions. It is thus hardly surprising that the edited extracts in the *computi* follow suit.

The extracts placed in the *Computus'* chapter on the signs of coming storms, *De praesagiis tempestatum,* are taken at some length from Pliny's Book 18, chapters 77 onwards, but without acknowledgement of their source. The selection has a brief introductory statement that attention will now be turned to further means of forecasting storms, and that those relating to the Sun will be dealt with first. The coverage here is full, and attention is paid especially to the Sun's appearance at its risings and settings, and to the colour and arrangement of clouds that then surround it. These are also related to the key points within the solar year that Pliny had set out in an earlier chapter. The following passages move on to predictions from the Moon, claiming the authority of 'the Egyptians' and quoting the Roman writer and polymath, Varro (116–127 BCE). The extraordinary range of Varro's knowledge and writing had been recorded by St Jerome.[18] Strikingly, of his impressive output only his work *On Agriculture* survives in full, in a medieval copy, testifying to the status of this work, which was also quarried by Virgil and Pliny themselves. The compilers of the *Computus* are thus displaying considerable research into surviving sources of information; however, their material stays very much in the prevailing mainstream. As with the signs to be gathered from the Sun, it is the appearance of the Moon that is most used, not its astronomical (or astrological) position. Predictions based on the appearance of the moon's horns on the fourth day of a lunar month, which Bede had criticised, are included here as unproblematic. Once again, key dates are provided for observations, these all cited by their place in a lunar month. The predictions based on the Moon are once again short-term, covering only two or three days, with only one real exception. This is the statement that 'if the Moon only becomes visible on its fourth day, and the west wind is blowing, the whole month will be wintry' (*Si ante quartam non apparuerit vento favonio flante, hiemalis toto mense erit*).

Next comes observation of 'the stars', based on Pliny, chapter 80, paras. 351–353. No planets are here mentioned by name, with most weather signs being related to the overall visibility and stability of the stars, especially at key dates. There is nothing on interactions between

---

[18] Jerome, Letter 33, to Paula: see W. Fremantle and P. Schaff, Ed. and Trans., *The Principal Works of St Jerome,* New York, Christian Literature Publishing, 1892, pp. 111–112. It is noteworthy that Jerome here comments on the fact that Latin speakers found long lists of informative works in Greek tedious.

stars and planets. Only one prediction relates to the planets at all. This is the statement that: 'if any of the planets is surrounded by a halo/circle, [this signifies] rain' (*si stellarum errantium aliquam orbis incluserit, imbrem*). It is immediately followed by the information that the 'sign' (i.e., constellation) of Cancer includes two stars called Little Asses, and that they bracket a small grouping called the Manger. This latter is significant because, if it ceases to be visible whilst the sky is clear and untroubled, a fierce storm is coming. The Little Asses are also important, since if either of them is covered by mist there will be gales from a specified direction. This then is astronomical and meteorological knowledge at a simple level, aimed at scholars dependent upon direct observation of the heavens. The first two chapters of Book 5 have already provided helpful information on the identification of the constellations; users are expected to be aware of the months during which each sign/constellation was visible from their location.

This raises the question of more technical astronomical knowledge in this period, and the place of meteorology in relation to it. It is unfortunate that no image is known to survive of Charlemagne's silver 'table', which supposedly depicted the spheres of the heavens, the stars, and the courses of the planets.[19] However, links have been made between surviving, luxury copies of astronomical texts and members of the Carolingian courts. A volume now known as the Leiden *Aratea*, is believed to have links with the court of Louis the Pious, and one of its images depicts the positions of the planets as calculated for a specific date. Which date this was has been debated, but it is now generally agreed that it was the day of the full Moon following the vernal equinox (in other words the Paschal full Moon) in 816. It would thus be 16 April according to modern calculation, but 17 April for those using Carolingian calendars.[20] To understand the significance of this volume in relation to astronomically based weather prediction in the court of Louis the Pious, it is necessary to look further at this image, and its textual context.

The group of texts now collectively known as *Aratea* played an important role in the transmission of classical astronomical knowledge to the Carolingian world. Versions survive in several luxury manuscripts from the earlier part of the Middle Ages, as well as in numerous plainer copies. Its popularity dwindled in the twelfth century, although it experienced a

---

[19] Views on this table vary, but it is accepted as having displayed a map of the heavens. See: F. Estey, 'Charlemagne's Silver Celestial Table', *Speculum*, XVIII, 1943, pp. 112–117; and M. Innes, 'Charlemagne's Will: Piety, Politics and the Imperial Succession', *English Historical Review*, 112, No. 448, 1997, pp. 833–855.

[20] See E. Dekker, 'Carolingian Planetary Observations: The Case of the Leiden Planetary Configuration', *Journal for the History of Astronomy*, 39.1, No. 134, 2008, pp. 77–90.

major revival in the fifteenth century, when it was rediscovered by classicising scholars.[21] The *Aratea* were based on Latin versions of a long Greek poem on astronomy and meteorology, written probably in Athens and by Aratus, in the third century BCE. Aratus' model of the heavens set out the geocentric spheres expounded by Greek astronomers and philosophers, and placed the planets in order around a central Earth, but gave little attention to technical details. Its long concluding section in fact deals with meteorology and weather signs. It was already rather old fashioned in its handling of constellations and star groups by the time it was transmitted to Roman scholars of the late Republic. Nevertheless, it was highly successful in its new milieu and was translated by several notable writers, including Cicero. This popularity continued at the courts of the early Roman emperors. The work also came highly recommended to the Christian world, having been used by Virgil in his *Georgics,* and quoted by St Paul in a speech given in Athens (according to the *Acts of the Apostles*). Jerome mentioned the numerous translations in his Commentary on St Paul's Epistle to Titus.[22] It is likely that Varro used its section on meteorology and weather signs when compiling his own coverage of these topics. The version that was most widely distributed in the Carolingian Empire, especially under Louis the Pious, was that attributed to the Emperor Germanicus. However, an independent translation of the whole poem, in Latin prose, was also made in Gaul, in the seventh or eighth century, and is known as the *Aratus Latinus.*

As with the computus, a good deal of research was put into the creation of expanded editions of the *Aratea* textual corpus, and the results are found, in varying versions, in the surviving luxury copies.[23] It does not appear that the texts were perceived as literary classics, but rather as repositories of authoritative information on technical subjects. One reason for the popularity of the Germanicus translation may have been that, unlike Aratus' original, it describes the constellations and star groups as they are seen from Earth, rather than as seen from outside the universe (and thus in mirror image). However, it is rather shorter than the original poem, and omits some potentially important astronomical information, as well as parts of the meteorological section. This problem was dealt with by the use of material from other sources, including

---

[21] See notes 12 and 13 above.

[22] See Katharina Volk, 'The World of the Latin *Aratea*' in T. Fuhrer and M. Erler, Eds., *Cosmologies et cosmogonies dans la litterature antique*, Vandoeuvres, Fondation Hardt, 2015, pp. 253–289.

[23] For details see Dolan, *Astronomical Knowledge Transmission*, esp. pp. 185–227.

varying versions of the established weather signs, to produce expanded editions of this text. Given the borrowings noted above, it is unsurprising that the weather signs found in the *Aratea* are very close to those recorded by Pliny; once again, special importance is accorded to the appearance of the Sun and the Moon. For instance, if the Moon appears 'slender and clear around its third day' this is a sign of good weather, but a red appearance on the same day foretells wind.[24] The fourth day is again significant, and if the Moon then appears faint and with 'blunted horns' this means that a south wind, or rain, are close. Related information is also given by Virgil in *Georgics I*, (lines 351–514), which includes the statements (at lines 429–33) that a pink blush on the horned Moon predicts wind, and that the Moon's appearance and visibility on the fourth day of each lunar month are especially significant.[25]

A more technical account of both astronomical and astrological knowledge was provided by the work usually known as the *Astronomica*. This long, didactic poem of the early first century CE was the work of one Manilius, of whom little is known. It was studied at least by a few experts in Ottonian Europe, although it never achieved the status or popularity of the works already discussed. It gave clear, if somewhat individualistic, expositions of most of the technical concepts applied in both cosmological and astrological texts. The most celebrated scholar to discover it and to request a copy was Gerbert of Aurillac, the future Pope Sylvester II. Gerbert wrote in 988 to the archbishop of Rheims to report that he had discovered 'eight volumes' of work on *astrologia*, which he believed to be by Boethius (ca. 480–524 CE). Boethius' full name was Anicius Manlius Severinus Boethius, which helps to explain Gerbert's excitement. Like Isidore he played a major role in transmitting classical knowledge to the medieval West; and his work on *The Consolation of Philosophy* was widely read throughout the medieval period.[26] Gerbert was staying in the northern-Italian monastery of Bobbio at this time, and it was from Bobbio that he later requested a copy of the work by 'Manilius or

[24] For the original version see Aratus, *Phaenomena* in A. Mair and G. Mair, Trans., *Callimachus, Lycophron, Aratus,* Loeb Classical Library, Cambridge, Harvard University Press, 1921, pp. 262–263.

[25] *Georgics,* Book I, in H. Rushton Fairclough, Ed and Trans., *Virgil: Eclogues, Georgics, Aeneid I-VI,* Loeb Classical Library, Cambridge, Harvard University Press, 3rd edition, 1999, pp. 98–135.

[26] On Boethius' own knowledge and handling of astronomy see: S. McCluskey, 'Boethius' Astronomy and Cosmology', in N. Kaylor and P. Phillips, Eds., *A Companion to Boethius in the Middle Ages,* Leiden, Brill, 2012, pp. 47–73; and M. Fournier, 'Boethius and the Consolation of the Quadrivium', *Medievalia et Humanistica,* N.S., 34, 2008, pp. 1–21.

Manlius' on *astrologica*.[27] The misattribution to Boethius helps to explain the acceptance of this work. However, study of the poem appears to have dropped when new translations of clearer versions of astrological material became available in the twelfth century.[28]

Manilius was unhelpful for anyone wishing to make a weather forecast, or to understand the scientific basis on which such a forecast could be made. The poem is also frustrating for those interested in late-classical astrological ideas, since it gives a detailed account of the construction of astrological charts whilst scarcely mentioning the roles or positions of the planets. The comments on weather assert that regional climates and local weather patterns are determined by the stars and are in harmony with the overall, rational design of the universe – but he gives no details. Much more traditional in its views, and more popular in the Carolingian period, was a shorter *Poetica astronomica*. This was believed to be the work of Hyginus (ca. 64 BCE–17 CE), the superintendent of the Palatine Library under the Emperor Augustus. The literary standard of this work is not high, but it was widely quarried as well as being copied in full. No fewer than 11 versions of it survive from the Carolingian period alone, most of these found together with *Aratea* material.[29] However, Hyginus added nothing new to the overall body of knowledge in relation to meteorology and weather prediction.

It is now important to turn to the astronomical knowledge actually transmitted by these works, and to the question of whether the planetary positions depicted in images like that in the Leiden *Aratea* could have been worked out by astronomical calculation. Disappointingly, but in accord with the preceding analysis of astronomical texts, the planetary positions prove to have been worked established using very simple techniques.[30] The position of the Sun in the Leiden example can be found by consulting a calendar showing the dates on which the Sun entered each zodiac sign, and then counting off the appropriate number of days. The position of the Moon is that of a full Moon, in other words at 180 degrees to the Sun, and could thus be very simply worked out. All the planets are depicted in the image as being either at the start, the end, or the centre of a zodiac sign. There is thus no question of exact calculation. Moreover, direct observation on a clear night in April 816 would in fact have shown Saturn, Jupiter, Mars, Venus and Mercury visible in the sky. Each would

---

[27] For the poem itself see *Manilius, Astronomica,* Ed. and Trans. G. Goold, Loeb Classical Library, Cambridge, Harvard University Press, 3rd edition, 1997. On Gerbert's letters see ibid., p. cviii. The most recent discussion is: K. Volk, *Manilius and His Intellectual Background,* Oxford, Oxford University Press, 2009; the medieval transmission is outlined at pp. 1–2.

[28] Dolan, *Transmission,* pp. 99–105.   [29] Ibid., pp. 105–110.   [30] See note 20 above.

also have been visible against the constellation related to the zodiac sign within which they are placed in the planetary diagram. Basic computus and direct observation appear to be all that was needed.

The use of very simple methods is further confirmed by the computistical work of the Carolingian scholar, Hrabanus Maurus (ca. 780–856 CE). This pupil of Alcuin became a great scholar and teacher in his own right, whose works were widely copied, as well as attaining the positions of abbot of the great monastery of Fulda and archbishop of Mainz. Hrabanus' *De computo* gives approval to the study of astronomy within the overall scope of computus, and provides a set of planetary positions, stated to be those of 9 July 820. Hrabanus does not explain how the calculations were made. However, once again the positions of the Sun and Moon can be simply established using the techniques of computus, while those of Venus and Mercury are stated as not available since the planets could not be seen. The latter point strongly suggests the use of direct observation; and the placings of Saturn, Jupiter and Mars in Aries, Libra and Pisces respectively could all be achieved in that way. It thus appears that astronomical knowledge remained largely theoretical in nature, and literary in expression, in this period. Identification of constellations and star groups, with the names and myths attributed to them by classical authors, was accepted as part of scholarship within the classicising milieu of the imperial courts. For Church leaders, and monks in particular, more practical knowledge of the relationships between celestial bodies and timekeeping was also of considerable value. However, planetary positions were primarily established by direct observation, and there was little advance on Bede's techniques for establishing the positions of the great luminaries, the Moon and Sun.

All this is, of course, in contrast to the astronomical and mathematical knowledge brought together in the work of the celebrated astronomer and geographer, Ptolemy of Alexandria (ca. 85–ca. 165 CE). Ptolemy had been able to make a series of observations of planetary positions from Alexandria in the period 127–141 CE, and united these with sophisticated mathematics to produce a model of the movements of the planets that had the great merit of being able to explain and predict to a high level of accuracy the complexities of these movements. However, Ptolemy's great work, the *Mathematical Compilation* (known from the medieval period on as the *Almagest*) appears not to have been translated into Latin until the twelfth century. It is true that a short work known as the *Preceptum canonis Ptolomei*, which was a Latin translation of part of Ptolemy's fundamental *Canons* or *Handy Tables*, seems to have been known in Italy in the sixth century. The best evidence for this comes from Cassiodorus (ca. 480–ca. 575 CE) the politician, scholar, and founder of the great monastery of Vivarium, in southeast Italy. Cassiodorus' work, *The Institutes*, was recommended reading for monks, and includes descriptions and reading lists for the seven liberal arts. Astronomy is listed as the most advanced of these, and Ptolemy is given as the author of three major works on the subject.[31] It is not clear that Cassiodorus had studied these himself; but comments elsewhere in his works hint at knowledge of something like the 'notes' recorded in the *Preceptum*. However, even this would have been of no real help in actual astronomical calculation aiming to go much beyond that already outlined. The *Preceptum* made it possible to calculate the positions of the Sun and Moon, and the dates of eclipses, and explained how to allow for the difference in calendar and location between Alexandria and Rome. However, it gave no data for the other five planets. Moreover, it appears to have been unused until the end of the tenth century.[32]

Nevertheless, it does seem that at least some amongst the computists had an additional tool available, in the form of a text beginning *In quo signo versetur Mars*. This is found in a small number of surviving Carolingian manuscripts.[33] It expounds a method for calculating the positions of the planets, based upon three pieces of information. The first is the officially accepted date in the solar calendar on which the planets were believed to have been first created (as discussed by Bede). The second is the date for which planetary positions are to be calculated, expressed in terms of the year of Creation or *annus mundi*. The final factor is the course and speed of each planet, as set out in texts such as Pliny and the *Seven Book Computus*. With this information it was possible to reach a calculation of the sector of the zodiac within which each planet should be found; and presumably direct observation could be used as a check when possible. This method is approximate, to say the least, but it appears to have found an audience. Three surviving collections of computistical texts, all produced in northern France in the ninth century, contain this treatise. Given the relatively low survival rate of such manuscripts this suggests that the method was fairly well known in Carolingian monasteries. One of the manuscripts is now Melk, Stiftsbibliothek

---

[31] Eastwood, *Ordering the Heavens*, p. 3.

[32] See S. McCluskey, *Astronomies and Cultures*, p. 115. For the text, and a more positive view of Carolingian use, see D. Pingree, 'The Preceptum canonis Ptolomei', in J. Hamesse and M. Fattori, Eds., *Rencontres de Cultures dans la Philosophie Medievale: Traductions et Traducteurs de l'Antiquite Tardive au XIVe Siecle*, Louvain-la-Neuve, Publications de l'Institut d'Etudes Medievales-Textes, 1990, pp. 355–375.

[33] See D. Juste, 'Neither Observation nor Astronomical Tables. An Alternative Way of Computing the Planetary Longitudes in the Early Western Middle Ages' in C. Burnett et al., Eds., *Studies in the History of the Exact Sciences in Honour of David Pingree*, Leiden, Brill, 2004, pp. 181–222.

Ms 412 (370. G 32), and is important because it was consulted by an expert in the field of computus. This was Helperic, monk and teacher of Auxerre and Grandval, who produced his own textbook on computus in the late ninth century.[34] This was well received and continued to be used well into the twelfth century, perhaps because it promised to make computus more accessible to pupils new to the subject. More than eighty manuscripts containing it have been identified.[35] In practice it added little to Bede's work; but this in itself provides evidence as to the state of meteorological knowledge ca. 900.

This enquiry has shown that considerable study of astronomy took place in the ninth century, even if the actual gains in knowledge were limited. What has emerged is that belief in the power of celestial bodies over earthly phenomena was well established, although attempts at weather forecasting continued to be dependent upon lists of old-established weather signs. This continued to be the case in the tenth century, although it is important to recognise the impact of the subdivision of what had been the Carolingian Empire. The increasing localisation of power and scholarship that characterises this period makes it necessary to adopt a new approach. This will be to consider the evidence of individual manuscripts, in order to establish whether new knowledge was incorporated into new editions of the relevant works. No attempt will be made to catalogue all the manuscripts that contain versions of the main corpus of material, but some figures can be given. Dolan has identified at least sixty manuscripts containing *Aratea* texts.[36] King lists seventy-one manuscripts with all or part of the extracts from Pliny.[37] An important finding is that the main new development was the increasingly sophisticated use of complex images, diagrams and tables to convey central concepts in visual form. This is significant since the dedication of so much effort to communication and reinterpretation in itself demonstrates the perceived stability of the knowledge on which they were based.[38]

---

[34] The main edition of this work is still that in Migne, Ed., *Patrologia Latina*, vol. 137, cols. 17–20.

[35] P. Nothaft, *Scandalous Error: Calendar Reform and Calendrical Astronomy in Medieval Europe*, Oxford, Oxford University Press, 2018, p. 34.

[36] See note 12 above.   [37] King, Investigation, pp. 70–73.

[38] B. Eastwood, *The Revival of Planetary Astronomy in Carolingian and Post-Carolingian Europe*, 1st edition, Ashgate, 2002; 2nd edition, Abingdon and New York, Routledge, 2018; and with G. Graßhoff, *Planetary Diagrams for Roman Astronomy in Medieval Europe, c800–1500; Transactions of the American Philosophical Society*, Vol. 94, Part 3, Philadelphia, American Philosophical Society, 2004. A list of manuscripts with such diagrams is given in the latter, at pp. 149–156.

An example of the scholarship that went into re-edited versions of the material is provided by a volume whose script and illuminations suggest an origin in the late tenth century, at the monastery of St Bertin, at St Omer.[39] Its core text is closely related to the Leiden *Aratea,* but further astronomical material from Isidore, and also Martianus Capella, is added. Martianus was a poet and scholar of the fifth century CE, whose long and elaborate poem, *De nuptiis Philologiae et Mercurii (On the Marriage of Philology and Mercury)* was popular with scholars from the sixth to the twelfth century. At least 241 manuscripts of the work are known, with the earliest datable to the ninth century.[40] Martianus provides detailed descriptions of the subject matter covered by the seven liberal arts, and his account of astronomy favours the view that Mercury and Venus circle the Sun, which itself moves around the Earth. The St Bertin compilation pays special attention to Aratus' weather signs, which appear on folios 30v to 33r. The compiler makes the coverage of Aratus' information complete by adding lines from the fourth-century Latin 'edition' and translation composed by the aristocrat and scholar, Avienus.[41] A reader could find detailed instruction here about the effects of each zodiac sign, and each planet, on the weather during the relevant season of the solar year. Actual forecasting was not possible on this basis; but the interest in factors affecting weather is clear. This 'extended edition' of Aratus represented an advance of knowledge that was prized, since it was re-copied ca. 1000 for St Mary's, Strasbourg, and presented there by Bishop Werinhar (1001–1028).[42]

Equally significant is the fact that the information on weather signs was sought out and added into manuscripts that did not originally have it. The volume now London, British Library, Ms Harley 647, was produced in the ninth century at an unknown centre, and contains Cicero's version of the *Aratea.* It has a set of the usual weather signs added in the margins of the astronomical section, possibly copied from a computistical collection.[43] It appears to have been brought to England, in this state, by the tenth century. Much more 'modern' is Harley 2506, which is entirely

---

[39] This is now Boulogne-sur-Mer, Bibliotheque Municipale, Ms 188.

[40] R. Copeland and I. Sluiter, 'Martianus Capella, *De Nuptiis Philologiae et Mercurii* CA 420–490', in their edited volume *Medieval Grammar and Rhetoric: Language Arts and Literary Theory, AD 300–1475,* Oxford, Oxford University Press, 2012, pp. 148–166, at p. 149.

[41] On Avienus' *Phaenomena* see E. Gee, *Aratus and the Astronomical Tradition,* chapter 6. For text and commentary see J. Soubiran, *Aviénus: Les Phénomènes d'Aratos,* Paris, C.U.F., 1981.

[42] For discussion, and description of the manuscript (now Bern Ms 88) see K. Lippincott, 'The textual tradition of the Germanicus *Aratea*' at www.kristenlippincott.com/the-saxl-project/manuscripts/classical-literary-tradition/revised-aratus-latinus/ (accessed February 2018).

[43] King, Investigation, pp. 83–85.

tenth century, appears to have been produced in England, and also contains the Cicero *Aratea*. Here the weather signs section is integrated as a chapter, and draws on other sources in addition to those found in Harley 647, some of them recent. The range of research that went into this volume is shown by the fact that it contains works not only by the established authorities, in the form of Hyginus and Martianus Capella, but also by the Carolingian commentator on those authors, Remigius of Auxerre. Coming completely up to date, it also contains work by the monk, teacher, and scholar, Abbo of Fleury (ca. 945–1004). Abbo established a reputation for his expertise in theology, astronomy, and mathematics, as well as his contribution to the movement for monastic reform. It was very probably Abbo himself who transmitted much of the meteorological knowledge collected in Harley 2506, whilst teaching at the monastery of Ramsey, 985–987.[44] Its influence in England is shown by the fact that one section of the compound volume, now British Library Ms Cotton Tiberius B V, was probably copied in England in the early eleventh century, and combines computistical material with the Cicero *Aratea* and Pliny's information on weather signs. It seems that in England this combination of texts was also long-lasting; related versions are still found in a computistical volume produced at Peterborough ca. 1100.[45]

Evidence from surviving, ninth-century manuscripts produced in France shows that the established computistical and meteorological texts retained their authority in mainland Europe.[46] The dominant 'edition' of this material was based on selections from the 7 Book Computus, and simply had Pliny's information on weather signs in Book 5, as usual. This reached the powerful abbey of Fulda in the tenth century, perhaps from St Gall, as is shown by a fragment now comprising pp. 177–224 of Einsiedeln Ms 266.[47] It can thus be argued that there was an 'old meteorology', which proved very long-lived, and which continued to be transmitted with computistical material, even as new work was done in the latter field. This is evidenced, for instance, by Paris, BnF, Ms 12117, a manuscript from St Germain des Près and datable to 1031–1060. To a

---

[44] On Harley 2506 see Dekker, Observations, p. 146; and M. Lapidge, 'Abbot Germanus, Winchcombe, Ramsey and the Cambridge Psalter', in M. Korhammer et al., Eds., *Words, Texts and Manuscripts; Studies in Anglo-Saxon Culture Presented to Helmut Gneuss*, Woodbridge, Brewer, 1992, pp. 99–129.

[45] The volume is now divided between BL, Cotton Tiberius C I (fols 2–42) and BL Harley 3667.

[46] For instance, Montpellier, Bibliotheque Municipale, Ms H. 334 (origin unknown) and Paris, BNF, Ms. Lat. 5543 (from Fleury).

[47] This can be viewed online at: www.e-codices.unifr.ch/de/sbe/0266/177/0/Sequence-998 (accessed June 2019).

selection from the Seven Book Computus this adds the newer computistical works of Abbo of Fleury and Helperic of Auxerre; but the meteorology is still that of Pliny's weather signs. Still more surprising is Rome, Ms Vat. Reg. Lat. 123, a collection of astronomical texts and information. This is datable to 1056 and is probably from Ripoll, well established by that time as a centre for the reception of Greek and Arabic science. Its astronomical texts are impressively wide-ranging and 'modern' and yet Pliny's information on weather (wrongly attributed to Macrobius) is still combined with material from Bede to form a chapter on 'Signs of Storms and Fair Weather'.[48]

This survey has demonstrated that the established, classically derived information on weather signs was sought after and respected. Knowledge of authoritative signs of coming weather clearly formed a part of the expert knowledge of computists. The ancient weather signs are also found added into other scientific collections, as late as the middle of the eleventh century, such as the extensive astronomical collection from Ripoll. Even in the twelfth century, they still appear as appendices to much newer work on subjects such as geography and natural philosophy.[49] They thus appear to have been an uncontested part of natural philosophical knowledge, and it might appear that 'superstitious' beliefs such as those recorded by Agobard in the early ninth century had long been rejected by ca. 1000. However, evidence from Anglo-Saxon England suggests that there at least this was not the case.

In the case of Anglo-Saxon England, many monastic houses were destroyed, shrunk, or radically restructured during the long wars and invasions of the ninth century. A widespread movement of re-foundation under royal and aristocratic patronage followed in the tenth century, and teachers and leaders were brought into England from highly regarded European centres. A central figure for this enquiry is Aelfric, monk of the Old Minster, Winchester, in the 970s, Abbot of Eynsham ca. 1005–1010, and prolific author of instructional works for monks, priests, and laity. His reputation was such that he was asked by Wulfsige, bishop of Sherborne, and Wulfstan, archbishop of York, to write Pastoral Letters for dissemination to clergy in their dioceses. Much of the emphasis in these writings was on the duty of clerics to give care and instruction to the laity, as well as to be fully educated themselves. The distribution and the survival of his works suggest strongly that they proved both useful and

---

[48] King, Investigation, pp. 115–17.
[49] See, for example, the volume now Paris Ms 11130, which unites materials from Bede with new works by William of Conches, and adds eight chapters that are actually the Pliny text on weather.

hard to replace. For meteorology the key text is his *De Temporibus Anni* (*The Divisions of the Year*). This is a very short primer on computus, written in Old English despite its Latin title, and intended to help priests to understand the liturgical year and to inform lay people on matters related to the calendar.[50] Aelfric clearly did not assume that his readers would be literate in Latin, and he did not attempt to teach them to make independent calculations on the movements of the planets or even on the dates of movable feasts. Nevertheless, the work is frequently found within collections of computistical and liturgical pieces.[51]

Aelfric expounds very basic topics. The account of the seasons is a shortened version of Bede's, where the reader is again told that it is the Sun that brings both light and heat to the Earth. The extreme example is Egypt (remote and exotic to Anglo-Saxon Christians, yet familiar from the Bible), which, due to its position in relation to the Sun's path, never experiences rainfall or winter. That it is nevertheless fertile and habitable is due to the presence of the Nile, and its annual floods. A simple account of cosmology follows, explaining also that the Earth has five distinct climatic zones. Much of Bede's information on factors determining actual weather (as opposed to more general climates) is omitted. The exposition of the lunar calendar that follows includes a clear condemnation of any attempt to predict the future by the Moon.[52]

Aelfric spends a relatively long time on the phases of the Moon and how they relate to the position of the Sun. He stresses that any belief that the Moon can turn itself in relation to the Sun, and that this can be used to predict the weather, is erroneous. Informed observation of the colour of the Moon, the Sun and the sky is the preserve of experts, who can judge 'what kind of weather is approaching'. The following sections deal with the stars and the winds. Aelfric is at pains to state that the courses of the seven planets are very complex, and the details of their movements would be unbelievable to the unlearned. He does give examples of selected stars and constellations that can reliably be observed from the northern hemisphere, and considerable space is given to the explanation of the air, its necessity for human life, its extent and the fact that it contains the clouds and storms as well as constituting the winds, when it is stirred up. A version of the standard list of the main winds, their characteristics and the types of weather conditions that they bring, follows. Thus the easterly wind is 'very moderate', whilst the southerly brings clouds, lightning and plagues. The westerly is essential for life, since it brings warmth and moisture, ending winter with its annual

[50] See *Aelfric's De Temporibus Anni*, Ed. M. Blake, Cambridge, D.S. Brewer, 2009.
[51] On the surviving manuscripts, ibid., p. 41.   [52] Ibid., pp. 90–91.

arrival, and finally the north wind brings cold, snow and dry clouds. Of the eight intermediate winds Aelfric comments that it would be tedious and over-complex to give details, but does note that the north-easterly counters the effects of the southerly wind, since by being high, cold, and very dry it drives away the plague brought by the south wind.

Rain is important enough to have a section of its own, which first points out that it too is part of God's system. The usual scientific explanation that the air draws up moisture from the earth and the sea, until it becomes saturated, and then lets it fall down as rain is briefly expounded. This pattern is also affected by wind and by the heat of the Sun. Biblical examples are used to support all this. Aelfric feels called upon to stress that it is perfectly explicable that salty sea water can be turned into un-salty rain through the action of the Sun and the air. All this is part of the fact that God's omnipotence encompasses power over the weather. Similarly, hail is simply rain that has been frozen before falling, whilst snow results when moisture is frozen in a semi-vaporous state, before it forms drops. The treatise concludes with an explanation of thunder. The air has the capacity to draw both heat from the Sun and water from the earth into itself, and when they are forced together by this process they 'struggle' and burst out as thunder and lightning. If the heat prevails, fiery lightning will be produced, to the detriment of crops; but if the water is stronger rain will result. This explains why a hot summer will produce more thunder storms than a cool one, we are told. Overall, Aelfric makes it clear that amateur interpretation of events such as thunder storms should be condemned, and a particularly fierce thunderstorm is not to be immediately seized upon as a portent. Such storms may be loud and bright enough to produce fear, but they are still to be accepted first and foremost as natural phenomena. And here the whole work ends.

This strongly suggests that prediction and interpretation of weather were matters of contention between learned ecclesiastics and those whom they sought to inform and educate. Further evidence comes from Aelfric's homilies. His 'Sermon on the Octaves and Circumcision of Our Lord' was to be delivered on 1 January.[53] It launches an attack on the foolish, pagan practice of carrying out 'divinations' (*wigelunga*) on this day. Once again the Moon features heavily, and once again the separation of the natural and scientific from the superstitious is a major

---

[53] See *Aelfric's Catholic Homilies; The First Series: Text*, Ed. P. Clemoes, Oxford, Oxford University Press for the Early English Text Society, Supplementary Series, 17, 1997, at pp. 228–229.

concern.[54] A custom of 'regulating travel' by the Moon is specifically rejected, but it is a scientific fact that every living creature on earth, including trees and plants, is affected by the phases of the Moon. The link between the Moon and the tides is also stressed as natural, and nothing to do with divination. That 'scientific' prediction of the weather did not come under suspicion as divination or magic is confirmed by Aelfric's 'Sermon on the Greater Litany', known as *De auguriis*.[55] Here the forbidden questions focus on things such as health, travel, marriage, brewing, making a journey, and timing personal decisions; no mention is made of attempting to forecast the weather.

This suggests a perceived need to establish acceptable knowledge on matters of cosmology and meteorology. However, Aelfric himself does not emerge as an expert on scientific matters. Indeed, his emphasis on the difficulty of computus perhaps helps to show how much the scholarship and scientific expertise brought to England by Abbo of Fleury were needed. Abbo had studied at Rheims, alongside Gerbert of Aurillac (the future Pope Sylvester II), and gained a grounding in mathematics and cosmology. When he entered the influential abbey of Fleury he would have found there one of the largest libraries in western Europe, with a collection of classical texts started in the ninth century.[56] Abbo was one of the select company of scholars in the late tenth century who understood complex arithmetical and geometric calculations. His own work on computus embodies a thorough revision of the Carolingian collections. It had not only carefully selected tables, but also clear explanations and instructions. The result could, it has been argued, be used by a 'reasonably well-educated priest', not only by a specially trained monk.[57]

Abbo's teaching in England was restricted to the years 985–987, at Ramsey.[58] However, he had an enthusiastic pupil in Byrhtferth, monk of Ramsey, whose works made Abbo's instruction more widely available. Byrhtferth wrote: a newly edited work on computus (which survives only in twelfth-century versions); and the commentary known as his

[54] For further discussion, and comparison, see L. Chardonnens, 'Aelfric and the Authorship of the Old English De diebus malis' in C. Giliberto and L. Teresi, Eds., *Limits to Learning; The Transfer of Encyclopaedic Knowledge in the Early Middle Ages*, Leuven/Paris/Walpole, Peeters, 2013, pp. 123–154. On divisions of the year in Anglo-Saxon England see also E. Anderson, 'The Seasons of the Year in Old English', *Anglo-Saxon England*, 26, 1997, pp. 231–263.

[55] Aelfric, *Aelfric's Lives of Saints*, Ed. W. Skeat, E.E.T.S., 76, London, 1881, pp. 364–383.

[56] See M. Mostert, *The Library of Fleury: A Provisional List of Manuscripts*, Middeleeuwswse Studies en Bronnen, 3, Verloren, Hilversum, 1989, Introduction.

[57] Ibid., p. xlv.

[58] For details see R. Wright, 'Abbo of Fleury in Ramsey (985–987), in E. Taylor, Ed., *Conceptualising Multilingualism in England, c800–c1250*, Brepols, Turnhout, 2011.

Enchiridion.[59] These offer instruction on such technical matters as how to calculate the dates of eclipses (both lunar and solar), unusually high tides, the first risings of specified stars and full Moons. This was combined with information on the winds, much more detailed than that of Aelfric. Sadly, his *Enchiridion* has very little to say on meteorology. It begins, as would be expected, with the structures and component parts of the various years, and the cosmological factors that determine them.[60] Further details on the zodiac and the Sun's course through it are given in the section on 'The Twelve Months'.[61] Data relevant to meteorological matters is largely restricted to the entries for the beginnings of spring, summer, autumn and winter. The only additional entry is in May, which is described as 'blooming and fruitful'.

Pedagogic intent is shown in the following section, which is addressed to 'young priests' and emphasises how they in turn should instruct their clerks. A key theme here is that the year, the natural world, and aspects of human life and experience are all held together in an ordered pattern. Central to this are the four seasons, themselves based on the equinoxes and solstices. Assigned to each season are two qualities that relate the seasons to the humours and the elements as well as the type of weather to be expected. Thus spring is wet and warm, summer is warm and dry, autumn is dry and cold, and winter is cold and wet. The idea that all natural things are harnessed into this structure is emphasised by a diagram, in which these basic correlations are set out. It is accompanied by a short text stating that the learned may find such things contemptibly simple, but that they are helpful in showing to the unlearned what computistical knowledge can do.

The insistence that correct understanding of the weather was part of the full understanding of God's creation, and that this was reserved for highly trained clerics, is clear. Whether the technicalities of computus were in tension with the short, 'prognostic', texts that offered instant information on a range of coming events remains a matter of debate. These texts were long categorised as magical and superstitious by modern scholarship, and have thus been kept very separate from the history of science. However, both Byrhtferth's works and contemporary computistical collections from mainland Europe contain numerous examples, which demonstrate that their status in the tenth and eleventh

---

[59] Byrhtferth, *Byrhtferth's Enchiridion*, Ed. M. Lapidge and P. Baker, Oxford, Oxford University Press for E.E.T.S., Supplementary Series, 15, 1995. It has been estimated that Byrhtferth quotes in all from over 100 classical and patristic writings. See M. Lapidge, Introduction, in *Byrhtferth of Ramsey: The Lives of St Oswald and St Ecgwine*, Ed. and Trans. M. Lapidge, Oxford, Clarendon, 2009, at p. xxiii.
[60] Ibid., p. 5.   [61] Starting at pp. 56–57.

centuries was high.[62] A twelfth-century 'edition' of Byrhtferth's computus, now Oxford, St John's College, Ms 17, contains a widely copied prognostic known as the *Revelatio Esdrae* (Prophecy of Esdras).[63] This and related prognostics also occur in a series of volumes belonging to leading individuals within the English Church.[64] Moreover, the other textual contents of these manuscripts range from liturgical works, through medical treatises and computi, to collections of sermons. This suggests that prognostics formed part of the knowledge primarily available to, and mediated by, senior members of the clergy, and were not simply relegated to the classroom.

Prediction of the weather in this period was thus required to conform to a strong belief in the rationality and order of God's created universe. It is this that provides the clearest context for the prognostic texts, which themselves depend crucially upon the acceptance of reliable, and thus predictive, connections between different levels of God's world. The weather signs, which simply consisted of long lists of very disparate phenomena, each linked to a particular meteorological outcome, made no attempt to explain causes or patterns. They thus resisted being satisfactorily integrated into the structured world so triumphantly brought together by the computists. For the same reasons they were incapable of being reduced to diagrammatic or tabular form, again in contrast to the prognostics. This was problematic, given that such visual and technical presentations were increasingly popular in works on computus, perhaps because they demonstrated the integrative power of this world view at the same time as offering practical tools for its application. The lack of clear structure, together with the absence of aids such as metre and rhyme, would also mean that accurate memorisation would require a considerable effort, even in a period when memorisation was a standard part of education. The long lists of weather signs certainly tend not to appear in volumes designed to be portable and to be used in a variety of situations, whereas the prognostics are found in such contexts. However, their long-lasting transmission in computistical collections suggests that this was

---

[62] There is a growing literature on this subject. For discussion see especially: R. Liuzza, 'Anglo-Saxon Prognostics in Context: A Survey and Handlist of Manuscripts', *Anglo-Saxon England*, 30, 2001, pp. 181–230; Liuzza, *Anglo-Saxon Prognostics: An Edition and Translation of Texts from London, British Library, MS Cotton Tiberius A iii*, Woodbridge, Brewer, 2010; and L. Chardonnens, *Anglo-Saxon Prognostics, 900–1100: Study and Texts*, Leiden/Boston, Brill, 2007.

[63] On this see especially M. Cesario, 'Weather Prognostics in Anglo-Saxon England', *English Studies*, 93, 4, 2012, pp. 391–426. For other weather prognostics see Cesario, 'An English Source for a Latin Text? Wind Prognostication in Oxford, Bodleian, Hatton 115 and Ashmole 345', *Studies in Philology*, 112, 2, 2015, pp. 213–233.

[64] For contemporary continental examples see Cesario, 2012.

not seen as a reason to reject them in more scientific and academic contexts.

The fullest Anglo-Saxon collection of prognostics is found in BL Cotton Ms Tiberius A iii, which was probably produced in Canterbury Cathedral Priory in the middle of the eleventh century. Overall, its contents are those required for the running of the priory. The prognostics included range from fairly long works providing interpretations of things seen in dreams, via a group tabulating how the Moon affected human affairs and the human body across a lunar month, to predictions based upon or related to the weather. Of the latter, two are versions of the *Revelatio Esdrae*, one offers predictions of the characteristics of individual months, and two use the occurrence of thunderstorms as the basis for offering predictions of a range of affairs and events. Similarly comprehensive is the collection gathered together in the volume known as 'Aelfwine's Prayerbook', now also in the Cotton Collection, as Mss Titus D xxvi and xxvii.[65] The Aelfwine in question was a monk of the New Minster, Winchester, in the early eleventh century, before becoming its abbot in 1031 or 1032. The volume contains a collection of computistical material to which is added a version of the *Revelatio Esdrae*. A separate section contains medical texts, together with information on how human activities were related to days in each month. It is this later section that includes a special collection of prognostics, one of which uses acceptable signs to forecast coming weather, including the colour of the sun and the moon. Short as it is this text draws upon multiple sources, one of them either Aelfric, or his own source, Bede. The *Revelatio Esdrae* appears here again, as does another set of predictions based upon the observation of thunder. Also included in the volume are such matters as discussions of the measurements of Christ's cross and body, and the significance of the numbers involved. Once again, the prognostics seem to emphasise that the created world could be understood in complex, yet rational and Christian, ways by those with the skills required.[66]

How then would such a person understand matters such as climate, season and the forecasting of weather? Given the completeness of the materials in Aelfwine's Prayerbook, the starting point will be that

---

[65] The manuscripts have been digitised and can be viewed on the British Library website. See: www.bl.uk/manuscripts/FullDisplay.aspx?ref=Cotton_MS_Titus_D_XXVI; and www.bl.uk/manuscripts/FullDisplay.aspx?ref=Cotton_MS_Titus_D_XXVII (accessed June 2019). See also B. Günzel, Ed., *Aelfwine's Prayerbook: B.L. Cotton Titus D. xxvi +xxvii*, Woodbridge, Boydell and Brewer for the Henry Bradshaw Society, 108, 1993.

[66] For a related argument, and discussion of the choices made by individual compilers, see R. Liuzza, 'What the Thunder Said: Anglo-Saxon Brontologies and the Problem of Sources', *Review of English Studies*, 55, no. 218, 2004, pp. 1–23.

volume. Its calendar provides notes of the beginning of each season and of the sun's entry into each zodiac sign. Spring begins on 7 February, summer begins on 9 May, the ninety-two days of autumn on 7 August, and the ninety-one (or ninety-two) days of winter on 7 November. However, the vernal equinox is placed as usual on 21 March, the autumn equinox on 20 September, the summer solstice on 20 June and the winter solstice on 21 December. The dates of the sun's passage from each sign to the next are listed, and the medically dangerous Dog Days are noted from 17 July to 5 September. Notes at the top and bottom of the pages comment on characteristics of each month, such as whether they are hot or cold. On folio 25r comes the *Revelatio Esdrae*, in a version whose predictions are based on the weekday on which 1 January falls in a given year, something that could easily be calculated from this calendar. The 'Revelation' provides three types of information about each year in the seven-year sequence: a weather forecast divided by seasons, forecasts for agricultural yields, and forecasts for human health and affairs. As might be expected, a year with 1 January falling on a Sunday has positive predictions. Winter will be good, spring windy and summer dry; there will be abundance of wine, cattle, and honey; and there will be peace for humanity. A 'Monday' year is more mixed, while Tuesday years are to be dreaded, as are years determined by Saturn's day.

The volume in its original form continued with matters of chronology (past, present and future) up to the coming of Antichrist. The intricate interaction of earthly and heavenly matters is again emphasised by the provision of a text intended to accompany a diagram on the measurements of the Cross and of Christ's body, and their significance. Following this diagram comes information on the distances from the Earth to the Moon, from the Moon to the Sun and from the Sun to the belt of the zodiac. Next we learn that, if the Moon on its fourth day is warmed in colour as if gold, then the wind will blow strongly, but if its colour is clear then the weather will be calm. A dark shadow on the upper horn of a crescent Moon is a sign of rain, as is a cloud covering the rising Sun. If the Sun at this same time shines redly then the day will be clear, but if it pales the air will be stormy. If it rises clear but turns red early in the morning then the day will be stormy, and if it reddens towards evening then the following day will be calm. This latter pair of points is related to the well-known, and biblically attested, prediction about red skies (Matthew 16:2–3.)

Equally biblical is the interest in the rainbow that dominates the next section. This 'arch also known as iris' was, of course, referred to several times in the Bible, and was attested as a possible sign from God. Aelfwine's book notes that the rainbow has four colours (as stated by

Bede) and is formed when the sun shines 'against' the clouds (a slightly obscure version of Bede's account). Newer assertions are that the four colours are derived from the four elements, and that the rainbow only appears when the moon is full. The next set of entries offer further prognostics, including one that interprets thunder as a sign, according to the hour of the day or night at which it is heard. Thus meteorological events can be predictors as well as the subjects of prediction, and here thunder can predict both weather and crop yields. The next text, headed 'Signs of Times' (*incipiunt signa de temporibus*) is a better version of the *Revelatio Esdrae*, again using the weekday of 1 January as the basis for its predictions. Who then could doubt that a trained priest could interpret and predict the weather as well as help the sick and calculate appropriate times for medical treatments?

Also relevant is a tenth-century Psalter, frequently linked to Winchester but possibly from Glastonbury or Abingdon.[67] It is now BL Royal 2 B v, and has computistical and prognostic texts added in a slightly later hand on folio 190 (r and v). These combine another thunder prognostic with information on the age of the world, its size and the measurements of Noah's Ark, the Temple and St Peter's. Another example is provided by the surviving sections of a late eleventh-century volume from Christ Church, Canterbury, now divided between BL Cotton Caligula A xv (folios 120–153) and BL Egerton 3314 (folios 9–72).[68] The Egerton section is in Latin, and links computistical extracts with information on the heavens, on winds and on rain, amongst other topics. The compiler has drawn upon the work of Bede, Isidore and Hrabanus Maurus, as well as Aelfric, and added a long extract on the months on fols. 14r–17v. The latter is attributed to the monk and mathematician of Reichenau, Hermannus Contractus (1013–1054).[69] Further information on matters relevant to weather, on folios 45r–72, was striking enough to lead a fourteenth-century librarian to insert the subheading: *Libellus de aeris inpressionibus* ('Treatise on the Weather'). This term was usually applied to (later) works on weather forecasting, and its introduction here suggests that all potentially reliable guidance on this subject was worthy of special notice.

---

[67] D. Dumville, *English Caroline Script and Monastic History*, p. 14.

[68] See P. Willetts, 'A Reconstructed Astronomical Manuscript from Christ Church Library, Canterbury', *British Museum Quarterly*, 30, 1965–1966, pp. 22–30.

[69] Hermannus' work on astronomy and the astrolabe has been more studied than his computus. His treatise on eclipses, *Prognostica de defectu solis et lunae*, and his 'Rules for Computus', *Regulae in computum*, have not been edited. For his work on the lunar month, *De mense lunari*, see A. Borst, 'Ein Forschungsbericht Hermanns des Lahmen', *Deutsches Institut für Erforschung des Mittelalters*, 40, 1984, pp. 379–477, at 474–477.

Further evidence of ongoing contest over meteorological knowledge and its possessors is provided by works on 'wisdom', such as the *Dialogue of Solomon and Saturn*. This survives in two manuscripts, now Cambridge, Corpus Christi College, Mss 41 and 422.[70] Ms 422 is also known as the 'Red Book of Darley', and is a complex liturgical compilation of the later eleventh century, which belonged to Darley by the late Middle Ages. The *Solomon and Saturn* texts are in a separate quire at the start of the book, apparently placed there in the twelfth century, and of uncertain origin. Here Solomon stands for the Judaeo-Christian tradition of learning, whilst Saturn stands for the inferior erudition of pagan peoples. Saturn poses challenging questions on subjects including why snow falls, why the waters of the Earth are in constant movement, and how fire and light behave. In each case Solomon knows more, and understands more deeply, than the pagan Saturn. Sadly, the loss of folios means that Solomon's explanations of snow and of the movements of the sea are lost, along with what may have been exchanges on earth and air.

Overall, the long period discussed in this chapter saw the establishment of a widespread and distinctive belief about the nature of the universe as a comprehensible and rationally explicable system. Crucially, this system was both intricately linked to religious doctrine and capable of being depicted as a complex, yet coherent, mechanism. As has been shown, the system brought together versions of classical meteorology, and techniques for weather forecasting of varied origin, and placed them in structured relationships with much else. Its intellectual ambition and spiritual certainty are both striking, as is the fact that modelling and predicting weather had an important place within it. And yet, as the next chapter will show, the narrowness of the knowledge base on which the whole system rested was about to be revealed – with transformative effects.

---

[70] D. Anlezark, Ed., *The Old English Dialogues of Solomon and Saturn*. New ed., Woodbridge, Boydell and Brewer, 2009.

3 Exploratory Encounters with the Work of Arab Astronomers and Meteorologists

The Alchandrean Corpus and Ptolemy's Tetrabiblos

As previous chapters have shown, the early Middle Ages saw considerable interest in both astronomy and meteorology, which was driven by two main groups of users. The first comprised monastic experts on computus, whose works linked the calculations involved in full understanding of the Church's calendar to broader studies of the Earth and its human occupants. The second centred on secular rulers and their advisers, for whom knowledge of the heavens and the Earth was prestigious, associated with power and a potential source of privileged information about the future. However, the knowledge base upon which these studies were constructed was narrowed by the absence of full Latin translations of key works on astronomy, geometry and mathematics. In the late Roman Empire these had been highly specialist subjects, largely the preserve of those who read Greek.[1] Moreover, aristocratic translators such as Cicero had focused on more literary and philosophical texts, such as the work of Aratus, which gave more scope for the display of erudition and style.[2] Boethius' planned series of translations was cut off by his execution, as has been seen.[3] Historical records show astrologers in high demand in the fourth and fifth centuries, but these were practitioners

---

[1] For a thoughtful survey of the debates concerning Roman astrology and the imperial court see S. Green, *Disclosure and Discretion in Roman Astrology: Manilius and His Augustan Contemporaries,* Oxford, Oxford University Press, 2014.

[2] See Chapter 2. On translators and their choices see D. M. Possanza, *Translating the Heavens: Aratus, Germanicus, and the Poetics of Latin Translation,* Bern and New York, Lang, 2004.

[3] References to a work on astronomy by Boethius are found in early medieval sources, as discussed in Chapter 2. Boethius himself wrote, in *The Consolation of Philosophy* and his surviving work on Mathematics, in a way that hints at a planned treatise on Astronomy, but no such work has been found. For discussion see: S. McCluskey, 'Boethius' Astronomy and Cosmology' in N. Kaylor and P. Phillips, Eds., *A Companion to Boethius in the Middle Ages,* Leiden, Brill, 2012, pp. 47–73; and M. Fournier, 'Boethius and the Consolation of the Quadrivium', *Medievalia et Humanistica,* N.S. 34, 2008, pp. 1–21.

whose livelihood depended upon claims to exclusivity, not writers of astronomical textbooks.

A development that radically transformed the world of scientific scholarship as well as international politics, from the seventh century on, was the rapid rise of the Arab Empire. The conquest of a huge zone extending around the southern and eastern coasts of the Mediterranean, north into Spain, and east to the Caspian, the Caucusus and the Indus Valley, brought into being a new culture as well as a new world power. This new society was far less influenced by the structures and values of Roman culture as well as of the Christian religion, and its rulers consciously collected and patronised experts in the important subjects that made available knowledge of the workings of the Earth and the universe. From the eighth century onwards significant investment was put into both the study and the practice of astronomy, geometry, mathematics and all their associated subjects. Symbolic of this is the semi-legendary House of Wisdom created by the ruler al-Ma'mun (813–833 CE) in Baghdad.[4] The products of this investment included not only the composition of a tide of scientific treatises, but also the construction of observatories and laboratories, the making of scientific instruments, and a movement to make available in Arabic the fundamental works of earlier scholars. A growing central conviction was that the planets and the stars played a crucial role in all aspects of human life on Earth. This was not because they were the embodiments or representatives of deities, but because of their scientific function as transmitters and mediators of the powers and forces structured into the universe by its Creator, and their ability to further the wishes of that Creator. By the late tenth century schools for the study of this great body of knowledge were well distributed across the Empire, and the new science was so strongly established as to survive increasing political tensions and fragmentations. Meanwhile, however, in western and northern Europe very little of this work was either available or of interest.

It was not until the end of the tenth century that a few bold seekers of knowledge, such as Gerbert of Aurillac, ventured from Latin, Christian Europe into the borderlands of the Arab world, in the form of northern Spain and Catalonia. Gerbert's own career also gives testimony to the highly divisive nature of the knowledge that he gained.[5] On the one hand

---

[4] See J. al-Khalili, *The House of Wisdom: How Arabic Science Saved Ancient Knowledge and Gave Us the Renaissance*, New York, Penguin, 2011.

[5] See: P. Riché, *Gerbert d'Aurillac, le pape de l'an Mil*, Paris, Fayard, 1987; and A. Schärlig, *Un portrait de Gerbert d'Aurillac: inventeur d'un abaque, utilisateur précoce des chiffres arabes, et pape de l'an mil*, Lausanne, PPUR Presses Polytechniques, 2012.

his new and scarce expertise was welcomed by rulers who fast-tracked his promotion and asked him to teach chosen pupils. On the other hand he was the target of accusations of having fraternised with magicians and even of having become a devil worshipper. It would of course be naïve to regard these accusations as simply a reaction to Gerbert's scientific and mathematical knowledge, since they were led by rivals within the Church hierarchy. Nevertheless, it is equally clear that the nature and the source of Gerbert's expertise provided his enemies with a powerful weapon.

If attention is now turned to the accepted body of knowledge available to those who shared Gerbert's interests in the early eleventh century it becomes clear that it remained restricted and somewhat incoherent, despite increasing sophistication in its deployment. A central element was the set of short texts now known as the Alchandrean Corpus, which was brought together in Catalonia in the late tenth century, and which appears to have drawn on the work of the Cordoban scholar, al Majriti (d. 1007) amongst others.[6] Al Majriti himself was an expert in all the constantly expanding branches of the new science of the stars, who wrote on the accurate calculation of the movement of the planets; the mathematical principles and technical construction of the astrolabe; and the applications of planetary data in the fields of medicine, astrological prediction and weather forecasting. Of course, such work drew upon a large and already compound body of texts and teachings brought together from Greek, Alexandrian, Persian and even Indian sources, as well as Arabic ones, and was aimed at those with related expertise. For travellers from northern Europe equipped with none of the above it posed formidable challenges, especially as fundamental primers and textbooks were apparently not available to them. With the hindsight of what had been translated into Latin and studied by 1200 the Alchandrean Corpus of ca. 1000 appears extremely fragmentary and lacking in practical understanding. Nevertheless, difficult as it was, it had the effect of opening the eyes of would-be scientists to what might be available to be known.

This Alchandrean Corpus included texts on astronomical tables and the more detailed calculation of planetary positions; the making and uses of astrolabes; and medical and astrological applications of this data. It gained prestige from association with the great Alexandrian astronomer, Ptolemy, although it took its name from an introductory outline of astrological procedures attributed to one Alchandreus. For those unable

---

[6] For texts and full discussion see D. Juste, *Les 'Alchandreana' Primitifs*, Brill, Leiden, 2007. C. Burnett, 'King Ptolemy and Alchandreus the Philosopher; the earliest texts on the astrolabe and Arabic astrology at Fleury, Micy and Chartres', *Annals of Science*, 55, 1998, pp. 329–368, is also helpful.

or unwilling to draw up full astrological charts it also offered instructions on how to allocate numerical values to letters, and then to use these to produce answers to various questions. In this it remained linked to some of the texts of prognostication that were already well-known in the Carolingian Empire.[7] However other parts of the collection were much more directly based upon Islamicate astronomy and astrology, as is seen in their detailed calculations of planetary positions for the 'hours' in which questions were posed and, even more clearly, in the importance given to the subdivisions of the moon's observed orbit known as the lunar mansions.

These texts were being studied and copied in northern Europe by ca. 1000, as is shown by various surviving manuscripts. The oldest known manuscript is now Paris, BNF, Ms lat. 17868, which is late tenth century. A copy of the simplified planetary tables that were attributed to Ptolemy survives in B.L. Harley MS 2506, which was produced ca. 1000, perhaps in the abbey of Fleury. The now-destroyed manuscript, once Chartres MS 214, was copied in the early eleventh century and contained both planetary tables and texts on the astrolabe. The same information was also being studied and copied at Reichenau and other centres in what had been the Ottonian Empire, where scholars such as Ascelin of Augsburg and Hermannus Contractus were working to produce better versions of the texts and their contents. Hermannus in particular showed a concern to increase the astronomical accuracy of instruments such as the astrolabe, and to find ways of reconciling the growing gap between the calendar as calculated by computus and the actual movements of the sun and moon. His treatise on the astrolabe, *De mensura astrolabii*, proposed a more accurate scheme for setting out a solar year, and tracking the position of the Sun, on the back of the instrument. He also used a more astronomically accurate, 'modern' date of 18 March for the vernal equinox, rather than continuing to use the Roman date of 25 March (or the Greek one of 21 March).[8] Hermannus also made important advances in mathematical knowledge, which he applied both to innovative versions of the sundial and the quadrant and to his analysis of the measurement of the circumference of the Earth.[9]

---

[7] On such prognostics see Chapter 2.

[8] See S.C. McCluskey, *Astronomies and Cultures in Early Medieval Europe*, Cambridge, Cambridge University Press, 1998, pp. 179–180. The text of *De mensura astrolabii* is edited by R.T. Gunther in *The Astrolabes of the World*, Vol. 2, Oxford, Oxford University Press, 1932, pp. 404–408.

[9] J. Hamel, 'Hermann the Lame' in V. Trimble et al., Eds., *Biographical Encyclopedia of Astronomers*, Vol. 1, New York, Springer, 2007, p. 489. For comment on Hermannus' computistical work see Chapter 2.

Evidence of the advance in astronomical knowledge can be obtained by comparing Hermannus' works with those of Abbo of Fleury, another acclaimed scholar whose teaching on computus had a considerable influence. Abbo found it necessary to write a short explanation of geometry and its application to astronomy for his pupils, which included a technical definition of the difference between a circle and a sphere. Another pedagogic piece that found an audience amongst computists was his explanation of the courses of the Moon and the other planets through the zodiac. This offered a more precise method for finding the position of the Moon than those discussed in Chapter 2.[10] However, Abbo's technique for finding the zodiac sign occupied by any planet remained effectively that based on combining the planet's rate of movement with the period elapsed since the date of its creation. His short explanations of the risings of the signs, and the five climatic zones of the Earth, remained popular into the twelfth century, and are found in collections of computistical materials such as that from Thorney, now Oxford, St John's, Ms 17. Like other computists discussed in the previous chapter, Abbo recommends direct observation as the most reliable means of identifying celestial objects. To help in this he provides notes on the colours, positions in relation to the Sun, and speed of movement of planets. Further certainty is to be gained by observing over several months. If the body under observation moves in relation to the fixed stars then it is a planet.[11] Abbo's main source seems to have been Pliny, and his treatises still depend upon assuming that each planet moves at a uniform speed, even though he also discusses factors that would result in varying speeds.[12] Perhaps most striking is Abbo's unique computistical table in the form of an acrostic poem. This both reads as a poem and provides the data for establishing matters such as the age of the Moon for a chosen date, and its zodiac sign.[13] The combination of erudition and

[10] R. Thomson 'Two Astronomical Treatises of Abbo of Fleury' in J. North and J. Roche, Eds., *The Light of Nature (International Archives of the History of Ideas, 110)*, Dordrecht, Nijhoff/Springer, 1985, pp. 113–133. See also A. van der Vyver, 'Les plus anciennes Traductions latines médiévales (Xe –Xie siècles) de Traités d'Astronomie et d'Astrologie', *Osiris*, 1936, 1, pp. 658–691.

[11] Thomson, 'Two Astronomical Treatises of Abbo of Fleury', p. 115.

[12] Eastwood argues that Abbo knew Pliny's data on astronomy through the Seven Book compilation on computus, although he also made use of Calcidius' *Commentary* on Plato's *Timaeus*. See Eastwood, *Revival of Planetary Astronomy*, chapter two, 'Abbo of Fleury and Calcidius'. For Calcidius' text see *Calcidius: On Plato's Timaeus*, Ed. and Trans. J. Magee, Cambridge, Harvard University Press for Dumbarton Oaks Medieval Library, 2016.

[13] For the poem see M. Lapidge and P. Baker, 'More Acrostic Verse by Abbo of Fleury', *Journal of Medieval Latin*, 7, 1997, pp. 1–27. A digitised image of the acrostic, with commentary, is given by F. Wallis, on the Calendar and the Cloister website:

ingenuity is extraordinary, and the acrostic is also visually striking. It carries to an extreme level the capacity of computus to express its grasp of the workings of heaven and Earth in tabular form; and yet it adds nothing to the body of scientific knowledge.

Scholars needed more data than was provided even in the Alchandrean corpus if real innovations were to be made, and this required further transfer of knowledge from the Islamicate world. An early step was made by Adelard of Bath, when he undertook extended travels through France into Italy, Sicily and Syria in search of scientific knowledge.[14] He seems to have been supported by very powerful patrons, once again demonstrating the perceived advantages which astronomical and meteorological advance could bring. His early career was promoted by John, the bishop of Bath and Wells (d. 1122) who had been a doctor to William the Conqueror, and who undertook a major programme of building work at the site of the Roman baths in Bath.[15] When he returned to England, Adelard seems to have joined the retinue of Henry, son of the Empress Matilda, since he dedicated his own work on the astrolabe, *De opere astrolapsus*, to a young man called Henry, of royal descent and closely related to a king, who was expected to achieve political power. As Haskins first pointed out, this strongly suggests the future Henry II, since candidates with the right name, at the right place and time, are not many.[16]

Adelard did not himself write on astronomy or meteorology, but rather on natural philosophy and on the fundamental importance of advancing understanding of the cosmos and its workings. His address to the young Henry argued that it was the duty of rulers to gain such knowledge. That this was a serious belief is shown by the fact that Adelard also made available in Latin a fundamental body of scientific materials. His text on the astrolabe incorporated new knowledge acquired during his travels, but perhaps of even greater value for his contemporaries were his translations of Euclid's *Elements*, al-Khwarizmi's planetary tables, and Abu Ma'shar's *Abbreviation of the Introduction to Astrology*.[17] Together with his

---

http://digital.library.mcgill.ca/ms-17/folio.php?p=25r&showitem=25r-26r_5Computus TablesTextsII_9EphemeridaAbbonis (accessed June 2019).

[14] For Adelard's statement about his travels in search of Arabic learning see *Quaestiones naturales* in C. Burnett, Ed. and Trans., *Adelard of Bath, Conversations with His Nephew*, Cambridge, Cambridge University Press, 1998, at p. 90.

[15] Ibid., p. xiii.

[16] C.H. Haskins, 'Adelard of Bath and Henry Plantagenet', *E.H.R.*, XXVIII, CXI, July 1913, pp. 515–516.

[17] See C. Burnett, 'Adelard of Bath and the Arabs' in *Rencontres de la culture dans la philosophie medieval; Traductions et traducteurs de l'antiquite tardive au XIVe siècle*, Louvain-La-Neuve, Cassino, 1990; and also, 'The Introduction of Arabic Learning

treatise on the abacus this provided a battery of materials and techniques of use for moving scientific study forward in many fields, not least in those of meteorology and weather forecasting.

Still other innovations were made possible by the arrival north of the Pyrenees of Petrus Alfonsi, a converted Jew from Huesca in the expanding kingdom of Aragon. The exact dates of his career are not known, but he travelled to England as well as to France, and certainly did so before 1135.[18] This is recorded in a treatise written by Walcher of Lorraine, who was Prior of Great Malvern 1120–1135, and who was described in his epitaph as a scholar, philosopher, astrologer, geometrician and abacist. Already in the last years of the eleventh century, Walcher had made observations of eclipses, using his astrolabe to make calculations of the Moon's movements. Building on this he compiled lunar tables based on his own calculations, and primarily intended to be used by physicians. It was in his treatise on the nodes of the Moon, *De dracone*, that Walcher recorded and applied the astronomical teaching he had received from Petrus Alfonsi ca. 1120.[19] This work shows a scholar grappling enthusiastically with complex mathematical and astronomical data – and at points not fully understanding all the issues arising in the problems he was tackling. Nevertheless, there is a real process of transmission and absorption of new knowledge recorded here. Petrus Alfonsi's own open letter, addressed to the scholars of France, expounded on his ability to teach advanced astronomy and its applications. Walcher's text supports this, and mentions 'the tables of Petrus Alfonsi'.[20] The latter have been identified as an early translation of al-Khwarizmi's tables, apparently made in 1116, and drawing on Petrus Alfonsi's education in Aragon. These tables, like the related work of Adelard, incorporated flaws but were still considerably in advance of anything previously available in northern Europe. They also demonstrate an awareness of the interests of northern European users, in that they provide tables showing the dates of major biblical and historical events according to various calendrical eras.[21] Moreover, whilst those tables

into British Schools' in Butterworth and Kessel, Eds., *The Introduction of Arabic Philosophy into Europe,* Leiden, Brill, 1994, pp. 40–57.

[18] See J. Tolan, *Petrus Alfonsi and His Medieval Readers,* Gainesville, University of Florida Press, 1993, esp. p. 10; and M. Lacarra, Ed., *Estudios sobre Pedro Alfonso de Huesca,* Huesca, Instituto de Estudios Altoaragoneses, 1996, esp. p. 12.

[19] For full discussion see P. Nothaft, *Walcher of Malvern, De lunationibus and De dracone,* Turnhout, Brepols, 2017, pp. 46–55.

[20] Ibid., p. 50; and R. Mercier, 'Astronomical Tables in the Twelfth Century', in C. Burnett, Ed., *Adelard of Bath; An English Scientist and Arabist of the Early Twelfth Century,* London, Warburg Institute, 1987, pp. 87–118.

[21] Tolan, p. 55.

would be of special interest for chroniclers and chronologists, another set would be helpful for computists and astronomers. These are the tables of mean motions for all seven planets, of retrograde motions, and of corrections to be applied to anomalous movements.[22] It is unclear whether Petrus Alfonsi was equipped to teach on the techniques of astrological calculation, but expert users of Adelard's translations would certainly have been able to do so. In these ways the ground was prepared for the large-scale arrival in north and west Europe of the translations of astronomical, astrological, and meteorological works, which played such a central part in the intellectual revolution known as the 'twelfth-century renaissance'. Crucial parts of this renaissance involved the translation and study of the long-awaited works of Ptolemy on astronomy and astrology, which were fundamental to the medieval versions of scientific weather forecasting.

The persistence and pre-eminence of the name of Ptolemy are demonstrated by the special enthusiasm with which his works were tracked down and translated in various centres. Moreover, his very challenging work on the structure and calculation of planetary orbits, known even in Latin Europe as the *Almagest*, was sought as much as his simpler and more astrological work, known by the Greek title of *Tetrabiblos* and the Latin one of *Quadripartitus*. It should be noted that the distinction between astronomy and astrology being made here is a modern and not a medieval one. For western medieval scholars as much as for those in the Roman Empire and in the medieval Arab world, the modern distinction between astronomy as a 'real' science and astrology as a pseudo-science did not exist. The study of the planets (and stars) their movements in relation to one another and to the Earth, and the terrestrial and human effects of all this, was one large, if disputed, body of knowledge. The crucial distinction was that between acceptable and unacceptable branches of this complex subject. More will need to be said on this in later chapters, but for the moment it can simply be noted that the central idea that the planets and stars had effects on all the matter of the Earth was not in itself controversial.

What a would-be forecaster of the weather, applying techniques based on this advanced knowledge, needed was to be able to identify the key celestial and terrestrial bodies involved. Data on their natures and qualities, as well as their positions and movements, and their relative degrees of power, was also crucial. Further knowledge of how to interrelate all this information, and how to judge which factors would have the greatest

---

[22] Ibid., p. 57.

impact in a given location at a given time, was also necessary. For all this the key work, much more practically useful and also much more intellectually prestigious than anything previously available, was Ptolemy's *Tetrabiblos*. It is hardly surprising then that this text was sought out and translated into Latin relatively early; the work itself was done by Plato of Tivoli, translating from Arabic and in the 1130s.[23] It seems that Plato of Tivoli was something of a specialist in astronomical translations, since he also worked on the complex planetary tables of al-Battani (compiled ca. 901–918), producing a Latin version under the title *De motu stellarum*.[24]

Much of the basic information found in the *Quadripartitus* was already in (limited) circulation.[25] However, the name of Ptolemy and consequent association with the advanced and revolutionary calculations set out in the *Almagest*, as well as clarity of organisation and presentation, all made the *Quadripartitus* far more authoritative and useful. With the full translation of this work, and its circulation in Latin Europe, the new science of astrometeorology, which was to continue to dominate understandings of weather until the end of the seventeenth century, had arrived. Given the importance of this work from ca. 1140 onwards it is unfortunate that the only modern, critical edition of a medieval Latin translation is a study of the thirteenth-century work of William of Moerbeke, which was itself based on a Greek text. This makes the Hervagius edition of 1533, and its availability via the Warburg Institute website, very helpful. Other editions, and translations into modern English, focus on the original Greek text, or on the abridged version known to modern scholarship as the 'Proclus Paraphrase'.[26]

The four-part structure of this book needs to be taken into account, since materials for the theory and practice of astrometeorology are found in various sections. The first 'book' is devoted, as is logical, to the main

[23] Plato of Tivoli's translation was printed in 1533 by Johannes Hervagius of Basel. This version has been made available via the website of the Warburg Institute, London, at: https://warburg.sas.ac.uk/pdf/fah750pto.pdf (accessed 11 June 2017).

[24] On these tables see E. Kennedy, 'A Survey of Islamic Astronomical Tables', *Transactions of the American Philosophical Society*, 46, 2, 1956, at pp. 32–34.

[25] A source available in western Europe since the later eleventh century at least was the work of Maternus. See Firmicus Maternus, *Matheseos Libri VIII, Ancient Astrology Theory and Practice*, Trans. J. Rhys Bram, Park Ridge, NJ, Noyes, 1976.

[26] The standard modern edition of the Greek text is that of Boll and Boer, updated by W. Hübner as *Claudii Ptolemaei opera quae exstant omnia, Vol. III, 1, post F. Boll et E. Boer secundi curis*, Stuttgart and Leipzig, Teubner, 1998. However, no complete English translation based on this edition exists. The standard English translation, accompanying an independent edition, is that of Robbins: Ptolemy, *Tetrabiblos*, Ed. and Trans. F.E. Robbins, Cambridge, Harvard University Press, 1940. For William of Moerbeke's version see G. Vuillemin-Diem and C. Steel, Eds., *Ptolemy's Tetrabiblos in the Translation of William of Moerbeke*, Leuven, Leuven University Press, 2015.

entities to be considered and their various natures and powers. Most fundamental of all are the planets, and it is of obvious relevance that, for instance, Saturn is dry and cold and has a related effect on other bodies and on the Earth whenever its influence is strong. However two of the planets, the 'luminaries', in other words the Sun and Moon, have special importance. Chapter 8 of Book One moves on to set out how the powers and effects of the other planets are themselves affected when they come into significant relationships with the Sun. Perhaps even more important than the Sun, although less powerful, is the Moon. This closest neighbour of the Earth had been carefully studied by the computists for centuries, and its powers over waters and tides were well known. However, Ptolemy adds far more detail to this basic picture, expounding the effects of the Moon on the atmosphere between it and the Earth. These are fundamentally modulated by the Moon's phases, in such a way that the Moon can generate heat or dryness in the atmosphere at certain times, as well as the more obvious moisture and cold at others. The same is true of the other planets, whose own qualities of heat or cold, moistness and dryness, are all inflected by their position in relation to the Sun. Thus, as Ptolemy observes, 'it is clear that when the planets are in significant associations with one another they produce very many variations in the quality of our atmosphere, with the intrinsic force of each remaining but being altered in its strength by the forces of the bodies with which it is configured'.

With this summary of the planets in place, Book One moves on to consider, in chapter 10, the effects of the seasons and of the four cardinal points (of the Earth's surface). This too will have been familiar material for computists, since the qualities attributed to seasons, and their resonances with the stages of human life, and the climatic zones of the Earth, were also well established. Once again part of this field of knowledge is the outline of the four key winds that blow from the four main compass points, and of the effects that they bring to bear. The reader is now at a point where the possibility of making a 'complete judgement' (in other words an actual forecast) is at least coming into sight. They will be now able to judge how the core effects of the celestial bodies will be strengthened or weakened, both by interrelationships with one another and by earthly factors such as season and geographical location. However, there is in fact a considerable way yet to go, since chapter 17 and its exposition of Houses, and chapter 19 and its explanation of Exaltations and Depressions are both yet to come. These set out the details of how the planets are individually boosted in power in the zodiac signs that are their own 'houses' or their 'exaltations' and contrastingly weakened in opposite signs. To understand this idea it is important to remember that the signs were (and are) equal divisions of the circular belt of the zodiac that runs around the outer boundary of the geocentric sphere of the universe. Thus any one sign (equivalent to a thirty-degree arc of the circle) will have another exactly opposite it. These ideas also had related concepts within computus, where writers such as Bede had set out the signs within which each planet was located when first brought into being on the fourth day of Creation, and were thus not as alien as they might appear. As has also been seen, the days on which the Sun moved from one sign into the next were routinely marked (sometimes with symbolic images) in ecclesiastical calendars.

The territory covered in Book Two was slightly more debatable for Latin Christians, since it moved on to the techniques and concepts needed for making annual predictions for specific regions and territories (and their inhabitants). Within this, chapter 10 deals with the idea of the 'New Moon of the year', a concept that further emphasises the special role of the Moon. Ptolemy has already expounded (in Book One) the idea that the power of the Moon is greatest whilst it is waxing, and thus the exact and agreed calculation of New Moons was an important matter for astronomers (just as it was for computists). Of all the New Moons of any year however, the most significant were those closest to the key points in the solar year – the equinoxes and solstices. The correlation of New Moons and new solar years was thus an important question, although as Ptolemy says there was no universal agreement as to when any solar cycle should be considered to begin. The compromise position was to look at the New Moons, which most closely preceded each of the four key solar dates, and this is recommended. Making an interpretation requires detailed knowledge not only of the zodiac position of the Sun but also (a much more complex question) that of the far faster-moving Moon.

In meteorological terms this is because, whilst the Sun 'creates the general qualities and conditions of the seasons', more variable factors such as winds require the additional consideration of the zodiac signs occupied by the luminaries at the time of conjunction and equinox/solstice. Further details are to be deduced from the positions and signs of all the other planets, and the relationships between the planets and the signs in which they are located. Still further information comes from the angular relationships between the signs containing important planets (as outlined above) since these determine the positive or negative inter-actions (aspects) between the planets. A final element relates to whether the planets are moving forward in their orbits as seen from Earth, or whether they appear stationary or moving backwards (retrograde). 'This' as Ptolemy says, 'might be called monthly investigation' and should thus, if accurately done, provide warning of key meteorological conditions and events for each month of the year.

For those who wish to make forecasts in greater detail, or for more precise time periods, still further calculations are needed, and these are covered in the following chapters. Book Two, chapter 11, deals with the zodiac signs and their effects on the weather, since each sign also has a distinctive type of weather related to it. Aries, for instance, is characterised by thunder and hail. However, each sign is further subdivided into portions, and each of these portions has its own characteristics. Thus, while Pisces is cold and windy overall, its 'leading portion' is temperate, its 'middle portion' is moist, and its 'final portion' is hot. As well as these three portions, each sign also has both a northern and a southern part, adding further qualifications. To take Pisces again as an example, its northern part is windy while the southern part is watery. If the position of the Sun is taken as central to the application of these details then we are here approaching weekly forecasts, since the Sun takes approximately one day to move through one degree of a zodiac sign, and will thus take ten days to pass through a ten-degree 'portion'.

The culmination of the instruction on matters relating to astrometeorology comes in chapters 12 and 13 of Book Two. Chapter 12 turns to 'The Investigation of the Weather in Detail'. The first procedure is a more detailed version of the one centred on New Moons that has already been outlined. The instruction here is to take the day of the New Moon and to draw up a full chart for a specific locality. This is interpreted in a manner analogous to that of a horoscope for a person, and thus to judge as to the weather for a quarter of a solar year. If it is desired to judge the weather for a specific month, then special attention should again be given to New Moons, again as above. The other planets and their positions in signs and portions of signs come next, in order to gain further information about winds and general weather conditions. The third step, for those aiming at even greater detail, is to consider not just New Moons and Full Moons but also 'half Moons' and the positions then occupied, including planetary aspects, in order to find the times at which conditions are likely to change. Finally, daily forecasts can be made by bringing the fixed stars into the calculation. The morning or evening rising or setting of major stars, and the specific positions occupied in relation to the Sun, will further intensify or modulate the conditions imposed by the planets on the days in question. Ptolemy's statement is that 'the hour by hour intensifications and weakenings of the weather vary in response to such positions of the stars' through the effects of the latter on the 'air currents'. However, in making an overall judgement, the would-be meteorologist must always remember that the primary factors will always have the strongest impact, with secondary factors acting as moderators only. However, when the secondary factors exactly repeat the effects of the primary factors, then extremes can be expected.

This exposition has shown just how revolutionary the new, scientific astrometeorology, based on Ptolemy's instructions, could be. Taken together with the same author's very precise and accurate tables, and their accompanying calculations for judging as to planetary positions, a chart could be drawn up for any location on any day of any year. There was no longer any need to depend upon short-term and highly localised observations of the appearance of the sky or the behaviour of birds and animals, as readers of earlier meteorological works needed to do. Moreover, use of an astrolabe made it possible to add more precise and universally agreed information as to the positions of the fixed stars, whether or not a significant one was actually visible in a particular location on a particular day. This might suggest that the older collections of 'weather signs' would be rejected as old fashioned – but this was not the case. Once again a lead was given in this by Ptolemy himself, who devotes chapter 13 of Book Two to a discussion of 'The Significance of Atmospheric Signs'. As in older, Greek and Roman works on this subject, the forecaster is here dependent upon direct observation, correlated with authoritative information as to the significance to be attributed to whatever phenomena might occur. In the case of the Sun, observations are to be made at sunrise and/or sunset for conditions that will apply to the coming day or night. The language is technical, and suggestive of a shared, scientific vocabulary, as in the statement that if the rising or setting Sun has 'haloes' around one side, or is accompanied by 'parheliac clouds' on both sides, and gives out rays affected by these, then storms and rain are signified. However, the reader is back in familiar territory when told that a Moon that appears thin and red when crescent (or waning) indicates winds, and that 'the direction in which the Moon is inclined' gives information as to the direction of the winds.

The tone of this chapter is difficult to judge, partly due to the complexities surrounding the medieval versions. On the one hand, the information is given with the same certainty and technical precision as the whole work, and thus carries the same authoritative air. On the other, the material itself is considerably shortened in relation to the space allocated to weather signs in older works on meteorology, and the writing shows a tendency to phraseology that suggests that Ptolemy is summarising the work of others. It seems that this is a topic on which Ptolemy is happy to summarise, rather than give full details. This is especially evident at the end of the chapter. Here, a brief list of comments on shooting stars, 'woolly' clouds and rainbows leads into a short and not entirely clear statement that the variously coloured appearances of phenomena in the atmosphere 'indicate outcomes similar to those brought about by their specific occurrences, as previously explained'. This is not further explained, but seems to say that, while weather signs are still important, they will mostly only agree with the more detailed and technical information already provided. The summary statement seems also to relate to chapter 9, where the appearance of comets was discussed rather briefly. No further discussion of these signs is deemed necessary, since the chapter and the book are brought rapidly to a close. The things fundamental to 'the investigation of general questions' have clearly all been dealt with.

This summary of Ptolemy's weather-related material has been deliberately nontechnical. Even so, two things should be emphasised. The first is the sophistication with which Ptolemy envisages the cosmos. Standard astrological charts, including the detailed ones outlined in the *Quadripartitus*, work by envisaging the cosmos as a complex geometrical system of which a diagrammatic snapshot can be taken. In other words they freeze a moment of time so that it can be analysed. However, an intrinsic part of Ptolemy's presentation of his material is that this geometrical system is constantly, and very complexly, in non-uniform motion. Thus the geometrical networks and patterns being produced are constantly shifting, and this requires the astrologer to analyse which elements in the system are increasing in power and which are decreasing. A further layer of the calculation involves whether individual bodies (predominantly the planets) are moving towards or away from others, and also the direction of their travel; it matters whether they are direct or retrograde in their movements. The second key point, partly the result of the first, is that Ptolemy's outline of the requirements and procedures for making a prognostication concerning the weather is not for the faint hearted. The calculations required would take several hours at the least, and it is clear that the scope for misjudging the constantly shifting patterns of forces at play was considerable. This point is worth emphasising since it may help to explain something that is otherwise rather surprising – namely, that astrologers who drew upon Ptolemy's work in the medieval period frequently saw a need to produce their own, usually simplified, treatises on astrometeorological weather forecasting.

Astrometeorology and Islamicate Astronomers

It has already been shown that scholars seeking for greater knowledge of astronomy than that available in Latin Europe in the eleventh century discovered a promising, if dangerous, source of such information in the Spanish Marches. It was through this connection, at first sporadic and tenuous, that revelations such as detailed planetary tables, the mathematical techniques required to use them, and the astrolabe, were brought into northern Europe. However, the names of Ptolemy's works, let alone their teachings, were scarcely known even to experts. Thus, the acquisition and translation of knowledge, new technologies and texts was at first a very individualistic process, dominated by the contacts made during the travels of a few pioneers. These journeys were undertaken into regions that either were still parts of the Arab Empire or had been so until very recently, and thus the astronomy that the travellers encountered was first and foremost that which had been built by Arabic-speaking scientists upon the basis supplied by Ptolemy. A very brief account of the material available to be encountered, in the first half of the twelfth century, is important at this point.

A major undertaking of the ninth-century, Islamicate astronomers was to build the most accurate possible models and tables of celestial structures and motions. This was partly a philosophical project, since it involved developing and testing analyses of how the cosmos functioned, and partly practical, since hypotheses were compared with observations made and recorded in state-of-the-art observatories. A fundamental contribution on this level was made by al-Battani, mentioned above, who supplemented and updated Ptolemy's *Almagest*, drawing upon his own astronomical observations. Moreover for these scholars, with contacts reaching into India as well as Persia and parts of the old Roman Empire, the works of Ptolemy were not the sole source of authoritative knowledge. Thus, while the astronomer al-Farghani composed a relatively elementary textbook, summarising the *Almagest* but reducing the technical detail, others produced surveys and encyclopaedias that considerably broadened the coverage of astronomy and astrology.

An important contribution of this latter type was made by Abu Ma'Shar, whose classic textbook was translated into Latin in 1133 as the *Introductorium in astronomiam* (also known as the *Introductorium maius*). His own *Abbreviation* of this 'Introduction' was translated earlier, as the *Isagoge minor*, but sometimes circulated under the names of different authors. The name given to the translation also led to further confusion. Similar problems were attached to his works on major astrological conjunctions of planets and on the concept known as 'revolutions of years'. These were both used in the prediction of major and widespread events, including drought, floods and famines as well as war and political crises.[27] They were translated under the rather confusing titles of *De magnis coniunctionibus et annorum revolutionibus* and *Flores astrorum sive liber de revolutionibus annorum.*[28] Both works are potentially relevant for making predictions of forthcoming weather, but both were challenging in the techniques and concepts invoked as well as in the technical vocabulary employed. Moreover, whilst Abu Ma'shar covered much of the material also presented in Ptolemy's *Quadripartitus* his preferences and emphases were different. For instance, he gives considerably more space to geometrical subdivisions of the zodiac signs, and to the planets that were regarded as their 'Lords'. He also covers the various sorts of 'Lots', calculated by counting degrees from significant points on the circle of the zodiac, which were used in detailed astrological predictions. It was for such reasons, together with their own lack of background information, that the early and wandering scholars of the eleventh and twelfth centuries encountered a vast and complex intellectual terrain for which they did not have adequate maps.

Nevertheless there is evidence that the Latins gave a special place within their studies to treatises on astrometeorology and on weather forecasting. Islamicate astrologers had made new contributions to this subject already, with Abu Ma'shar dedicating a section within his *Flores* to methods of making such predictions. Another astronomer whose works were eagerly read in western Europe, Masha'allah (known in Latin as Messahalla) wrote encyclopaedic works such as a *De Scientia motus orbis* (on the movement of the celestial sphere) and an influential treatise on astrological prediction of major events. Translators sought out not only these but also a short work or 'letter' on wind and rain (*Epistola in pluviis et ventis*). Further evidence of the importance of such knowledge is that the great philosopher and astronomer, al-Kindi, wrote several short treatises and letters on the causes of meteorological phenomena, which are closely related to chapters from his work *On the Revolutions of the Years of the World.* The latter was only translated in full into Latin (from Hebrew) in 1278.[29] However, an edited version of Al-Kindi's exposition

---

[27] On some of the complications that arose in the circulation of translations of these and related works see M. Robinson, 'The heritage of medieval errors in the Latin manuscripts of Johannes Hispalensis (John of Seville)', *Al-Qantara*, XXVIII 1, 2007, pp. 41–71.

[28] Roughly: *On the Great Conjunctions and the Revolutions of Years;* and *Flowers of the Stars or Book of the Revolutions of Years.*

[29] See G. Bos and C. Burnett, *Scientific Weather Forecasting in the Middle Ages: The Writings of al-Kindi*, London, Kegan Paul, 2000; and C. Burnett and D. Juste, 'A New Catalogue of Medieval Translations into Latin of Texts on Astronomy and Astrology', in F. Wallis and R. Wisnovsky, Eds., *Medieval Textual Cultures*, Berlin and Boston, de Gruyter, 2016, pp. 63–76.

of astrometeorology was translated much earlier; this was so highly regarded in the Latin West that he remained respected as an expert on weather forecasting through the early modern period. This Latin 'edition' was known as *De mutatione temporum* and is believed by its modern editor to be taken from a lost Arabic summary of al-Kindi's works. These latter have survived in later Hebrew translations, although not in the original.[30] It has been shown that the terms and ideas in this work accord with those in al-Kindi's works; but the Latin treatise draws upon other works as well. The translator is not named in most of the surviving manuscripts, although two give the name 'Azogont'.

What was it that made al-Kindi's work so important?[31] As Charles Burnett showed, it was the Islamicate astronomers and philosophers of the ninth century who first made a 'serious attempt to create a science of weather-prediction that is distinct from meteorology'.[32] This is a fundamental breakthrough, and was not the achievement of al-Kindi alone. However, his status as a leading scientist and philosopher meant that his espousal of the subject was crucial. He made it part of the new understandings of the universe, its structure and its workings, which were opening up intoxicating insights into the works of the Creator. Combined with the obvious practical importance of advance knowledge of major weather events and changes, this made the subject one highly likely to attract the interest of patrons, as well as enticing to scientists. The Latin treatise in eight chapters, which circulated under the name of *De mutatione temporum*, has been shown to be a compilation of two of al-Kindi's longer letters on weather forecasting, as noted above. It also incorporates some material not from al-Kindi, which may have been added by an editor of the Arabic texts. Neither the date of the translation nor the name of the translator is recorded, but the treatise was being copied and circulated in the first half of the thirteenth century. Its popularity is shown by the fact that thirty manuscript copies have been identified, a relatively high total for such a work. Indeed, this is one of the

---

[30] See also C. Burnett, 'al-Kindi, Latin Translations of', in H. Lagerlund, Ed., *Encyclopedia of Medieval Philosophy*, Vol. 1, New York, Springer 2011, pp. 676–678.

[31] On all this, see C. Burnett: 'Weather Forecasting, Lunar Mansions and a Disputed Attribution; the *Tractatus pluviarum et aeris mutationis* and *Epitome totius astrologiae* of "Johannes Hispalensis",' in A. Akasoy and W. Raven, Eds., *Islamic Thought in the Middle Ages (Studies in Text Transmission and Translation, in Honour of Hans Daiber)* Leiden, Brill, 2008, pp. 219–266; 'Lunar Astrology: The Varieties of Texts Using Lunar Mansions with Emphasis on "Jafar Indus"', *Micrologus* 12, 2004, pp. 43–133; and 'Weather Forecasting in the Arabic World', in E. Savage-Smith, Ed., *Magic and Divination in Early Islam*, Aldershot and Burlington, Ashgate, 2004, pp. 201–210.

[32] Burnett, 'Weather Forecasting in the Arabic World', p. 5/205.

most influential texts within the new genre, and thus central for this study.

It opens with a promise to give a clear explanation of meteorology overall, together with the operations of the atmosphere and the weather, and the causes of heat, cold, dryness and wetness. The conceptual framework and terminology are all very Aristotelian, as is the central idea that the fundamental driving force of such processes is heat, which is itself the outcome of planetary movements and the energy they generate (effectively by friction, though the term is not used). The most powerful driver of this heating process, and of changes and variations within it, is the Sun, both because of its intrinsic power and because of its regularly changing position and speed in relation to any given part of the Earth's surface. However, the detailed effects of the Sun are modulated by its interactions with the other planets, brought about by their movements in relation to one another. Within this, certain positions and certain pairings or groupings of planets are especially powerful. To aid in deriving practical applications from this concept, a means of tabulating planetary combinations and calculating the level of heat each will generate is also given, with details of the effects of the combination of each individual planet with the Sun. Additional factors to be added into the calculation are whether other planets are also involved, and whether periods of high heat follow one another (which will intensify their effect). It will be clear already that this text focuses on providing useful knowledge set out in practical ways.

The next most powerful planet is the Moon, as would be expected. The Moon is here treated as especially powerful in relation to earth as well as to water. Its powers are modulated most strongly by its position in relation to the Sun, calculated as it passes through twelve key points in each monthly cycle. Once these calculations have been made, the forecaster will be able to judge concerning the strength and direction of winds, since heated air will expand into zones where cooler air has contracted. However, more than one type of planetary combination is possible, and more than one may take place at any given time. It is thus important to be aware of the geometrical angles formed by the positions of the planets and their combinations, and of how these 'planetary aspects' should be interpreted. In coming to an actual forecast, the natures of the planets themselves, and the qualities and elements with which they have affinities, must also be taken into account (as in the *Quadripartitus*). Another layer of complexity is added by the fact that each of the 'signs' into which the circle of the zodiac is divided has its own set of qualities and affinities. An important concept here is that of planetary 'houses' or 'domiciles', which identified the signs within which each planet would have its own powers strengthened (and, in the signs placed opposite, weakened).

If all that were not enough, there is also the question of the direction of movement of each planet, and of whether they are moving towards or away from one another. This is clearly related to Ptolemy's arguments, but here is formalised in the concept of 'openings of the doors'. Put simply, this idea identifies specific combinations of planets, and their movements to or from one another, as especially likely to cause rain. It happens when a lower, faster-moving planet 'applies to' (roughly, comes close in its zodiacal position to) a higher planet, if the planets concerned have 'houses' placed opposite one another in the zodiac.[33] Once again this idea draws on concepts set out in Ptolemy's work, where both planetary houses and applications are defined in Book One of the *Quadripartitus*. However, Ptolemy does not identify the specific pairings, based upon opposing houses, emphasised by al-Kindi and other Islamicate writers, nor use the term 'openings of the doors'. This idea, together with the central emphasis placed upon the forecasting of rain, seems to be an innovation. A new, and manifestly more astronomically based, method of weather forecasting had thus been created. However, the tradition of weather signs was not entirely rejected. Like Ptolemy, al-Kindi also provides a list of selected signs of this type, for those who wish to use them, even though they can predict weather events only in the short term.

It will already be clear that, whilst each element in this system might be clearly set out, the process of drawing together all the necessary information, let alone that of making an overall evaluation of outcomes, depended upon expertise and confidence. However, still further technicalities are to come, firstly in the form of the 'lunar mansions'. These 'mansions of the Moon' were not mentioned by Ptolemy. They were accepted in the medieval period as having been identified by Indian astrologers, and were based on twenty-eight fixed stars or star-groupings, each occupying a sector of the belt of the zodiac through which the Moon passed monthly.[34] For many medieval students of the science of the stars they were more important than the Moon's twelve points in relation to

---

[33] For further detail see Burnett, 'Weather Forecasting, Lunar Mansions and a Disputed Attribution', pp. 231–233.

[34] For brief comments see J. Tester, *A History of Western Astrology*, Woodbridge, Boydell, 1990, pp. 81–84, 162–164, 174–175, 180–181. They were rather vaguely mentioned in the *Alchandrean Corpus*. An introductory account was given in the ninth-century *Book of Thirty Chapters* or *Elements of Astronomy*, a summary of the *Almagest* by al Farghani or 'Alfraganus' (in chapter 20). This work was translated into Latin at least twice in the twelfth century.

the Sun (mentioned above). Each was given a name, related to that of the relevant star(s), and like the planets and the signs they were believed to have individual characteristics. Given that al-Kindi, and the Latin version of his work, are dealing with weather forecasting it is unsurprising that the mansions are here characterised as moist, wet, moderate and dry. Together with the Moon itself they emerge as of special importance, since they make it possible to identify four key times each month when the position of the Moon will have particular power in relation to weather. Thus the forecaster can concentrate on the Moon at one of these times, its mansion and any planets with which it is in a relevant relationship, and rejoice that this provides the key to the weather until the next such point is reached. As an example, if the Moon is entering or already in a wet mansion then the outcome would be expected to involve rain, but a powerful aspect with the strongly dry planet, Saturn, would greatly weaken this. If there is an aspect with the disruptive force of Mars then storms, with thunder and hail, are likely.[35]

Commentators on al-Kindi's expositions of weather forecasting have noted that he appears here to contradict his philosophical system. The problem is that al-Kindi, like Aristotle, accepted that the planets were literally above the spheres of the four sublunary elements and the qualities and processes associated with them. Thus they caused effects within the terrestrial zone but could not themselves be stated to have natures or qualities of the types found in that zone. This view is clearly in tension with the assigning of natures and characteristics to the planets, as is found in the texts summarised above. The problem is real, since al-Kindi set out brief arguments to support the view that weather forecasting is in accordance with advanced natural philosophy, and is actually at a high level within it, due to the range of complex knowledge it requires. However, in other works al-Kindi provides an overall model of the proportions and harmonies that dynamically hold together all the component parts of the universe, and this model helps to remove the apparent contradiction. The means by which the planets and their movements bring about specific effects on Earth are discussed in complex detail in several works, and do not in themselves require the assigning of sublunary characteristics to the celestial bodies. Nevertheless, for the purposes of writing practical manuals on a technical subject, it would be acceptable to simplify or remove some of the philosophical complexities.[36]

---

[35] Burnett, 'Weather Forecasting in the Arabic World', p. 9/209.

[36] For discussion see P. Adamson, *Al-Kindi*, 2007, esp. chapter 8, 'The Heavens: Prediction and Providence', Oxford, Oxford University Press, pp. 195–196.

Of course, al-Kindi was not the only expert on the new science of the stars to write on either meteorology or weather forecasting, and for those who were not also engaging directly with Aristotelian philosophy these theoretical problems were much less important. The importance of the weather, and its effects on human life, ensured that most of the leading experts on this exciting new field of science engaged with it. Some wrote treatises setting out the principles of the new, astronomically based meteorology; others dealt with it within broader textbooks. Given the philosophical and technical complexities involved, the range of sources on which they could draw, and their own different levels of astronomical practice, it is also unsurprising that their views differed. Important writers whose work is relevant include Masha'allah and Abu Ma'shar, as already shown. Nevertheless, for the purposes of understanding the process of reception of this new science in northern Europe, it is important to remember that medieval scholars in that region were pursuing their own goals. Accurate and scientifically based weather forecasting was certainly amongst them, as was full, critical knowledge of the battery of scientific and philosophical work of which it was a part, but comparative study of the views of individual Islamic writers was of interest only as a tool in the pursuit of these ends. It is thus time to move on, and to look more closely at this process of reception, and at how the new forms of weather forecasting were transmitted and interpreted. The result of this process was to be the creation and consolidation of a form of scientifically accredited weather forecasting that would dominate until the seventeenth century, at least.

4   Meteorology, the New Science of the Stars and the Rise of Weather Forecasting

The subject matter of this chapter is of fundamental importance for its contribution to the emergence of scientific weather forecasting, but it is often found embedded in texts that have received little scholarly attention until very recently. This chapter will attempt to bring this material together in order to supply a clear account of the transformation that took place in understandings of what constituted meteorology. The evidence to be considered will frequently be somewhat technical, but the picture that emerges is no less compelling for that. The first point to make is that, once the extent of Islamicate astrometeorology became known north of the Pyrenees, leading translators paid special attention to works on the subject. They rapidly made direct translations of such treatises, and since each was usually working individually they often made duplicate translations of the same work, under varying Latin titles. To add to the resulting confusion, they also compiled summaries of the teachings and procedures involved, which circulated as new works under their own names. These patterns of translation and adaptation add to the complexities of putting together a clear outline of the content and dissemination of the growing body of knowledge, but this chapter will make the attempt.

A helpful place to start is with the scholar discussed in the previous chapter, Petrus Alfonsi. He made an early translation, in 1116, of the planetary tables compiled by al-Khwarizmi.[1] These tables were important because they provided not only the mean (or simplified) motions of the planets but also instructions for correcting these to take account of periods of retrograde motion for individual planets.[2] For anyone accustomed only to the basic calculations expounded by writers like Abbo of Fleury this would already be revolutionary. Added to the tables

---

[1] See J. Tolan, *Petrus Alfonsi and His Medieval Readers,* p. 55 and N30.

[2] For the tables see: O. Neugebauer and H. Suter, *The Astronomical Tables of al-Khwarizmi,* Copenhagen, Munksgaard for Danske videnskabernes selskab Historisk-filosofiske skrifter, vol. 4, No. 2, 1962; and H. Suter, *Die astronomischen Tafeln des Muhammad ibn Musa al-Khwarizmi,* Frankfurt am Main, Institute for the History of Arabic-Islamic Science at the Johann Wofgang Goethe University, 1997.

themselves was an explanatory text, providing both a philosophical over-view of the workings of the universe and an exposition of the various parts of the science of the stars.[3] This exposition of the expanding science of the stars argued, as was usual, that it had three parts, with the first being knowledge of the structure of the universe and the second being the mathematical models required to understand its complex patterns of movement. The third focused on the analysis of the effects of these celestial structures and patterns upon terrestrial things. It is this third, practical division that includes understanding of the weather. No sum-mary is given of this part of the science, but we are informed as to the impact of the Sun upon the seasons on Earth, and comments are made for instance (and as usual) on the fact that the dry planet, Saturn, will bring drought when it is strong and in a zodiac sign of the Fire group.[4]

Petrus Alfonsi made the radical move of travelling to France and probably to England to spread the word about the new science and its attractions; but more scholars travelled in the opposite direction. Among them was Hermann of Carinthia, an early specialist in the translation of works on astrology, who compiled and issued an astrometeorological treatise, entitled 'Book of Rains' or *Liber imbrium*.[5] It is not clear at what stage in his career Hermann produced this text, but his total knowledge of astronomy and astrology was certainly extensive. He translated not only the work of al-Khwarizmi but also that of Abu Ma'shar (787–886 CE). The latter, usually known in Latin as Albumasar, was one of the most widely respected and influential astrologers of the medieval period. Perhaps the one that had the greatest impact on Latin Europe was his *Book of the Great Introduction to the Science of the Judgements of the Stars* (usually known as the *Great Introduction*), which was translated in 1133 by John of Seville and in 1140 by Hermann of Carinthia. Her-mann's translations of fundamental works also included the *Planisphere* of Ptolemy. His source for this work was the version edited by the tenth-century, Andalusian astronomer and mathematician, Maslama al-Majriti. Even so, such translations required expert knowledge of the

---

[3] Unfortunately the Latin translation was based on a recension made in Spain in the late tenth century (attributed to al-Majriti), which introduced a serious error into the calculations. On this see A. Kennedy and W. Ukashal, 'Al-Khwarizmi's Planetary Latitude Tables' *Centaurus*, 14,1, 1969, pp. 86–96. However, this does not affect the arguments made here.

[4] Tolan, p. 59.

[5] See C. Burnett, 'Arabic into Latin in Twelfth Century Spain: The Works of Hermann of Carinthia', *Mittellateinisches Jahrbuch*, 13, 1978, pp. 100–134.

material being translated, and it is clear that Hermann was himself an expert in all branches of the science.[6]

Moreover, Hermann was not working alone. An important colleague was Robert of Ketton, later Archdeacon of Pamplona, who translated al-Kindi's textbook on making astrological judgements (the *Judicia*). Hermann and Robert were both working to acquire sufficient expertise to undertake a translation of Ptolemy's *Almagest*. This ambitious plan was made possible due to the recent conquest of territory in Spain that had been under the rule of the Banu Hud dynasty until 1110. From 1118 their city of Zaragosa became part of the Christian kingdom of Aragon and the contents of their library were made available to scholars from northern Europe.[7] Hermann and Robert were prominent amongst this group; but other translators were also making use of the same resource. One such was Hugo of Santalla, a translator active in Tarazona in the middle of the twelfth century, working under the patronage of Bishop Michael of Tarazona. Hugo worked on another *Book of Rains*, this one attributed to Hermes, but said to have been abbreviated by 'Jafar Indus'.[8] Its astrology is partly non-Ptolemaic, since it makes fundamental use of the lunar mansions in a way that Ptolemy did not. The demand for the work is shown by the fact that it has been identified in more than thirty manuscripts, as well as having been printed twice in the sixteenth century.[9] More will be said on it below.

It will be clear from what has already been said that, despite the enormous progress that has been made in tackling the complex problem of just what these early translators encountered and what they made of it,

[6] On the basis of the latter see Sidoli and Berggren, 'The Arabic version of Ptolemy's *Planisphere* or *Flattening the Surface of the Sphere*; Text, Translation, Commentary', *SCIAMUS* 8, 2007, pp. 37–139; and P. Kunitzsch and R. Lorch, *Maslama's Notes on Ptolemy's Planisphaerium and Related Texts*. Munich, Bayerischen Akademie der Wissenschaften, 1994.

[7] C. Stalls, *Possessing the Land: Aragon's Expansion into Islam's Ebro Frontier under Alfonso the Battler, 1104-1134*, Leiden, Brill, 1995.

[8] This was first identified and discussed by C. Haskins in 'The Translations of Hugo Sanctelliensis', *The Romanic Review*, Vol. II, No.1, 1911, pp. 1–15. See also Haskins, *Studies in the History of Medieval Science*, Cambridge, Harvard University Press, 2nd edition, 1927, chapter 1.

[9] C. Burnett, 'The Translation of Diagrams and Illustrations from Arabic into Latin', in A. Contadini, Ed., *Arab Painting; Text and Image in Illustrated Arabic Manuscripts*, Brill, 2010, pp. 161–177; and M. Reichert, 'Hermann of Dalmatia and Robert of Ketton: Two Twelfth-Century Translators in the Ebro Valley', in M. Goyens, P. de Leemans, A. Smets, Eds., *Science Translated: Latin and Vernacular Translations of Scientific Treatises in Medieval Europe*, Leuven, Leuven University Press, 2008, pp. 47–69.

further clarification remains to be done.[10] An example of the challenges presented by the material is given by Thorndike's pioneering study of Latin translations of works by the astrologer known in Latin Europe as 'Messehalla'. This was Masha'allah (ca. 740–815 CE), who rose to prominence in the Abbasid court at Baghdad from the time of its foundation in 762. A widely circulated text was the *Epistola* or 'Letter', which set out key teachings, in twelve chapters, on the significance of eclipses, conjunctions and revolutions of years.[11] The majority of the surviving manuscripts attribute the translation to John of Spain. Chapters 6 to 12 of this work are relevant for weather forecasting, and Thorndike found that a text titled *Messehalla de imbribus* ('Messehalla on Rains') is in fact a version of these chapters of the *Epistola*. This is found in a fourteenth-century copy in Paris, B.N.F., MS 7316A (folios 51r–52v). The compiler of this volume was clearly interested in weather forecasting since folios 69v to 71v also contain a treatise headed *Epistola Messehalle in pluviis et ventis* ('Letter of Messehalla on rains and winds'), which is stated to have been translated by one Drogo. Neither the translator nor the origin of the text have been clearly identified, but it is further evidence of the amount and complexity of material available by the fourteenth century. The same applies to the contents of folios 68r–69v of the same manuscript, which contain another short text, this one headed *Modus alius Mesehalla de aeribus* (loosely, 'another work by Messehalla on the weather').

Equally problematic is the short text, mentioned above, which went under the title of *Liber ymbrium* ('Book of Rains') and was said in some manuscripts to have been 'produced' or 'edited' by Hermann of Carinthia.[12] Its importance is demonstrated by the analysis of Charles Burnett, who has made a detailed study of the works of Hermann of Carinthia and adds a further eleven copies of this text to those previously identified.[13] However, confusion on the part of copyists and scholars as to authorship and translation is found in several of these manuscripts. The confusion was mostly between Hermann's work and one on a closely related subject by the author known in Latin as 'Jafar Indus' or simply 'Jafar'. In some manuscripts the works are copied one after another and

---

[10] For an overview see C. Burnett, 'Translations, Scientific, Philosophical and Literary (Arabic)' in E.M. Gerli, Ed., *Medieval Iberia, An Encyclopedia*, New York and London, Routledge, 2003.

[11] See L. Thorndike, 'The Latin Translations of Astrological Works by Messehalla', *Osiris*, 12, 1956, pp. 49–72.

[12] This was edited by Sheila Low-Beer in 1979, in her unpublished PhD thesis for the City University, New York.

[13] See also M.L. Colker, 'A Newly Discovered Manuscript of Hermann of Carinthia's *De essentiis*', *Revue d'histoire des textes*, 16, 1988 (1986), 213–228.

each under the correct name, but elsewhere Hermann's work becomes an addition to, or part of, the treatise of Jafar. Perhaps most confused is Paris, B.N.F. MS nouv. Acq. Lat. 3091, where one section of Hermann's work is copied into the middle of Jafar's treatise, while the rest follows after. Parma, Bib. Palat., MS Pal. Fondo Parm. 720 has Hermann's work, without a title, on folios 430r to 432r, with Jafar's treatise following. Both these manuscripts are thirteenth century, which suggests that copies of these short works on weather forecasting were circulating rapidly and via various intermediaries, since a high level of confusion had been created in a relatively short time.

Hermann's preface, edited by Burnett, suggests that he himself had read widely on weather forecasting and had found a lack of clarity in the available works. He says that he has attempted in his 'edition' to give a clear summary of what 'Indian authority' has handed down, and to reconcile divergent views. This has clearly not been easy, since he complains that some scientific authors use a 'multitude of words' to 'hide' what they are actually saying, whilst many others 'adulterate' the subject through their discords, and still others produce 'interminable ramblings'. No names are given, presumably for obvious reasons. It was perhaps the mention of 'Indian authority', which led to the medieval assumption that Hermann's work was effectively a version of that of 'Jafar Indus'. This latter was translated both by Hugo of Santalla and by an anonymous translator.[14] To make matters still more confused, it is possible (as Burnett notes) that the name Jafar was itself a misunderstanding of the full name of Abu Ma'shar, who also made reference to the expertise of Indian astronomers, and one of whose works was known as *Liber mutationum temporum*. It is certainly clear that Islamicate work on astro-meteorology made reference to previous studies by Indian astrologers, and that a sprinkling of information on the latter subject thus reached Latin Europe.[15]

The work attributed to Jafar itself was translated into Latin at least twice, as noted above, with Hugo of Santalla's version being the longer.[16] Both translations open with a reference to Indian expertise, which is closely linked to knowledge of the key role played by the Moon. Calculation is again needed of the mansions of the Moon, together with its aspects, or angular relationships, with other planets. It is explained that the Moon plays a fundamental role in the bringing of rain, both through

---

[14] Burnett, 'Arabic into Latin' p. 123.
[15] On this see D. Pingree, 'The Indian and pseudo-Indian Passages and Elements in Greek and Latin Astronomical and Astrological Texts' *Viator*, 1976, pp. 141–196.
[16] Burnett, 'Arabic into Latin', p. 124.

its own nature and because it acts as mediator of the influences of the other planets and the stars. The anonymous version even suggests that the speed with which rain falls is determined by the current movement of the Moon.[17] However, the anonymous translation, in keeping with its brevity, deals mainly with general principles and with meteorological theory. Hugo of Santalla's version is much longer and much more practical. It offers, for instance, a very useful list of each possible combination of planet and zodiac sign, with the effects thereof. It then continues with information on major changes, both physical and political, which can be affected by weather and climate.[18] This perhaps explains why the work of Jafar, as translated by Hugo, dominated over that of Hermann of Carinthia; Hermann's attempt to summarise and shorten had made his work less recognisable as a complete treatise and less helpful for scholars new to this complicated subject. The confusion between the two is also made more understandable by Burnett's observation that the terminology used by Hermann and Hugo is very similar, even though Hermann's work is not taken directly from Hugo's and uses material not in Hugo's.

Equally confusing, though less widely circulated, was a treatise headed *Experta cognitio imbrium et ventorum*, identified in only two manuscripts and attributed to another scientist and translator, known as Hermann the German. This individual, named in surviving manuscripts as Hermannus Alemannus, was active as a translator in Toledo in the middle of the thirteenth century. The manuscripts containing the meteorological treatise are both from the later Middle Ages, making the early transmission of the text impossible to trace. Whether Hermann was translator, compiler or author is equally unclear. Another factor leading to problems in the accurate identification of texts on astrometeorology is that interest in the subject, combined with the brevity and technical complexity of the works themselves, led to their collection (often anonymously) in groups within volumes assembling material on astronomy, astrology and medicine. An example is the late thirteenth-century manuscript now Cambridge, Clare College, MS 15 (Kk. 4. 2). This is a highly practical assembly of works of varying length and origin, focusing on weather forecasting, medicine and veterinary practice.[19] Its first three items bring together a wide range of information on astrometeorology. The first is a compound version of the

---

[17] Ibid.   [18] Ibid.
[19] See M.R. James, *A Descriptive Catalogue of the Western Manuscripts in the Library of Clare College, Cambridge*, Cambridge University Press, 1905, pp. 28–34. James dates the manuscript to ca. 1280. Its origin is uncertain, but it was in English ownership in the fourteenth century.

Liber imbrium. Also included is a very recent work by Bartholomew of Parma, a respected expert on astrology and the first recorded teacher on astronomy at the University of Bologna (active 1280–1290 CE). The treatise in question focuses on specialised weather forecasting, *Iudicium particulare de mutatione aeris,* and is datable to the third quarter of the thirteenth century. The Clare College manuscript's section on weather forecasting ends with a comment that suggests that the material has been collected in response to a special request. Astrometeorology thus has a special place in this volume, whose other works on the science of the stars are mostly broad surveys, including the compilation known as the *Book of Nine Judges.*

The *Book of Nine Judges* itself made a significant contribution to the spread of knowledge on astrometeorology, as well as on much else, and is worth detailed consideration for that reason. It included the work of more than one translator, as well as bringing together the techniques and theories of the nine experts promised by the title. Its texts were probably extracted and assembled by Hugo of Santalla, and it was an expansion of an earlier *Book of Three Judges.*[20] It was especially popular in the twelfth and thirteenth centuries, after which it appears to have been superseded by longer works providing fuller instructions on technical matters. The greater part of the compilation deals with the methods by which the astrologer can produce guidance and answers for clients who bring specific questions and problems. However, its final, long chapter provides an impressively thorough coverage of astrometeorological techniques, taken primarily from al-Kindi and Masha'allah, as well as 'Dorotheus' and 'Umar'. The name Dorotheus usually refers to Dorotheus of Sidon, who studied and wrote in Alexandria in the first century CE, and whose five-book poem on astrology only survives in later translations.[21] However the use of the name here appears to be confused, since the information attributed to Dorotheus is largely based on the work of Masha'allah.[22] The Umar referred to is 'Umar al-Tabari, also known in Latin as Omar, a colleague of Masha'allah in Baghdad. The material on weather forecasting attributed to him is taken from his *Book of Questions in the Judgement of the Stars.* The title of the compound chapter translates as 'On Weather and Disasters', and its opening section provides general

---

[20] The *Book of Three Judges* appears to have been compiled by Hermann of Carinthia and Hugo of Santalla, and dedicated to Michael, bishop of Tarazona. Only three manuscript copies are known. See C. Burnett, 'Scientific Translations from Arabic: The Question of Revision', in Goyens, de Leemans and Smets, *Science Translated,* pp. 11–34, at p. 18.

[21] See D. Pingree, Ed., *Dorothei Sidonii Carmen Astrologicum,* Leipzig, Teubner, 1976.

[22] B. Dykes, Ed. and Trans., *The Book of the Nine Judges,* Minneapolis, Cazimi Press, 2011, p. 6.

pointers on making a prognostication concerning 'the corruption and detriment of things' in any year. After this minatory start, the chief subject is given as 'rain' although wars and plagues are also dealt with.[23]

A complicating factor with this chapter is that the material, being taken from different authors, can be contradictory or repetitive. All the instructions, it should be said, are technically demanding and assume a reader familiar with the basics of astrology. It appears that the collection was intended for practitioners able to test the various techniques and choose whichever they considered best. The compilation starts by presenting extracts mainly attributed to Umar. The first instruction is to look at the 'assembly' of planets at the time of the Sun's entry into Aries. This in itself raised technical problems by the middle of the twelfth century, since the assumption that it should coincide with the Spring equinox was no longer accurate (as already reflected in the Anglo-Saxon calendar discussed in Chapter Two). The accumulated error due to the precession of the equinoxes meant that by this time the Sun was still near the middle of the preceding sign, Pisces, at the equinox. The practitioner is left to decide on this question, but the assumption appears to be that the day of entry into Aries is what matters. In interpreting the chart once drawn up, a key question is the identification of the Lord of the Ascendant, another concept with which the reader is assumed to be familiar. The term 'Ascendant' relates to the eastern horizon as represented on the astrological chart, and was the point where that horizon intersected the ecliptic (the plane of the apparent path of the Sun around the Earth). It was one of four key points, at ninety-degree angles to one another, which were fundamental to constructing the astrological 'houses' in relation to any chosen point on Earth. The zodiac sign in this key position at the chosen moment was 'on the Ascendant', and therefore any planet located in it was of special importance, as were planets opposite it, and those with significant relationships to the sign. The chapter informs the reader that, if Saturn is in this position, or in a powerful relationship to the Lord of the Ascendant, or otherwise strengthened, the effect on the weather will be baleful. The atmosphere will be obscured and even corrupted, and the weather will tend to be unseasonal. However, a weak Saturn will lead to a year of standard weather patterns.

---

[23] For an English translation, see ibid., pp. 600–624. Dykes' translation is based primarily on two manuscripts and on the 1509 printed edition by Peter Leichtenstein. For details, see p. 8. A digitised copy of the 1509 version, now Bibliotheca Electoralis [Konvolut: 4 Math. VII, 10] in the Landesbibliothek, Jena, is available online at: https://archive.thulb.uni-jena.de/hisbest/rsc/viewer/HisBest_derivate_00000033/BE_0050_0105.tif?logicalDiv=log000003 (accessed 24 June 2019).

This emphasises the power of Saturn as the strongest 'malefic' planet; but the text goes on to expound the related, though lesser, effects of the next most negative planet, Mars. If Mars is placed in any of the ways just described for Saturn, and especially if it is at the Midheaven of the chart, then hot seasons are likely to be especially hot, and even cold seasons are likely to be warmer than usual. By contrast, if Jupiter, Venus or the Moon are in any of these strong positions then the air will be calm and clement, and the weather will be kind at the seasons for planting and sowing. Mercury is important if placed at the Midheaven and in a sign of the Air group (Libra, Aquarius and Gemini), especially if Saturn or Mars is in the same sign. A year marked by such a grouping would suffer from storms, strong winds and unhealthy weather. Similarly, if Mercury is strengthened by its angle with a negative planet, it will echo the effect of that negative planet.

It is next repeated that planets in the eastern sector of the horoscope dominate the reading; but a special case is also given for the effects on such planets of being in negative 'aspects' or angular relationships (such as 180 degrees, or 'opposition') with Mars or Saturn. If there is such a relationship with Mars, and Mars itself is in a fire sign (Aries, Leo or Sagittarius) then both hot and cold seasons are likely to reach extremes and to have damaging effects. However, a beneficent aspect, such as 120 degrees, will moderate this effect. If Saturn is the planet in question then the dominant effect will be unusually cold weather, especially if Saturn is in a cold sign. The indications are less bad if Saturn is in a hot sign, especially if the planet on the Ascendant is itself positive and strengthened by other factors, since this is likely to produce a balance overall, and even to favour the growth of plants. Similarly, a powerful Mars can balance out factors that would otherwise lead to excessive cold or wetness, and thus is not necessarily negative.

The special interest in rain found frequently in Islamicate astrometeorological texts is found here also in the form of a section on the 'Lot of Rain'. As noted in the previous chapter, Lots were a subject of considerable interest in Islamicate astrology. The Lot of Rain explained here deals with winds; and once again the key element is the placing of Saturn and Mars. If either of these is located at the degree allocated to the Lot itself, or in a significant aspect with the Lord of that position, then they will have powerful negative effects, even if they are not otherwise powerfully placed. The calculation of the placing of the Lot depends upon the position of Mercury, and technical instructions are given for this. It is sufficiently important that the forecaster is advised to repeat the calculation for each time at which the Sun enters a sign at 90 or 180 degrees to the sign on the Ascendant, in order to discern characteristics of the weather in each quarter of the year. Moreover, the same calculation for the Sun's entry into each sign will give indications for the weather in the month in which that entry takes place. If forecasts for rain on individual days are desired, then instructions are also given for a 'Lot of one-day rains or winds'. This technique is credited to Abu Ma'shar, and involves calculating the degrees between the Sun and Saturn at the rising of the Sun on any given day, and then applying this to the Moon. If Mercury is at the point thus calculated then winds are likely on that day; and this is strengthened if Venus is also linked to the Lot and to the Moon. A calculation can also be made for the time of sunset, and looking especially at the Moon.[24]

Considerable attention is given to the chart for the day on which the Sun enters the twentieth degree of Scorpio, since it is stated that this gives the best warning of heavy rain, thunderstorms and strong winds. Here the judgement starts with looking at Venus, Jupiter and Mercury, and their positions in relation to the four cardinal points of the chart. If they are western then heavy rains and dews are indicated; and the meaning is the same if any of them are retrograde (moving backwards in relation to their usual course around the ecliptic). Conversely, if they are eastern, and especially if they are moving faster than usual, then dry conditions are likely. If Mars is at any of the key points and in an air sign, especially if it is in aspect with Mercury, then storms (especially thunderstorms) can be predicted, as can diseases caused by corruption of the air. If Mars is in the lowest point, in an earth sign (Taurus, Capricorn or Virgo) and in aspect with Mercury, then earthquakes and fires or eruptions are probable. Related conditions, but with Mars in a fire sign, will predict destruction by fire; and a water sign predicts drought as well as harm to everything dependent upon water. However, if Mars is balanced by influences from the fortunate planets then the damage caused by any of these positions will be moderated. We next move on to the still more negative planet, Saturn. If it is found at the first of the positions described for Mars then the air will be darkened and corrupted and there will be heavy and damaging rains. With Saturn in the second position there will not only be earthquakes but also destructive and polluted floods. Similarly its effects in a water sign will be still worse than those of Mars, with the drying up of wells added to the previous list; while in a fire sign the earth and its stones will be corrupted.

The next extract deals with the Moon, and especially whether it is moving away from Venus and going ahead of Mars (or vice versa). Either

---

[24] For problems of translation here see Dykes, *Astrology of the World*, 1, p. 606 and n.25.

of these portends heavy rain (as in the phenomenon of the 'opening of the doors' discussed in the previous chapter) as do similar positions in relation to Jupiter and Mercury. The power of the Moon and Saturn over the weather is so great that a movement of the Moon in relation to Saturn alone also signifies heavy rains. Moreover, the Moon's position in relation to the Sun is also significant for the forecasting of rain, even if there is no 'opening of the doors'. This is taken further in the next section, which sets out the angles between Moon and Sun that are designated 'posts' or 'foundations', and that relate to the phases of the Moon. New Moon and Full Moon are important, and the forecaster should calculate the Ascendant at these times, and the Lords of the Ascendant and of the sign opposite to it ('in opposition'). Significant relationships between these and with the Moon are important for predicting rain; and if Venus, Mercury, Saturn or Jupiter are moving retrograde or slowly at the same time, then rain is certain. Again, the Latin here is complex and hard to follow, which would require further expertise on the part of the forecaster.[25] The next extract discusses indications for rains, based on the position of the Lord of the Ascendant for that year at the times identified by the methods just outlined, and especially at the time when the Sun enters the twentieth degree of Scorpio. A powerful aspect at this point can intensify the rains; and even if this is absent, an aspect with the Moon predicts earthquakes and severe thunderstorms.

At this point the extracts from Umar conclude with a general section on disasters and their prediction, before attention turns to the works of al-Kindi. These were outlined in the previous chapter, since the philosopher's views were widely in demand, but their treatment in the *Book of Nine Judges* will be briefly considered here. Once again (in section 8) the key indicator for the year is stated to be the chart for the Sun's entry into Aries, and especially the Ascendant. Also a major factor in the chart is the position of Saturn, and the qualities of the sign occupied by Saturn on this day will set the tone for the weather during the whole year. The role of Jupiter in relation to the quarters of the year is again present, although here it is expounded less clearly, and the relationships between the Lord of the Ascendant and other planets at the start of each quarter are again important. For each month, the charts at New Moon and Full Moon must be consulted for shorter-term forecasts. Both here and in the exposition of special indicators for heavy rain this version is less easy to follow than that of 'Umar', although its statement that Venus is key for rain, Mercury for winds, Saturn for clouds and hail, Mars for hot

[25] See Dykes, pp. 609–610 and comments in Notes there.

winds, Jupiter for cool winds and the Sun for heat and dryness, is helpfully simple.

Next come the 'posts' of the Moon, and their importance in the identification of 'openings of doors' or times of heavy rain, together with the additional factors brought into play by the nature of any superior planet to which the Moon is 'applying'. The language here is rather compressed, and this is still more the case with the mention of points on the chart that emphasise moistness. No guidance is here given as to the locations of these points, leaving them somewhat enigmatic, although the following section, which explains that the times when the Moon is at one of its quarters are particularly significant, is more helpful. Equally reduced to the bare bones is the statement that the Sun and each of the other planets will have greater effects when at one of the key points of their respective orbits, although their strengths are not equal. The next and final group of materials from al-Kindi moves away from weather and on to the question of human health in the year to come. As this summary makes clear, this selection of extracts appears to place less dependence on al-Kindi than might be expected.

Sections 10 to 13 revert to weather forecasting but attribute the texts to Dorotheus, although they actually relate closely to Masha'allah's treatise on rains.[26] Section 10 takes up the importance of the Sun in Scorpio, although here the entry into the first degree of Scorpio is preferred to the twentieth degree. Venus' position at this time indicates the part of the year when rains will be heaviest (and lightest). Venus' position in relation to Mercury and the Moon at a key point of the year supplies further important information, especially if any of these are in water signs, and again if they are in aspect with any of the Lords of the chart. For instance, if the Moon is close to Mars, and especially if Venus is moving ahead of Mars, a dry year is forecast. In contrast, if Jupiter is in a water sign and has Venus and the Moon in positive relationships, then a year of good and healthful rains is likely.

Still in section 10, the text moves on to consider each planet's effects as 'ruler of rains' for a given year, and how this will be affected by the planet's own position and by its aspects with beneficent or negative planets. Once again, consideration must be given to the sign in which the key planet is located, and especially to whether it is airy, fiery, watery or earthy. By now it will be less than surprising to see that the Moon can overdetermine all these indicators. For instance, if the ruler of rains is in the same sign as Mars and the Moon is strengthening Mars, then the year

[26] Ibid. p. 618.

will be cloudy but with little actual rain – although if the sign is an air one then dews will be heavy.

Methods of forecasting rain for the quarters and months of the year are set out in sections 11 and 12. For the months, charts must be drawn up for New and Full Moons. Briefly, if the Moon is in a positive position in relation to one of the beneficent planets at one of these times then there will be rain in that half of the month. Even if Saturn, which usually brings dryness, is strengthened by the Moon at such a time, this can be counterbalanced if the Moon is close to Venus and Saturn itself is in a water sign. However, Saturn in a fire sign would be overpowering; and if allied with Mars there would be not only a dry month but also clouds, winds and corruption of the atmosphere. The issue reached in section 13 is that of rain on specific days, and here the days when the Moon reaches each of the four main points of the chart are key. For instance, if this happens when the Moon is in a water sign, and is positively placed in relation to Venus and Mercury, then it will rain on that day. However, the effect of the Moon will be greater if it is near the beginning of the sign in question and weaker at the end. Further factors indicate whether the rain will be steady or intermittent, and whether it will last for more than one day. This section also moves into a list of possible combinations of planets and positions on any day, and of the weather conditions that they forecast. Additionally, the hour at which the Moon enters a new sign, and the relationship between that sign and the planet ruling the hour of transition, can offer information as to possible extremes of weather.

This might appear to be a logical conclusion to the subject, but in fact a final section 'On rains' is given, which brings together points, especially relating to the Sun, not yet dealt with. These cover matters such as the Sun's entry into any of the Mutable signs (Gemini, Virgo, Sagittarius and Pisces) or reaching the later portion of Scorpio, and the special significance of Aquarius and Leo for rains and storms. The section has the possibly helpful effect of re-emphasising the roles of the water signs and the power of the Moon and Venus in relation to rain, but it is nonetheless oddly inconclusive as the final section of both the survey of weather forecasting and the whole book. No attempt is made to sum up the material covered, to deal with possible contradictions, or to give explicit preference to one authority over another. The reader is presented with a broad range of authoritative material, and is left to use it according to their own skill and judgement. The *Book of Nine Judges* thus demands careful thought, with practice and experimentation, from its users. It is perhaps not surprising that other, more straightforward works, even if less exhaustive in their coverage, had a wider appeal to those who wanted instruction in the basics of weather forecasting. Nevertheless, as this summary has shown, scholars of natural philosophy and astronomy in twelfth-century Western Europe had access to a range of works on astrometeorology through this one, compendious selection alone.

The observation that twelfth-century, Latin texts on astrometeorology were addressed to expert readers applies also to another relevant early translation, Hermann of Carinthia's version of the *Fatidica* (or 'Prognostics') of Sahl, made probably as early as 1138.[27] Sahl ibn Bishr was another ninth-century scholar in the court of Baghdad (and Khurasan). The *Fatidica* was primarily concerned with the methods for making predictions of large-scale events, such as harvests, famines, floods and wars, and thus part of it deals with extreme weather events. It is therefore not surprising that several of the surviving manuscripts partner the *Fatidica* with at least one short work on foreknowledge of rains and winds (Cambridge, University Library MS Kk iv 7, and Cambridge, Pembroke College, MS 227, are examples). The level of interest in these matters is demonstrated by the fact that still other approaches to the subject are found in works on the making of largescale predictions by calculation of the 'revolutions of years'. This, as in the extracts compiled in the *Book of Nine Judges*, involved the identification of a 'Lord of the Year' and special attention to planetary positions close to the time of the vernal equinox and the Sun's entry into the sign of Aries. An authority on this topic was Abu Ma'shar, both in his *Introduction* and in his books dealing with 'Revolutions of World Years', one of which was usually known in Latin translations under the title of *Flores* ('Flowers'). This was the subject of another early translation, this time by John of Seville, probably in the 1140s.[28] It was a popular, brief introduction to an important subject, as is shown by the fact that over forty manuscripts are known, and that it was printed six times in the early modern period.[29] It comprises roughly thirty short chapters, setting out the method for drawing up the horoscope for the 'revolution of the year', taken as the hour of the entry of the Sun into the first point of Aries. The information concerning the

---

[27] Burnett, 'Arabic into Latin', pp. 115–118.

[28] This translation was itself revised, perhaps more than once, by anonymous editors. See D.N. Hasse and A. Büttner, 'Notes on Twelfth-Century Translations of Philosophical Texts from Arabic into Latin on the Iberian Peninsula', 2017, at: www.philosophie.uni-wuerzburg.de/fileadmin/EXT00246/Hasse-Buettner_Menaggio_3_27_Feb_2017.pdf (accessed 13 November 2017).

[29] For comments, and reproduction of the edition of Johannes Sessa, Venice, 1488 or 1506, see D. Juste, 'Notice on Abu Ma'shar *Flores*', https://warburg.sas.ac.uk/pdf/fah820b2342376.pdf (accessed 13 November 2017). A digitised version of the Ratdolt edition of 1488 (*Flores Albumasaris*) is available at the website of the Biblioteca Digital Real Academia de la Historia, at http://bibliotecadigital.rah.es/dgbrah/es/consulta/registro.cmd?id=44564 (accessed July 9, 2019).

planetary Lord of the Year is as usual, but here the chapter on predicting rain (*De pluviis*) identifies Mars as the most important planet. If Mars is located in either of its own houses (Aries and Scorpio) at the significant hour then a period of heavy rain is signified. If it is in either house of the dry planet, Saturn (Capricorn and Aquarius) then drought is indicated. In all other positions Mars forecasts average rainfall.

This is clearly indicative of the importance accorded to weather predictions within the making of annual prognostications of major events. However it could hardly be claimed as a full weather forecast, and does not preclude the need for the detailed treatises under discussion. Whilst it would be tedious to attempt a detailed comparison of all such texts, it is important to demonstrate the increasing emphasis on providing detailed and scientific instructions. A brief account, for comparison with the *Book of Nine Judges*, will therefore be given of the specialised treatise on weather forecasting attributed to John of Seville, which draws on the texts and concepts already outlined. An edition of this text, with translation and commentary, has been made by Charles Burnett.[30] The first point is that the treatise, unlike al-Kindi's fuller coverage of the subject, avoids any philosophical discussion or explanation. It is presented purely as a set of instructions – though aimed at someone already familiar with the basics of the science of the stars. As already noted, this starts from the same point as the treatises on revolutions of the year. The forecaster should take the time of the new Moon or full Moon occurring closest to, but before, the Sun's entry into Aries, and draw up a chart. The making of the forecast begins with the highest planet, Saturn, and the first step in interpretation is to identify the zodiac sign in which Saturn is placed. The next step is the identification of the element to which that sign is assigned. A fire sign predicts heat, an air sign forecasts cold, a water sign means a wet year, and an earth sign brings dryness. However, Saturn's position within one of the subdivisions of the sign is also important, as is any planet placed close to Saturn, especially if it is in the same sign. The next step is to identify the planets in aspect with Saturn, and to calculate whether these will strengthen or weaken Saturn itself.

The forecaster now moves on to the next planet in sequence, Jupiter, and here has to look at new and full Moons occurring just before the Sun enters the signs of Aries, Cancer, Libra and Capricorn. These are the 'cardinal' signs, marking key points in the solar year. The position and aspects of Jupiter at these times will be significant for the quarter of the solar year that begins as the Sun enters the appropriate sign. Having

---

[30] Burnett, 'Weather Forecasting', pp. 239–265.

established the overall conditions for the year, and then those for the quarter, it is now possible to move on to individual months. Once again it is times of new and full Moon that are needed, and here the signifying planets are Venus and Mercury. Also important for the month is the sign on the ascendant (that is, rising on the eastern horizon) at the time of new Moon, since only a fixed sign in this position (Taurus, Leo, Scorpio or Aquarius) will guarantee that the forecast conditions will last for the full month.

Next come instructions on the Moon, and on the 'openings of the doors' that have already been discussed. The account of the latter given here is very brief, and would be easier to follow as a table rather than in the staccato clauses actually provided. Most important are conjunctions of: Sun and Saturn; Moon and Saturn; Jupiter and Mercury; Venus and Mars. Also to be calculated are aspects of the Sun and Moon with Saturn (if any) and those between the other pairs of planets (if any). The positions and strengths of aspected planets at these 'openings of the doors' will lead to specific predictions for temperature, winds (and their direction), clouds, rainfall, pleasant weather and storms. Thus, if Mercury is the significant planet then rain and wind are predicted. For Saturn, the outcome will be bad, but details are again affected by whether it is in one of its own signs. Further points on the importance of the Moon, both as a major influence on rain and as a transmitter of powers from the other planets, are next given. The ways in which this will be further nuanced by the direction and speed of movement of the planets concerned are once again set out only briefly. Once again, a reader already familiar with the procedures and terminology involved is being assumed.

It has already been noted that times and quantities of rainfall are important in astrometeorological texts, and that is supported once again here, since sections 21 to 34 (in Burnett's edition) all relate to further indications of rain. The moist and temperate planet, Venus, is second in importance to the Moon in this regard, and details of significant positions, times and aspects are given in several sections. A brief mention is made of the contribution of Mercury, and another of the effects of conjunctions of three planets in the sign of Aquarius. Sections 32 to 34 revert to the power of the Moon in relation to rain, and the levels of its effects for different cities, and this leads into a list of the regions of the earth over which the Moon has special influence. Regions assigned to other planets and to the zodiac signs then follow. The existence of competing views on Jerusalem and Rome is mentioned, but the treatise asserts that Jerusalem's sign is Aquarius, and that of Rome is Leo. These points are clearly important when making a forecast for a particular region or city, and once again the forecaster will need to exercise judgement and experience in order to allow for the differences of opinion.

With all this in place the text moves without preamble, in section 56, into its second part. The focus shifts back to the importance of the new or full Moon closest to the Sun's entrance into Aries when making prognostications of largescale events for a whole year. Amongst these major events, drought or floods are most clearly indicated if the Moon has a significant aspect with Saturn at the crucial time, although an aspect with Mars can bring excessive heat if the latter planet is in a warm sign (section 61). Sections 68 to 96 deal with the mansions of the Moon and their geometrical calculation, from the starting point of two large fixed stars called 'the Horns of the Ram'. The names and stars of each are listed, as is whether each is dry, temperate or moist. Section 97 gives a helpful list of the eleven mansions that signify rain, whilst 98 covers the six dry mansions. The whole treatise concludes with the techniques for using this information in a forecast for a specific time and place. The days of rain each month are indicated by the mansions in which all the planets are located, and the interrelations between them, at the exact times of new and full Moon each month. To judge as to the strength of the indication for a particular city or region then the factors affecting the appropriate rulers and signs (as listed earlier) should be analysed.

As before it is very clear from this outline that, once the basic assumptions as to the powers of the planets are accepted, the method of weather forecasting set out here is entirely scientific in its procedures. The techniques involved are those of astronomy and geometry, and the treatises are written in the voices of experts addressing other experts, or at least advanced students. It is equally clear that astrometeorology is taken for granted as an important part of this expanding and exciting new science. The assessment of the qualities, movements and changes of the atmosphere, driven by the highly complex patterns of interactions between the planets, the stars and the significant sectors of the heavens, emerges as a complex field of study in itself. The level of skill and difficulty involved bears a satisfying correlation to the complexity and notorious variability of the weather itself. The need for the forecaster to acquire and apply experience and skill is also logical, especially for the more localised and short-term forecasts that are envisaged as possible in this 'new' science. From this point of view, the collection of sometimes contradictory instructions and findings by the leading authorities in the field is in itself scientific in approach. Those able to follow the instructions would presumably keep records of their findings, and come to decisions as to which methods worked best. It appears that no one method was expected to be successful in every case; but that was not exclusive to medieval weather forecasting. Modern meteorologists and forecasters still need to call upon their judgement and can still make significant mistakes. The case of the 'great storm', which hit England in 1987 showed that this was still the case in the late twentieth century; and even with the data-processing power available in the second decade of the twenty-first century forecasts still require human judgement.

A further important point is that the production and dissemination of the texts surveyed in this chapter presupposes the existence in twelfth-century Latin Europe of scholars able and willing to engage in depth with astrometeorology. For some, it appears to have been a skill on which they wanted a succinct, but still specialised, textbook. For others it was part of a comprehensive study of the ever-widening fields of astronomy and astrology. However, what is not clear from the treatises themselves is how widespread such individuals were in northern and western Europe by the late twelfth century. The question of the reception and dissemination of astrometeorology within the courts of the powerful, and in fully developed universities, will be dealt with in later chapters. In the remainder of this chapter some examples will be given of the channels by which knowledge and debate were transmitted amongst networks of highly engaged scholars. A small case study is provided by Charles Burnett's analysis of a twelfth-century manuscript containing selected extracts from a broad range of astronomical works. This was presumably compiled by someone who had received advanced instruction in the subject area, although it may have been in the possession of a group of Dominicans in Scotland by ca. 1230. This suggestion is based upon the presence in the manuscript of an inscription linking it to 'Clement of the order of preachers' and the fact that it was brought into Scotland relatively early. These two pieces of information suggest a link to Clement, later bishop of Dunblane, who was part of the group of Dominicans invited into Scotland in 1230 by King Alexander II. The manuscript is now MS D. b. IV. 6 in Edinburgh University Library.[31]

The section analysed by Burnett makes up roughly the second half of the volume, and opens with the old-established names of Plato and Calcidius. More innovative is the inclusion of extracts from the *Introductorium maius* of Abu Ma'shar, in the translation made ca. 1140 by Hermann of Carinthia. Linking the selections from both the older and the newer works are interests in the positive and negative powers of the

---

[31] C. Burnett, 'The Arrival of Pagan Philosophers in the North: A Twelfth-Century Florilegium in Edinburgh University Library' in J. Canning, E. King, M. Staub, Eds., *Knowledge, Discipline and Power in the Middle Ages; Essays in Honour of David Luscombe*, Leiden, Brill, 2011, pp. 79–94.

planets, the human capacity to understand and analyse these, and the possibility of judging as to future conditions on this basis. A concern with the history of the science of the stars, in this broad definition, is also manifest. The effects of planetary movement are dealt with, and prominent within this is interest in the role of the planets in causing predictable changes in the weather. It is hardly surprising that no texts on the making of birth charts for specific individuals are included, given the theological problems that the activity raised. What is striking is that aspects of the new science, and of the powers that it potentially bestowed upon scholars, are here integrated into an intellectual framework inherited from the early medieval past. Both the central interest in understanding the actual workings of God's creation, and the concern with factors likely to impact on their management of their resources and responsibilities, are still clear.

The patterns of dissemination of new ideas in England in the later twelfth century remained heavily dependent upon personal histories and contacts, since scholars still found it necessary to travel in order to study. For this reason, the interests of individual scholars and their equally individual patrons continued to be crucial, as in the earlier period. A case in point is provided by Daniel of Morley, who provided a brief intellectual autobiography in the preface to his work on natural philosophy.[32] This was his *Philosophia* or *Liber de naturis inferiorum et superiorum,* written after his return to England following a period studying and translating in Spain, and at the request of John of Oxford, bishop of Norwich.[33] Daniel asserts that 'the wisest philosophers in the world' were to be found amongst the Arabs and that due to the obscurantism dominating the schools of Paris it was necessary for him to go to Toledo. This may have been facilitated, as Singer suggests, by the marriage of Alphonso VIII of Castille to Leonora, daughter of Eleanor of Aquitaine and Henry II of England. (Still further contacts were provided by the marriage of Richard I of England to Berengaria of Navarre in 1191, though Daniel was back in England by then.) It is not clear how long Daniel spent studying and translating in Toledo, but he returned with 'a valuable collection of books'. At first this deeply unfamiliar knowledge received a frosty response; but a fortunate encounter with Bishop John

---

[32] On this see C. Singer, 'Daniel of Morley. An English Philosopher of the XIIth Century' in *Isis*, Vol. 3, No.2, 1920, pp. 263–269.

[33] For the text, see K. Sudhoff, 'Daniels von Morley *Liber de naturis inferiorum et superiorum* nach der Handschrift. Cod. Arundel 377 des Britisches Museums zum Abdruck gebracht', *Archiv für die Geschichte der Naturwissenschaften und der Technik, Band 8,* 1917; and *Daniel of Morley, Philosophia,* ed. G. Maurach, *Mittellateinisches Jahrbuch* 14, 1979, pp. 204–255.

led to deep discussion of Arab teachings on meteorology and astronomy, and why it should be that sublunary bodies 'seem to obey the superior bodies by a necessary law'. As a result of this exchange, Daniel agreed to write up a survey of his new knowledge, to which he gave the title already mentioned. This is not a work of weather forecasting, nor was it widely copied, but it is nevertheless important in showing how the ground was prepared for the arrival of full astrometeorology. One of its most important sources was the *Introductorium maius* and it provided an effective, if somewhat idiosyncratic, outline of theories from that fundamental work, together with arguments taken from Aristotle's works on cosmology and meteorology.

One scholar who made more technical and practical use of the full battery of scientific knowledge on astronomy and astrology available in England in the late twelfth century was Roger of Hereford. The sources of his knowledge, and the locations of his training, are unknown. He is associated with Hereford partly by a set of astronomical tables for the meridian of Hereford (adapted from those of Raymond of Marseilles), which appear to have been drawn up in 1178, and are attributed to him. It is also likely that he is the 'Roger Infans' found in several Hereford charters of the last two decades of the twelfth century. The editing of the astronomical tables presumably sprang from his employment by Bishop Gilbert Foliot of Hereford to compile an ecclesiastical computus (for calculating the church calendar) in 1176.[34] However, Roger's expertise went considerably further than this, as is shown by his textbook on astrology, the *Liber de quatuor partibus judiciorum astronomie*. Here he shows knowledge of the work of Raymond of Marseilles mentioned above, as well as of Hermann of Carinthia's translation of Abu Ma'shar and Robert of Ketton's translation of Al-Khwarizmi.[35] This work was more successful than Daniel of Morley's, and has been found in more than twenty manuscripts (some containing only extracts).[36] The promised fourth part is not found in any of the manuscripts, but even so it is clear that the procedures dealt with here have to do with drawing charts and answering enquiries for individuals rather than making forecasts concerning the weather or other natural phenomena. As might be expected of a work on judicial astrology, no attention is given to

---

[34] Charles Burnett, 'Hereford, Roger of (fl. 1176–1198)', Oxford Dictionary of National Biography, Oxford, Oxford University Press, 2004, www.oxforddnb.com/view/article/23955 (accessed 16 October 2017), and references there.

[35] See N. Whyte, 'Roger of Hereford's *Liber de Astronomice iudicandi*: A Twelfth-Century Astrologer's Manual', M.Phil Dissertation, Cambridge, 1991, published online as a pdf, accessed 16 October 2017.

[36] J. North, *Horoscopes and History*, p. 39.

astrometeorological concepts such as the openings of the doors (or the mansions of the Moon). However, Roger's expertise in Islamicate developments of Ptolemaic science is shown by his tables of the natures and times of the signs, houses and planets, and of the latter's positions of strength and weakness.[37] Thus Roger clearly possessed the expertise required to make a weather forecast, if a client wished for this, and it is unfortunate that so little is known of his career.

An area within which knowledge such as Roger's was rapidly assimilated was that of medicine; and it is clear that Roger's own expertise was sought after in late twelfth-century England.[38] Later developments, in the growing university of Oxford, will be traced in a subsequent chapter.[39] Meanwhile, knowledge of the *Introductorium maius* was also spreading in England in the second half of the twelfth century. Indirect evidence is provided by the strictures of John of Salisbury against ambitious individuals who seek to foretell the future and to gain knowledge and power by illicit means. More positive is the testimony of Ralph of Cricklade, prior of St Frideswide's, Oxford, 1141 to ca. 1188, and author of a *Speculum fidei*. This work was compiled 1156–1160, and amongst its sources is the *Introductorium*, in the version of Hermann of Carinthia.[40] Ralph's quotations appear to be intended to make this alien author and book acceptable to Christian readers, and focus on how the stars 'guide' the natural world under the direction of God. He is also one of the first of many to argue that Abu Maʿshar's work gave information on the Incarnation and birth of Christ. His writing is very precise, and he says that he is quoting directly from the manuscript he read; and one interested patron was Robert, earl of Leicester. However, it is likely that Ralph's work was also known to the cleric, Peter of Blois, a writer who shows some slight knowledge of the *Introductorium*. Peter used a small part of what seems to have been the same version and referred only to the importance of the testimony on the birth of Christ.[41] Thus, despite anxieties as to both the sources and the uses of astrological knowledge, it was clearly spreading fast and far, especially (though not exclusively) amongst those with scientific interests.

---

[37] Roger's summary of these is: *ad quarum evidentiam tabulas de horis presupposuimus et naturis signorum et temporibus planetarum et domorum, debilitates planetarum, habitudines eorum adiuvium spatium, virtutum planetarum in signis et quantitatis virtutum*, see Whyte, ibid., p. 49. However Whyte also notes that the material is largely taken from Hermann of Carinthia's translation of Abu Maʿshar's *Introductorium maius*.

[38] See R. French, 'Foretelling the Future: Arabic Astrology and English Medicine in the Late Twelfth Century', *Isis*, Vol. 87, No. 3, 1996, pp. 453–480.

[39] See in particular R. French, 'Teaching Meteorology in Thirteenth Century Oxford. The Arabic Paraphrase', *Physis*, 36, n.s. fasc. I, 1999, pp. 99–129.

[40] Burnett, 'Arrival of Pagan Philosophers', p. 87.   [41] Ibid., p. 89.

This chapter has shown that responses to the implications and the applications of the new science, of which astrometeorology formed a part, were both complex and varied in the twelfth century. What is perhaps striking is the absence of the types of attack met by earlier pioneers. This can be explained by the fact that at the heart of the new science was a body of geometrical and mathematical tools and models that could be studied and applied in isolation from any specific religious or ideological debates. This new body of knowledge was central to what has been called the 'de-animation of the heavens', which arguably took place in both the Islamicate and Latin worlds across the medieval period.[42] Study of the illuminations to be found in astronomical manuscripts and calendars shows that there was no outright rejection of the classical imagery of deities, heroes and monsters used to identify the various celestial bodies. Nevertheless, the discussions of celestial matter, motions and powers that proliferated from the twelfth century on were conducted on a new, and highly technical, level. The universe was not yet routinely described as a mechanism, in the manner found in thirteenth-century textbooks on astronomy and cosmology; nor was it accepted that the structures that comprised the universe could continue to move along their divinely ordained paths without the presence of some form of intelligence or impulsion. Nevertheless, the rules outlined above for calculating the positions of the planets on a chosen date, and coming to a judgement as to the likely meteorological effects of their spatial inter-actions, could be followed without any need to engage in cosmological or theological debate. Moreover, it had been established at least since the time of St Augustine that things above exercise influence over material things below, and there was no doubt that the weather, complex as it is, was a phenomenon produced and experienced on a material level.

One thing that has emerged clearly from the evidence analysed in this chapter is that the range of knowledge required to carry out astrometeor-ological forecasting was just as extensive as that for making other forms of astrological prediction. Weather forecasts were thus likely to be produced by those with overall expertise rather than by astrometeorological spe-cialists; but the evidence discussed here has shown that interest in the subject was widespread and serious. Both in the form of short treatises on weather forecasting itself, and as dedicated sections within surveys of

---

[42] See especially R.C. Dales, 'The De-animation of the Heavens in the Middle Ages', *Journal of the History of Ideas*, 41, 4, 1980, pp. 531–550. Dales' views were powerfully challenged by E. Grant, *Planets, Stars, and Orbs; The Medieval Cosmos, 1200–1687*, Cambridge, Cambridge University Press, 1994, especially in the section 'Are the heavens alive?', pp. 469–487.

what was made possible by the new science, astrometeorology had a special place. An impressive amount of time and work clearly went into the translation, dissemination and reception of this body of knowledge. However, weather forecasting was not of interest only to scholars in the medieval period. The political, economic and military importance of the weather endowed foreknowledge with great value. At the same time, mastery of newly available knowledge on questions of natural philosophy gained in prestige. For both these reasons it is important to trace the routes by which the new, scientific weather forecasting was brought into the courts of the powerful. That task will be taken up in the next chapter.

5   The Contested Rise of Astrometeorology

The short outlines of the techniques and theories involved in the practice of astrometeorology set out in the preceding chapters have shown two things very clearly. The first is that this was not a specialism that could be learnt on its own; skill in making such forecasts depended crucially upon preexisting expertise in astronomy, together with knowledge of geography, mathematics and geometry and their associated instruments. The second is that, whilst the various available texts broadly agreed on the central ideas and techniques to be applied, they disagreed substantially on the degree of importance to be placed on the various factors in play when making a specific forecast. Thus the new science of weather forecasting was put into something of the same situation as the much older science of medicine. In other words, expertise was only acquired after substantial investment of time, money and effort, and was scarce, although growing, and for this reason experts expected to receive payment or other reward for their services. It could be added that the two areas of expertise were also comparable in that, whilst the rich and powerful might well pay handsomely in times of need, failures or mistakes could bring risks to the practitioners. In practice there was another, more direct, link between the two fields, namely that the astronomical expertise required for astrometeorology was also coming to be seen as central in advanced forms of medicine. Thus by the second half of the twelfth century the rather shadowy, and frequently changing, figures employed as royal doctors and physicians will also have had much of the knowledge required to make weather forecasts. However, in the absence of lists of their books or details of the services they provided for their powerful employers (the second of which is hardly to be expected) this is very hard to examine in detail.

What can be said is that a certain scepticism, or even fear, towards such professionals, and the exotic or downright dangerous knowledge that they possessed, is demonstrated in literature associated with the royal courts of Europe. John of Salisbury, supporter of Archbishop

Thomas Becket and later bishop of Chartres, wrote a well-known critique of what he perceived as the rise in the practice of various forms of magic both in the Church and in the royal court. Indeed, John's closeness to Thomas Becket gave him privileged knowledge of details such as Becket's consultation, whilst Henry II's Chancellor, of a palm-reader. The enquiry was undertaken in order to gain information as to the likely outcome of military actions in Wales. This surprising information is given in John's treatise on politics and government, the *Policraticus*, (Bk 2, chapter 27). Perhaps even more surprising is the link between expertise in palm-reading and knowledge of healthcare, which was accepted in late twelfth-century England. This is demonstrated by the prestigious manuscript known as the Eadwine Psalter, which is now Cambridge, Trinity College, MS. R. 17 1.[1] This psalter appears to have been made or commissioned by one Eadwine, who is depicted as a monastic scribe in a full-page miniature. It was subsequently given to the Benedictine priory of Canterbury Cathedral.[2] It is remarkable in many ways, but what is relevant here is that it contains, in addition to its main text, maps showing the system of pipes delivering clean water around the cathedral precincts and carrying away dirty water, a diagram and note on the identification of comets, a text on divination from a person's name and the earliest-known Latin exposition of palm-reading.[3] That such a combination of expertise was available in Canterbury in the second half of the twelfth century, and was so highly regarded as to be recorded in a volume also containing one of the fundamental texts of the monastic liturgy, perhaps helps to explain John of Salisbury's misgivings. However, John of Salisbury does not include astrometeorology in his descriptions of dangerously magical practices, and this is in accordance with the fact that the influence of the stars and planets over the physical world (including the physical body) was accepted as straightforward, scientific fact. From St Augustine onwards, what worried Christian theologians and moralists about the magic arts was the contact they opened up between vulnerable humans and predatory demons. This was not in question when the stars and planets were simply affecting the elements and their disposition on Earth.

---

[1] http://trin-sites-pub.trin.cam.ac.uk/james/viewpage.php?index=1229 (accessed 7 November 2017).

[2] For discussion see M. Gibson, T. Heslop and R. Pfaff, Eds., *The Eadwine Psalter*, Philadelphia, Pennsylvania State University Press, 1992.

[3] See C. Burnett: 'The Eadwine Psalter and the Western Tradition of the Onomancy in Pseudo-Aristotle's Secret of Secrets', *Archives d'Histoire Doctrinale et Littéraire du Moyen Âge*, 55, 1988, pp. 143–167; and 'The Earliest Chiromancy in the West', *Journal of Warburg and Courtauld Instititutes*, 50, 1987, pp. 189–195.

Analysis of the widespread medieval genre known as 'mirrors of princes', in other words treatises written by aspiring scholars and advisers offering information and guidance to rulers, leads to the same conclusion. These works may not always have been taken seriously by their recipients, but they nevertheless offer good evidence as to what was perceived as necessary or valuable knowledge for rulers, together with insights as to what was undesirable. John of Salisbury's *Policraticus*, mentioned above, may be placed in this category, but other examples were found all across medieval Europe, and persisted into the early modern period. An analysis of nearly fifty works found that four key themes are addressed in all of them, with the first two being the obvious categories of the practice of rulership and the personal qualities desirable in good rulers. It is perhaps surprising that religious ideas and principles come in only third in the list, with this being most marked in Christian works, and it is very striking that a close fourth position is occupied by knowledge of geography and of the natural world, including climate and weather.[4] A further relevant point is that this fourth major theme rose considerably in importance in Christian texts from the twelfth century onwards, and was more popular in such works than in Islamic ones from the end of the thirteenth century.

An early stage in the ascension of astronomical and meteorological study into the ranks of knowledge highly valued for rulers is represented by Adelard of Bath's treatise on the astrolabe, discussed earlier.[5] This is a specialist work rather than a wide-ranging treatise; but it is addressed to a youthful prince named Henry, and states that this prince is already aware of the importance of natural philosophy in general and the works of the Arabs on astronomy in particular. That such knowledge is not dangerous, but rather necessary for a good ruler, is emphasised by the principle that anyone who wishes to rule successfully needs to understand not just the physical nature of the world but also the rules that govern its wonders. Indeed, Adelard asserts that the young prince has actually commissioned him to write down in Latin what he has learned from

---

[4] L. Blades, J. Grimmer, and A. McQueen, 'Mirrors for Princes and Sultans: Advice on the Art of Governance in the Medieval Christian and Islamic Worlds', published as a pdf by Stamford University, 2014, and available from their website: http://stanford.edu/~jgrimmer/BGM_final.pdf (accessed 7 November 2017).

[5] See C. Haskins, 'Adelard of Bath and Henry Plantagenet', *The English Historical Review* XXVIII (CXI), 1913, pp. 515–516. There is no modern, published edition of the text, nor a modern English translation. For discussion see E. Poulle, 'Le traité de l'astrolabe d'Adelard de Bath' in C. Burnett, Ed., *Adelard of Bath: An English Scientist and Arabist of the Early Twelfth Century*, London, 1987, pp. 119–132. For translations of extracts see A. Lawrence-Mathers and C. Escobar-Vargas, *Magic and Medieval Society*, New York, Routledge, 2014, pp. 107–108.

the Arabs, in order to make this possible. Such statements cannot be taken as simple facts; but equally it would be bold on Adelard's part to make such an assertion without any basis. A further small piece of evidence for the importance and perceived usefulness of the new, Arabic and Islamicate, astronomy is provided by the survival of a set of ten 'political' horoscopes from the middle of the twelfth century. These are now bound up, without any clear provenance, in B.L., MS. Royal App. 85, folios 2r and 2v. They deal with questions such as whether a Norman army will come (presumably to England) and whether the barons of Anjou will be loyal, and appear to relate to the long civil war between Stephen of Blois and the Empress Matilda. Political analyses link them to both sides in the conflict; but there is cautious agreement that, if they were drawn up in England and at the time in question, then the most likely person to have created them is Adelard of Bath.[6] There is no record of Adelard or any other scholar or cleric acting as an astrologer (as opposed to a doctor) to the king; but it is hardly likely that there would be. The key points here are that individuals with the skills to draw up astronomical and astrological charts for chosen times and chosen questions were spreading across Europe by the middle of the twelfth century, and that ambitious rulers were being made aware of the expanding frontiers of available knowledge.

It could be argued that, since the maintenance of good health involved keeping the body in balance with external conditions, the making of weather forecasts was a part of the expertise required in a fully trained doctor.[7] That the duties of such professionals could include the giving of advice and even the interpretation of dreams is shown by a well-known narrative in the chronicle now known as that of John of Worcester. In his account of events in the Anglo-Norman realm in the years 1128–1133, John, a monk of the cathedral priory of Worcester, told how he had been present at Winchcombe when one of Henry I's doctors, a Lotharingian named Grimbald, told of a sequence of nightmares that afflicted the king.[8] It seems that Grimbald saw the terrified king leap out of bed and

---

[6] The main proponent of the idea that the horoscopes were drawn up for Henry Plantagenet is J. North. See especially 'Some Norman horoscopes', in Burnett, Ed., *Adelard of Bath*, pp. 147–161. Further discussion is given by N. Vincent, 'The Court of Henry II', in C. Harper-Bill and N. Vincent, Eds., *Henry II: New Interpretations*, Woodbridge, Boydell, 2007, pp. 278–334.

[7] Petrus Alfonsi's 'Letter' emphasised that astronomy was needed for use in medicine, in predicting eclipses, and in weather forecasting, and made it clear that experts like himself could offer all these.

[8] For these annals see: *The Chronicle of John of Worcester III: The Annals from 1067 to 1140 with the Gloucester Interpolations and the Continuation to 1141*, Ed. P. McGurk, Oxford, Clarendon Press, 1998, pp. 174–211.

prepare to defend himself against attack, but was able to convince Henry that he was simply dreaming. More than that, the chronicler states that Grimbald interpreted the dreams as warnings that the king should do penance; John even compares Grimbald to the prophet Daniel, who interpreted the dream-visions of Nebuchadnezzar, as told in chapter two of the Book of Daniel.[9] John's account presents Grimbald in a wholly positive light, but it is not hard to see how courtiers could be worried by the doctor's privileged position in relation to the king. It is this sort of anxiety that is reflected in Geoffrey of Monmouth's *History of the Kings of Britain*, which caused a sensation when it appeared in the 1130s by revealing a whole new view of the early history of Britain. Amongst Geoffrey's stories of good and bad kings those relating to King Arthur have attracted by far the most attention, but he also warns of the dangers posed by allowing relatively unknown physicians to have access to the king. A Saxon named Eopa who has some medical knowledge succeeds in fooling the British King Aurelius and his courtiers into believing that he is a monk and a doctor and is thus able to poison the king.[10] That the new science of interpreting the stars could also have powerfully negative military and political applications is shown by Geoffrey's account of the 'Spanish magician', Pellitus.[11] Pellitus' skills in reading the stars (and interpreting the flight of birds) mean that he is able to warn the Saxon King Edwin of the military and naval movements of his enemy, the British King Cadwallo, and thus ensure victory for Edwin. Clearly such expertise would be both highly dangerous and extremely valuable.

However, whilst Geoffrey's version of British history was taken very seriously from the twelfth to the sixteenth century, and accepted across all of Europe with only a very few critics, its negative view of the new scientific and medical knowledge contrasts with the positive approach taken in the works offering political and practical advice to contemporary rulers. These, as noted above, included natural philosophy and meteor-ology, in up to date forms, within the knowledge recommended for rulers. The central questions raised at this point are thus, whether astro-meteorology was reaching the courts of powerful patrons by the middle of the twelfth century, and how practitioners were perceived. It is clear that, despite the confidence of experts in the impeccable scientific cre-dentials of this new field, scholars in positions close to secular and ecclesiastical leaders had misgivings as to the applications and sources

---

[9] For discussion of these annals and the illustrations in Oxford, Corpus Christi College, MS 157, pp. 380–383, see A. Lawrence-Mathers, 'John of Worcester and the Science of History', *Journal of Medieval History*, 39:3, 2013, pp. 255–274, and references there.
[10] Geoffrey of Monmouth, *The History of the Kings of Britain*, viii, 15.   [11] Ibid., xii, 4.

of the new science of the stars. The technical instructions discussed in the preceding chapters were clearly aimed at practitioners rather than at their patrons and clients, and there is no evidence that copies of them were included in the libraries of rulers at this early stage. It is therefore necessary to look for less direct forms of evidence as to how and when astrometeorological knowledge and practice became available in medieval courts.

An early witness is provided by the *Dragmaticon* written by the scholar and philosopher, William of Conches. William appears to have been born in Normandy, and to have spent part of his career teaching at a cathedral school, possibly that of Chartres. His achievements as a teacher and textual commentator were celebrated by John of Salisbury; but William left this post after a disagreement with the bishop (whose name is not recorded). The *Dragmaticon* is presented as a learned discussion on natural philosophy with the duke of Normandy, rather than a technical treatise addressing an expert audience.[12] This work represents a major survey of up to date topics in natural philosophy, bringing together scientific knowledge with William's own philosophical and theological views. It was probably written in the 1140s, when its patron, Geoffrey Plantagenet, was duke of Normandy as well as count of Anjou. The *Dragmaticon* remained respected and widely read into the later Middle Ages, with at least eighty manuscripts of the Latin text still surviving.[13] It was also revised and edited by a rival, contemporary theologian, whose name is not known. This 'edition' was made to accord more closely with the views of Hugh of St Victor, the celebrated teacher and theologian based in the recently founded house of St Victor, in Paris. In this form the work is known as the *Compendium philosophiae* and survives in a further three known copies. By the 1140s William had had a long and successful, if controversial, career as a philosopher (in both the theological and the natural branches) in Chartres and Paris. His early views on philosophy, expressed in his *Philosophia* in the 1120s, were sufficiently emboldened by the latest medical and scientific knowledge arriving north of the Alps to attract condemnation from those powerful critics, William

---

[12] For the text see *Guillelmus de Conchis: Dragmaticon; Summa de philosophia in vulgari*, Eds. I. Ronca, L. Badia, J. Pujol, *Corpus Christianorum Continuatio Medievalia*, 152, Turnhout, Brepols, 1997. A translation based on this edition is given in *William of Conches; A Dialogue on Natural Philosophy (Dragmaticon Philosophiae)*, Trans. I. Ronca and M. Curr, Notre Dame, Indiana, University of Notre Dame Press, 1997.

[13] Fundamental research on this is presented in L. Thorndike, 'More Manuscripts of the *Dragmaticon* and *Philosophia* of William of Conches', *Speculum*, 20: 1, 1945, pp. 84–87. For a survey of later findings see J. Cadden, 'Science and Rhetoric in the Middle Ages: The Natural Philosophy of William of Conches', *Journal of the History of Ideas*, 56: 1, 1995, pp. 1–24.

of St Thierry and St Bernard of Clairvaux.[14] Two points that drew particular criticism were William of Conches' arguments on spirits and his assertion that Eve was not made from Adam's rib. Neither was based directly on astronomical treatises, but both show an openness to new understandings of the universe, the human body, and the power of human reason. In the *Dragmaticon* William carefully corrects the points on which he had been condemned, but still sets out a bold overview of the growing knowledge of the universe. Moreover, just like Daniel of Morley and Petrus Alfonsi, he criticises the priorities of contemporary European philosophers who are represented as valuing linguistic analysis and literary style more highly than the serious effort of understanding God's creation.

It has been generally accepted that the patronage that William of Conches apparently received from Geoffrey of Anjou shows that William was acting as tutor to the sons of Geoffrey and the Empress Matilda. Certainly there is evidence that both Geoffrey and his son, the future Henry II of England, were perceived as highly educated.[15] However this may not have been quite as unusual as it appears amongst the higher aristocracy in France at the time, at least amongst those families who aspired to rise even higher. Support for this suggestion comes from the poem of praise that Abbot Baudri of Bourgueil wrote for Adela, regent countess of Blois.[16] Adela was the daughter of William the Conqueror, wife of the count of Blois, and mother of the future King Stephen of England, and the poem demonstrates that she was very aware of her dynastic importance. The families of Blois and Anjou were rivals in France, the Holy Land and England, and Baudri's poem suggests that Adela was being encouraged to patronise advanced learning just as much as the duke of Normandy and count of Anjou. Adela's husband, Stephen of Blois, died on crusade in 1102, leaving her regent for their son, Thibaud. The poem is clearly not intended to be taken as a literal description of Adela's lifestyle and 'royal chambers' but nevertheless suggests that advanced knowledge of astronomy, geography, history (biblical and secular) and all the liberal arts was desirable for those aspiring to the higher echelons of power. It contrives to flatter Adela by stating that she is already a patron of all these forms of knowledge while

---

[14] See J. Leclerq, 'Les lettres de Guillaume de Saint-Thierry à Saint Bernard', *Revue Bénédictine*, 79, 1969, pp. 375–391.

[15] J. Cadden, p. 19.

[16] See L. Delisle, 'Poème adressé à Adèle, fille de Guillaume le Conquérant, par Baudri, abbé de Bourgueil', *Mémoires de la Société des Antiquaires de Normandie*, 28, 1870/71, pp. 187–224; and M. Otter, 'Baudri of Bourgueil, "To Countess Adela"', *Journal of Medieval Latin*, 11, 2001, pp. 60–141.

working to show that Baudri could offer induction into even greater mastery, as well as ensuring a fitting place for Adela's family in the historical record.

Returning to the *Dragmaticon* it is perhaps the case that William of Conches may have known more about astrometeorology than has previously been suggested. There is internal evidence in the *Dragmaticon* that William was familiar with Adelard's *Natural Questions* and it is striking that the *Dragmaticon* is frequently copied in manuscripts together with Adelard's treatise on the astrolabe – though this does not prove that William actually knew the latter.[17] Indeed, William's knowledge of recent discoveries in astronomy has been shown to be impressive, although William himself adhered to traditional, Platonic, views on cosmology rather than accepting the more Aristotelian concepts found in newly translated Arabic works. One of the more surprising recent discoveries concerning the sources used in the *Dragmaticon* is the demonstration that William knew and used a text usually attributed in the medieval period to Masha'allah and listed under the title *Liber de orbe*.[18] William is a very early witness to the dissemination of this treatise, and appears to have known an unusual version of it. The most popular Latin translation was that produced in Toledo by the prolific translator of scientific texts, Gerard of Cremona (d. 1182).[19] The version used by William may also have been produced in Spain, but was much vaguer as to the original author of the work. It is also curious that William used it for only two issues within his survey of astronomy: the orbit and movements of Saturn, and proof for the spherical shape of the Earth. However, the presence of such recently translated and technical material in William's book fits with his even earlier use of medical treatises also newly available from Arabic sources. It is thus possible to argue that William's scientific 'encyclopedia', compiled for the duke of Normandy, is representative of an important route by which new ideas about the weather and the possibility of accurate forecasting were being conveyed to rulers. For that reason it is worth detailed attention.

The *Dragmaticon* is organised in six books, and is in many ways an extended version of topics covered in classical works on meteorology.

---

[17] C. Burnett, *The Introduction of Arabic Learning into England*, London, British Library, 1998, 54.

[18] On this see: B. Obrist, 'William of Conches, Masha'Allah and Twelfth-Century Cosmology', *Archives d'Histoire Doctrinale et Littéraire du Moyen Age*, 76, 2009, pp. 29–87; and T. Mimura, 'The Arabic original of (ps.) Masha'allah's *Liber de orbe*; its date and authorship', *British Journal for the History of Science*, 48:2, 2015, pp. 321–352.

[19] See C. Burnett, 'The Coherence of the Arabic-Latin Translation Program in Toledo in the Twelfth Century', *Science in Context*, 14 (1/2), 2001, pp. 249–288.

Within this, Book Three deals with the heavens and the stars as well as with humans and animals, while Book Four moves on to a more technical discussion of the planets and the details of their movements. Book Five offers a more traditional version of meteorology, closely based on Seneca's *Natural Questions*. This work was relatively little known in the early Middle Ages, although there is evidence that excerpts, at least, were studied at Reichenau and in the circle of Alcuin in the ninth century. The full text was fairly widely distributed in the twelfth century, and its popularity rose further in the thirteenth.[20] However, in the books of the *Dragmaticon* based on more 'modern' science, the discussions of climate, seasons, and patterns of weather are conducted in more technically scientific language, just as William promised in his preface. For instance, in part 6 of Book Two, William sets out his explanation of the processes by which the movements of the Sun actually bring about seasonal change on Earth. The Sun is the source of heat for the sublunary atmosphere and the Earth below it, and a lowering in the degree of this heat can cause the elements of air and fire to contract and even to be turned into water or earth. Similarly an increase in heat can reverse the process. In relation to seasons on Earth, a crucial role in triggering the onset of summer is played by the Sun's passage across the Tropic of Cancer. This in turn is in contact with the temperate zone of the Earth below, and as the Sun moves and crosses the Tropic it actually sets part of the air alight, causing fire that warms water on the surface of the Earth. Some of the water is heated enough to turn into vaporous air, while the remaining water is still warm enough to heat the upper part of the earth and to liquefy some of it. Conversely winter is triggered when the Sun moves across the Tropic of Capricorn and these transformations are reversed.[21]

Further relevant points are made in Book Three, when the Philosopher and the Duke discuss the structure of the universe and the elements of which it is composed. The Duke is presented as learned and interested in the disagreements between Plato and Aristotle on these issues, whilst remaining more traditional in his views than the Philosopher. In part 6 of this book the conversation turns to the movement of the fixed stars, and the Philosopher is definite that they move with the Firmament, the outermost sphere of the universe. Thus they are carried with the Firmament around the Earth, moving from the East through the South to the West and on to the North before returning to the East. This leads into a slightly unclear account of the obliquity of the ecliptic in relation to the

---

[20] See H. Hine, 'The Manuscript Tradition of Seneca's *Natural Questions*: Addenda', *Classical Quarterly*, 42, 2, 1992, pp. 558–562.

[21] Ronca and Curr, pp. 32–33.

celestial equator. After this preparation, Book Four moves into a discussion of the roles of the other planets in relation to the seasons.[22] The first to be considered is the outermost, Saturn, which takes a slow thirty years to complete a circuit around the belt of the zodiac. The Philosopher states cautiously that it 'is said' to be cold and destructive; but goes on to expound the advanced theory that the cold of Saturn can diminish the effective heat of the Sun. Thus, if Saturn is close to the Sun at the time when the Sun is in Cancer and making its transit of the Tropic of Cancer, the heat will be reduced – and so, consequently, will the processes outlined above. The next planet, Jupiter, is also important for weather as well as other natural processes. This is because it is benevolent, and can moderate both the destructive cold of Saturn and the destructive heat of Mars when it is close to them.

The discussion becomes still more technical, though not always entirely clear, when the Philosopher moves on to the movements and effects of Mars. This planet moves quickly, completing a circuit in two years, and is harmful, hot and dry. This, like the basic idea of planets on eccentric orbits, could already be found in the traditional accounts of astronomy produced as luxury books in the Carolingian and Ottonian periods (see Chapter 2). However, the Philosopher now goes on to expound a version of the Ptolemaic theory of epicycles in addition to circular orbits with individual centres, and of how this helps to provide an explanation of planetary retrograde motion. Here William is attempting to summarise recent discoveries from Arabic astronomy; but he does not seem fully clear on the relationship between epicycles and eccentrics, despite his references to the views of the 'Chaldeans'. Next come the closer planets, Venus and Mercury, and it emerges, as in the astrometeorological works already discussed, that these lower planets are less powerful than the higher ones. Venus is benevolent and also temperate, and thus usually brings positive effects, but these are weakened when, at the highest point of its orbit, it comes close to Mars. This will happen relatively frequently, since Venus takes only one year to complete a circuit. Mercury moves slightly faster still, and is close to Venus (we learn) when Venus is at the lowest point of its own orbit.

However, the Philosopher notes that there is not yet agreement on the relative positions of Mercury, Venus and the Sun, and this acknowledgement leads into a further discussion of epicycles. Here, William seems to attempt to reconcile the newer astronomical views with the old-established ones. He says that an epicycle is a circle that exists wholly

---

[22] Ronca and Curr, pp. 58–68.

above the Earth, enclosing no part of the Earth. Moreover an epicycle itself revolves around a larger circle, and at least in the case of Saturn this is the eccentric circle of the planet's orbit.[23] In the cases of Venus and Mercury, William adheres to the view that their orbits go around the Sun rather than directly around the Earth. The assertion is made that Venus and Mercury move from West to East, whilst travelling with and close to the Sun. What he says is that their 'epicyclic orbits' are centred on the Sun, with Mercury's going around its middle and Venus' being placed above the middle of the Sun. However, when Venus and Mercury are at the highest points of their respective orbits both are higher than the Sun. Sadly, although this point, like the ensuing outline of the direction of movement of these planets and the closeness of the three, will have consequences for the weather, this is not pursued in this chapter. A final weather-related point comes in chapter 7 of Book Four, when the argument is made that the planets move around the Earth from West to East, thus balancing the firmament's opposite direction of travel. This prevents negative pressures on Earth, although the power of the firmament is such that it still exerts a force over the planets. In the case of the Sun it is this pull from the firmament that prevents it from being continuously above the Earth for six months, and thus moderates its heating effects.[24]

Some of these arguments are further reinforced in Book Four, where the seasons and their relationship to human health are discussed. An interesting point is raised in chapter 10, when the Duke points out that the Sun is the same distance from the Earth when it is in Aries, Taurus and Gemini as when it is in Leo, Virgo and Libra, and yet the latter period is usually warmer. The Philosopher's answer is that in Spring the Sun's heat is largely taken up in bringing moisture out from the earth, whereas by Autumn this moisture has been dried up, and thus it takes until the Sun reaches Libra in late September for the heat to fade again. A further good point is made by the Duke in chapter 11, when he asks how it can be that seasons vary from year to year in one and the same place. Here William draws on Arabic medical works translated by Constantine the African, and the astronomical works already outlined, in

---

[23] Ibid., p. 62.

[24] Adelard of Bath's *Natural Questions* cover related points, for instance in the discussion of the obliquity of the ecliptic and its effect on the seasons. See Adelard of Bath, *Conversations with His Nephew: On the Same and the Different, Questions on Natural Science, and on Birds*, Ed. and Trans. C. Burnett, Cambridge, Cambridge University Press, 1998, pp. 214–215.

putting together the Philosopher's answer.[25] Constantine produced a series of important translations of medical works during the second half of the eleventh century (he died before 1099) and was received as a monk at the great abbey of Monte Cassino. From Constantine's translations comes the statement that the planets too have seasons as they move around their orbits, and that these can affect the seasons caused on Earth by the Sun. From the astronomical treatise comes the alternative suggestion that this could be the result of other planets affecting the Sun directly when they are close enough to do so. Here William, like Constantine and other authors already discussed, states that any good physician needs to know not only the position of the Sun on the zodiac but also the positions of the other planets, and which ones are placed close to the Sun. A knowledge of their natural qualities is also vital. The detailed astronomical knowledge required for weather forecasting would exceed this, but the astronomical knowledge accepted as needed by skilled doctors is already clear.

After these explorations of new ideas and techniques, Book Five reverts almost entirely to Seneca for its outline of meteorology (in the classical sense), together with use of Pliny's *Natural History* and a very few references to Adelard's *Natural Questions*. However, William does convey a sense that he and his Philosopher-figure are reasoning out central issues rather than simply copying the unnamed sources. An example of this occurs when the Philosopher not only repeats the established view that winds are caused when air is stirred up and made to flow but also rejects the suggestion that the stirring is caused by a buildup of moisture particles in the air.[26] His preferred explanation is that the movements of the ocean cause changes in the air, though other factors, such as the formation and breakdown of clouds, can also be involved. Interestingly, in at least one manuscript of the *Dragmaticon*, this causes a rupture between text and illustration. The diagram of the wind rose inserted at this point follows Seneca's description of the winds, even though William's version differs from it.[27] Winds and their causes and effects, including on temperature and moisture in the air, are discussed for some time, but there is nothing here pertaining to astrometeorology. The arguments are conducted entirely in traditional, terrestrial terms.

The same conclusion applies to the discussions of rain, the rainbow, hail and snow, which follow in chapters 3–5. Careful thought has gone

---

[25] See I. Ronca, 'The influence of the *Pantegni* on William of Conches's *Dragmaticon*' in C. Burnett and D. Jacquart, Eds., *Constantine the African and Ali Ibn al-Abbas al-Magusi: the Pantegni and Related Texts*, Brill, Leiden, 1994, pp. 266–285.

[26] Ronca and Curr pp. 92–93.   [27] Ibid., p. 95.

into unifying and summarising the views of authorities, but there is no mention of the movements and interactions of the planets as causes of these phenomena. The lengthy analysis of thunder and lightning in chapter 6 conforms to the same approach, whilst demonstrating erudition by considering a wide range of arguments. In all these cases care is taken to provide explanations for the seasonal patterns and variations in occurrence and severity. It is such seasonal patterns, together with the physical causes that bring them about, which make the traditional signs of coming weather provided by the behaviour of animals and birds reliable. As in previous chapters there is no attempt to suggest that agreed answers have been reached to all questions and disagreements. Indeed, a tantalising list of phenomena not yet accounted for, such as how lightning can melt a sword whilst not harming its sheath, is set out. It is perhaps not coincidental that it is the Duke who wishes to discuss shooting stars, heavenly fires and comets, given that all these were potentially identifiable as signs of earthly events. Here again the Philosopher's answers are largely dependent on Seneca; and the established views on their roles as signs of coming weather are reinforced. However, the material on comets in particular does suggest a real attempt to offer a wide-ranging survey on this complex subject. The Philosopher is informed on the fact that comets, unlike planets, can appear outside of the band of the zodiac. Interestingly, he accepts that comets have a fiery nature and are recognisable by their long, 'hairy' tails, but he makes no mention of the established view that their appearances presage political upheavals. Instead he merely states that they are signs of stormy weather, strong winds and rains, before suggesting a change of subject.

Chapter 9 sees a shift to analysis of waters and tides, with the causative links between oceanic movements and winds again explored. A persuasive, physical model for this is propounded, and the natures and consequent meteorological effects of winds from each compass direction are dealt with. This leads the Duke to ask the important question of how winds can be so variable, if the ocean currents flow according to given patterns. The answer is once again conceived in purely terrestrial terms, since the Philosopher says that such variations are caused by variations in terrain on the ground and by differing temperatures in moving layers of air. Similar points arise in the discussion in chapter 12 of floods and other extreme weather events. The Duke again asks how such events can happen, and how they can be so varied in their occurrence, if weather is produced by regularly occurring causes. The answer is, in effect, that small variations in seasonal patterns can have cumulative effects, and that if these build up for long enough then an extreme will be reached. Equally, such effects can be magnified by subterranean shifts, such as underground rivers breaking through their 'banks' to cause floods, or disappearing into new rifts in the earth and leaving dried-out land above them.

However, a tentative step towards astrometeorology is also taken in this chapter. The Philosopher says that a possible cause of floods is that if all the planets 'rise at the same time', and are distant from the Earth, then they will draw less moisture from the Earth than usual, thus leaving a surplus. Equally, if they set at the same time their joint closeness to the Earth will lead to a conflagration. This explanation suggests a lack of familiarity with the newer calculations of planetary orbits, despite its interest in the powers of the planets. Further reinforcement of this conclusion is provided in Book Six, and its discussion of the Earth. A clear and confident discussion of the climatic zones on the surface of the Earth, and how these relate to the visible sky, is provided in chapter 3. Similarly, a clear outline of the zodiac constellations and their assigned positions in the heavens is provided. But equally there is no discussion of technical issues such as the precession of the equinoxes or the increasing dislocation between the portions of the zodiac assigned to the 'signs' and the actual positions of the constellations after which these signs are named. Once again, the chief authorities named are long-established ones such as Juvenal, Boethius and Virgil. Thus the overall impression of the *Dragmaticon* is that it is placed slightly uncomfortably on the boundary between the old science and the new. The cutting-edge science promised to the ambitious Geoffrey of Anjou is genuinely delivered in the senses that William strongly supports the growing move to allocate observable phenomena directly to divine intervention only when physical causes cannot be found, and he brings elements of the new science of the stars into certain, selected discussions. On the other hand, even though there is clear ambition to use newly available sources, pride of place in this category is given to Seneca's *Natural Questions* and thus to works that remain within the established world view.

Overall the *Dragmaticon* suggests caution in relation to the new science of the stars and its applications. There is evidence of interest in the possibility of astrometeorology, but no sign that William himself could perform it. However, there is clear evidence that expertise in astrometeorology was being demonstrated at this very time within Latin Europe by Abraham Ibn Ezra. Still more importantly, Ibn Ezra appears to have been active as a teacher of this technique, amongst other branches of the new science. This polymathic scholar was almost a contemporary of William of Conches and Petrus Alfonsi. Like the latter, Ibn Ezra was born in Tudela, in Muslim al Andalus (ca. 1090). Tudela was under Muslim rule at this time but was conquered by Alfonso I of Aragon in

1115. Unlike Petrus Alfonsi, Ibn Ezra did not convert to Christianity. He studied in both Saragossa (conquered in 1118) and Cordoba, and was an acclaimed expert in both the Hebrew tradition of Biblical commentary and the new sciences (studied primarily in Arabic). For reasons apparently having to do with the political and religious insecurity in his home region he left al Andalus in about 1140, and spent the next twenty years or more travelling in Latin Europe. His career has to be pieced together from brief references in his surviving works to places, dates and patrons, but there is broad agreement on the outline.[28] He travelled first into Italy, and stayed for a few years in Rome before moving on to Lucca, Pisa, Mantua and Verona. In one of his scientific works, the *Sefer ha-Olam (Book of the World)*, he recorded astronomical observations and astrological calculations made during this time in both Lucca and Pisa. One of his sets of planetary tables, the 'Pisan Tables', is datable to 1143, and was produced close in time to commentaries on these tables and to works on the astrolabe.[29] From Italy he took ship to Provence, and lived for several years in Narbonne and Béziers. At some point he visited Bordeaux and Angers, before settling for longer in Rouen. He is finally recorded in London, before disappearing in the 1160s. It is remarkable that during all this time he appears to have been supported by patrons, students and (probably) clients in the regions through which he passed.

One method by which Ibn Ezra was able to earn money seems to have been by issuing new versions of his key scientific works, presumably revised with differing audiences as well as different societies in mind. Throughout his travels Ibn Ezra seems to have been in close contact with local Jewish communities, and these would clearly have been the main readership for his works in Hebrew, which included poetry and treatises on the Jewish calendar as well as Biblical commentaries. However, his scientific works raise more complex problems as to their audience and patrons (and even their attribution). This is partly because of increasing evidence that Ibn Ezra himself may have been involved in the production of early Latin versions of these works as well as those in Hebrew. To make the situation still more complex, it has been shown that some of Ibn

---

[28] See S. Sela, *Abraham Ibn Ezra and the Rise of Medieval Hebrew Science*, Leiden and Boston, Brill, 2003.

[29] Argument continues on the precise details of Ibn Ezra's career. See for instance C. Burnett, 'Advertising the New Science of the Stars circa 1120-50', in *Le xiie siècle. Mutations et renouveau en France dans la première moitié du xiie siècle*, Paris, Etudes publiées sous la direction de F. Gaspari, 1994, pp. 147–157; and R. Smithuis 'Science in Normandy and England under the Angevins. The Creation of Avraham ibn Ezra's Latin Works on Astronomy and Astrology', in G. Busi, Ed., *Hebrew to Latin, Latin to Hebrew: The Mirroring of Two Cultures in the Age of Humanism*, Berlin, Institut für Judaistik, Freie Universität, and Turin, N. Aragno Editore, 2006, pp. 23–60.

Ezra's main textbooks on astrology have an extremely close relationship to texts and translations attributed to John of Seville.[30] The works involved are in fact those relating to weather forecasting and specifically to astrometeorology, and thus need discussion here.[31]

What is universally agreed is that Ibn Ezra composed an 'astrological encyclopedia' based on authoritative Arabic works of astrology but also drawing on his own expertise and calculations.[32] This began with a basic textbook on astrological terms and fundamental concepts, the *Beginning of Wisdom*, which followed established practice in the science. Much less standard, however, was the next treatise, a sort of theoretical commentary on the first work, entitled the *Book of Reasons*. Separate works were composed, sometimes in more than one version, on each of the main areas within astrology: 'Nativities' or birth charts; 'Elections' or guidance on decisions; 'Interrogations' or responses to specific types of questions; a *Book of Luminaries* that is mostly devoted to medical astrology; and the *Book of the World* (sometimes also called the *Book of Conjunctions*), which deals with what can most succinctly be called 'mundane astrology'.[33] Versions of all of these, in Hebrew, were issued in an impressively short time during 1148, whilst Ibn Ezra was based in Béziers. Together they offer a wide-ranging and highly practical induction into astrological techniques, and when combined with Ibn Ezra's works on planetary positions, astronomical instruments and Hindu-Arabic mathematics and numerals it becomes clear that the author was capable of both practising and teaching across all parts of the science of the stars.

As noted above it is the book on world or 'mundane' astrology that includes Ibn Ezra's handling of astrological weather forecasting, and that is extremely closely related to works attributed to John of Seville. Both owe considerable amounts to Ptolemy's *Quadripartitus* and even more to Abu Ma'shar's *On the Great Conjunctions* (whose full title can be abbreviated to the *Book on ... the Indications of the Celestial Bodies on Terrestrial Events* and that is sometimes known as the *Book of Religions and Dynasties*). The texts that currently go under the name of John of Seville are the

---

[30] A cautious view on this relationship is given by S. Sela, *Abraham Ibn Ezra: The Book of the World*, Leiden & Boston, Brill, 2010, p. 27 and references there.

[31] The arguments were first put forward by C. Burnett in a paper on 'John of Seville and the Authorship of the *Epitome totius astrologiae* (*Ysagoge* and *Liber quadripartitus*)', subsequently published in his 'Lunar Astrology: The Varieties of Texts Using Lunar Mansions, with Emphasis on *Jafar Indus*', *Micrologus*, 12, 2004, pp. 43–133.

[32] The term is that of S. Sela, in *Abraham Ibn Ezra and the Rise of Medieval Hebrew Science*, Leiden and Boston, Brill, 2003, p. 57.

[33] For discussion see Abraham Ibn Ezra, *The Book of Reasons (a Parallel Hebrew-English Critical Edition of the Two Versions of the Text)*, Ed. and Trans. S. Sela, Leiden and Boston, Brill, 2007, pp. 1–2.

Liber primus de gentibus, regibus, civitatibus, aeris mutatione, fame et mortalitate (or *First book on peoples, kings, cities, weather, famine and death*) and the *Tractatus pluviarum et aeris mutationis* the treatise on weather forecasting previously discussed, which circulated separately but was effectively an extract from the longer work.[34] It would be possible that these works were independent translations or versions of their sources, except for the fact that 'John of Seville' uses Latin words based in turn on Hebrew words that are themselves neologisms coined by Ibn Ezra in the works accepted as his.[35] This would suggest, at the least, that the work of Ibn Ezra came first, and that 'John of Seville' learnt from them.

Since it has also been argued that Ibn Ezra was able to issue at least some of his works directly in Latin, the question of authorship becomes very complex at this point.[36] However, what matters for the present study is that it appears that Ibn Ezra's works reached Christian readerships across Europe, in Latin, and from an earlier date than has often been supposed. Even if the works attributed to John of Seville are left aside, it is clear that Ibn Ezra would have been in contact with Jewish scholars familiar with both their local vernacular and Latin, and who could have acted as translators as well as pupils. When the distribution of the *Book of the World* is placed alongside that of the 'editions' of John of Seville the speed and extent of the spread are revealed as impressive. Perhaps even more important is the evidence that Ibn Ezra was, at the very least, transmitting his skills to regions of twelfth-century Europe that were parts of differing (and sometimes rival) polities. The tone of the 'astrological encyclopedia' is highly practical, and it seems likely that Ibn Ezra offered both consultations and instruction in the various parts of the science of the stars, as well as producing reference works and guides for the further use of pupils and patrons. Thus, whether the works attributed to John of Seville were or were not produced by a separate

---

[34] See n. 31 above.

[35] This was first demonstrated by R. Smithuis in her PhD thesis, 'Abraham ibn Ezra the astrologer and the transmission of Arabic Science to the Christian West', Manchester, University of Manchester, 2004; and is endorsed by S. Sela, *Book of the World*, p. 27.

[36] This argument has been made chiefly by R. Smithuis, see: 'Abraham Ibn Ezra's Astrological Works in Hebrew and Latin: New Discoveries and Exhaustive Listing', *Aleph, Historical Studies in Science and Judaism*, 6, 2006, pp. 239–338; and 'Science in Normandy and England'. J. Rodriguez Arribas accepts that Ibn Ezra issued one of his treatises on the astrolabe (written 1154, in Rouen) in Latin rather than Hebrew: 'Reading Astrolabes in Medieval Hebrew', in MacLeod, Sumillera, Surman and Smirnova, *Language as a Scientific Tool: Shaping Scientific Language Across Time and National Tradition*, New York and London, Routledge, 2016, pp. 89–112, at p. 92; and 'Medieval Jews and Medieval Astrolabes: Where, Why, How, and What For?' in S. Stern and C. Burnett, Eds., *Time, Astronomy and Calendars in the Jewish Tradition*, Leiden and Boston, Brill, 2014, pp. 221–272.

individual is less important here than the fact of the creation of versions that circulated under a 'Christian' name. There is no surviving evidence that Ibn Ezra received direct patronage from the dominant Christian communities in the cities and towns he visited – and yet his skills would have been of great potential value to them. Moreover it is unlikely that such a renowned, foreign visitor could arrive in a small Jewish community, teach, issue books and perhaps practise as a doctor and astrologer, without coming to the attention of the authorities. This is perhaps especially the case for Anglo-Norman territories, where Jewish groups were small and under the special control of the kings of England, and where Ibn Ezra's stays in Rouen and London would have drawn attention. It is significant that from 1153 the king was Henry II, the probable recipient of Adelard's treatise, and son of the 'Duke' of the *Dragmaticon*. High-level interest in the value of the knowledge and skills offered by Ibn Ezra would help to explain the scholar's ability to travel so widely and stay for extended periods wherever he went.

What exactly, then, was said on astrometeorology in the works issued under Ibn Ezra's own name, either in Hebrew or in Latin? An interesting point is raised by Sela, who observes that the fundamental Arabic works on the 'great conjunctions' and mundane astrology do not include lists of the numbers and types of conjunction actually possible. It seems likely that such information would be covered at a rather lower level. Ibn Ezra's *Book of the World* appears as consciously addressing a different, and less expert, audience, since it opens with such a list (as does the version of 'John of Seville').[37] A similar suggestion can be made in relation to the care given by Ibn Ezra to set out with mathematical precision the level of power to be attributed to planets that are in complex geometrical relationships to one another. Such combinations, particularly when several planets of varying general degrees of power are involved, require complex judgement for which previous experience is very helpful. What Ibn Ezra offers in the second, later version of the *Book of the World* is an extended calibration of the effects on individual planets of being placed in signs, divisions of signs, specific relationships to the Sun or other identifiable points, which impacted (either positively or negatively) upon their normal level of power. This is applied over four consecutive sections of the work to produce a guide to interpreting all possible combinations of planets, positions and interrelationships.[38] Such pedagogical materials, together with Ibn Ezra's expositions of his own observations and findings, have two important effects. Firstly they inculcate confidence in his

---

[37] Sela, *The Book of the World*, p. 28.   [38] Ibid.

expertise and qualifications, and secondly they make it possible for those less experienced to make use of this expertise. The comments on the errors made by Abu Ma'shar himself add still further to this while giving the reader the feeling of observing a dispute between two leading authorities.

Astrometeorology is dealt with at several points in the *Book of the World*, together with the various astrological procedures required and the authorities who have written on these matters before. The first relevant point comes early, and it is the assertion that, since the exact moment of the Sun's ingress into Aries will vary depending upon the location in question, and cannot be calculated with sufficient precision, it is more satisfactory to take the exact time of the new or full Moon immediately preceding, since this can be judged exactly. The positions of Saturn, Jupiter and Mars at this time are of special significance for weather as well as for economic and political affairs, and al-Kindi is quoted specifically on the forecasting of rain. The procedure starts with the calculation of the ascendant sign, and the element to which it is affiliated. A Water sign is a predictor of rain, and this is strengthened if the Moon is at the ascendant or Midheaven; it is strengthened further if the planetary ruler of the sign is in aspect with it, or in conjunction with the Sun or Moon. The timing of the rain is linked to the day on which the Moon actually reaches the ascendant. Factors affecting the heaviness and duration of the rain include whether significant planets are retrograde, whether the lower planets are close to the Sun, and whether they are placed between a pair of other planets and in a sign that is feminine, cold or watery. The signs of Aquarius and Leo are also significant in the prediction of rain, because of the qualities of certain powerful stars that they contain.

The whole final third of the *Book of the World* pays considerable attention to weather forecasting and, after the more general factors outlined above, the next relevant topic is a version of the concept already discussed as the 'opening of the doors'. Ibn Ezra gives it a related but different name, whilst citing the authority of al-Qabisi (Alchabitius in Latin). He explains that each superior planet has one other planet that is its 'key' in this regard. In each case this will be the planet that rules the sign placed opposite in the zodiac to that ruled by the superior planet. Where the superior planet rules two signs, it will usually have two such 'keys'. For example, Saturn rules the signs of Capricorn and Aquarius. The sign opposite Capricorn is Cancer, which is ruled by the Moon, and the sign opposite Aquarius is Leo, which is ruled by the Sun. Both are placed lower in this system than Saturn. Thus for Saturn the 'key' planets are the Sun and Moon, and for that reason an aspect between the Moon and Saturn at any new or full Moon will bring heavy rain in the relevant month. To calculate the actual days involved the forecaster should count the degrees between the location of the Moon and that of Saturn at the time when the aspect is complete. The predictive power of the calculation will be increased if the Moon is at one of its twelve key points at this same time. These twelve lunar 'key points' are based on the Moon's position in relation to the Sun, starting at new Moon (when the Moon is in conjunction with the Sun). Thus they relate both to the aspects between the Moon and the Sun and to the consequent phase of the Moon. Before taking this concept any further, however, Ibn Ezra goes back to the subject of planets in 'key' relations to one another. Next down from Saturn is Jupiter, which rules Sagittarius and Pisces, and thus the opposite signs are Gemini and Virgo. Both of these are ruled by Mercury, which is therefore the sole 'key' for Jupiter and which affects the air. Thus relevant aspects between Jupiter and Mercury mainly predict winds. A final issue is that of planets in the sign on the ascendant and the sign opposite it, and whether they are retrograde.

With all this set out, the text moves on to how to make a forecast for a month. First, the ascendant sign and its ruler are identified. If the latter is Jupiter or Mercury, and especially if they are in aspect or powerfully placed, then (as would be expected from what has already been said) strong winds are likely. To identify the locations most likely to be affected, Ibn Ezra's lists of affiliations between signs and planets on the one hand and cities and countries on the other should be consulted. For more detailed prediction, the positions of the lower planets, Venus and Mars should be considered, since their locations and interrelationships can affect the likelihood of rain, thunder and lightning, or hail. Another procedure makes use of the position of Saturn at the time of the Sun's entry into Aries, despite the observations noted above. The majority of indications here relate to human activities and health rather than weather. However, it is also stated that if Saturn is in a Water sign there is danger of destructive floods, and if Mars is in a Fire sign there is danger of equally destructive fires. If there is an enquiry about possible drought, then the positions at the time of a conjunction between Jupiter and Saturn should be considered. Key points here are the positions not only of Jupiter and Saturn themselves but also of Mars. Rules for 'progressing' the positions of the planets, and relating them to a new Moon, are given. This is not explained in detail, but would be valuable in relating the chart for the conjunction to a specific point in the year.

Attention next turns to other significant points on which forecasts can be based, and the day on which the Sun reaches the twentieth degree of Cancer is rejected as such a point. However, more is now said on the day of the Aries ingress, and the positions of the beneficent planets (Venus in particular) are discussed. This is the point at which the 'rules' for calculating the relative power of the planets are set out, together with Ibn Ezra's rejection (on the basis of negative experience) of one of Abu Ma'shar's views on the power of Mars in Aquarius or Capricorn at the time of the Aries ingress. Similar expertise, and informed doubts, are made clear in the final main discussion, that of the mansions of the Moon. As in John of Seville's version, the Indian origin of these mansions is mentioned, together with the fact that the Arabian astrologers accept them. If the reader wishes to follow suit, then they are to be calculated from the beginning of Aries, and the Tables of al-Battani are recommended. Ten of them are wet by nature, and so if the Moon is in one of these on the first day of a lunar month, and especially if it is in aspect with a retrograde planet, there will be rain. The indication is strengthened if the Moon is in a Water or feminine sign. By contrast, seven of the mansions are dry and so will have the opposite effect. Finally, for any monthly weather forecast it is the position of the Moon at the start of the month that is important; but the predictive power of the start of the month before the Aries ingress is greatest, followed by those for the entries into Libra, Cancer and Capricorn (the other equinox and the solstices)

At several points the importance of being exact about the latitude for which a chart is drawn up is emphasised. This may imply a suggestion that Abu Ma'shar and other earlier experts failed to take this sufficiently into account, or else that Ibn Ezra found his new pupils and patrons dependent upon outdated sources – although he does not quite say so. At the least, these strictures show awareness that the writer is taking complex knowledge into new territories for which it will need to be adapted, as well as pointing out that a textbook originally drawn up for a different country and century will not apply seamlessly in other territories and later times. Such an emphasis is found more explicitly in Ibn Ezra's works on planetary positions and tables, and seems to be something whose importance he wished to make known. His abilities to make updated and recalibrated charts, and to interpret them on the basis of extensive experience, were of course assets that set him apart from amateurs, students and those dependent on outdated textbooks.

This analysis would now lead to the question of whether Ibn Ezra's teachings did indeed reach outside the Jewish communities for whom they were first drawn up; but sadly this cannot easily be answered. As noted above, no twelfth-century manuscripts of Ibn Ezra's works are known to survive, either in Hebrew or Latin; and the 'official' translations into Latin, preserving the name of the author of the original works, were made only in the thirteenth century. All that can be said for certain is that Ibn Ezra's teachings would have increased the number of those in Jewish communities who were able to produce scientific weather forecasts, and to link these with advances in medical practice as well as with other branches of astrology. That such skills were in demand amongst the dominant Christian communities is also clear. The apparent production of 'plagiarised' versions of Ibn Ezra's work under the name of John of Seville adds to the evidence for interest in, and demand for, sources of this knowledge amongst twelfth-century scholars.

Further, supportive evidence comes from the production and reception of the scientific works of a near-contemporary of Ibn Ezra, Abraham bar Hiyya. He too was a product of the rapidly changing and multicultural environment of the northern part of the Iberian peninsula. His place and date of birth are not recorded, but he is strongly associated with Catalonia, and was active as a scholar by the early twelfth century.[39] It is likely that he died before 1140, although his work on *Calculation of the Motions of the Stars* is datable to 1136.[40] Like Ibn Ezra, bar Hiyya was highly skilled in Arabic science, and chose to write learned introductions to key branches of the subjects concerned in Hebrew. This suggests that he too was writing for Jewish communities or groups who were not familiar with Arabic, and who had little or no background knowledge of the 'new science'. Indeed, he remarks in some of his works that he had been commissioned to write by those in such circumstances. However, it is unclear whether he travelled at all, and it certainly does not appear that he became a peripatetic scholar and teacher as did Ibn Ezra. It should also be remembered that Catalonia in the early twelfth century had expanded both southward and northward, notably by the annexation of Provence in 1112. Jewish communities in the latter region might well have been interested in bar Hiyya's works, and it has been argued that he crossed into Provence late in his career.

In his writings, if not by personal instruction, bar Hiyya conveyed information of great economic as well as scientific value for contemporaries. An example of this is his survey of geometrical calculation and land surveying, within which he also gave instruction on advanced mathematics. That he was interested in making mathematical and scientific knowledge available in Latin as well as Hebrew is shown by the fact that the translator, Plato of Tivoli, recorded collaborating with bar Hiyya.[41] Unlike Ibn Ezra, he was more interested in astronomy than in its use as

---

[39] For a careful survey of what is known of his career see H. Töyrylä, *Abraham Bar Hiyya on Time, History, Exile and Redemption*, Leiden and Boston, Brill, 2014, chapter one.
[40] Ibid., p. 20.   [41] Ibid., p. 20.

the basis for astrological analyses; and none of his recorded works deals with astrometeorology. However, he provided important preparatory materials in his treatise on astronomical calculation. This is his *The Calculation of Planetary Motions*, and it provides both updated tables and explanatory instructions.[42] Would-be astronomers and chronographers in northern Europe, who struggled with translated works that incorporated unfamiliar mathematical and trigonometrical terminology, as well as giving dates for planetary positions according to the Arabic calendar, would find here a deeply helpful manual. The tables themselves are based on the work of al-Battani, and the explanatory material includes the arithmetical procedures needed for making calculations based on the tables, as well as techniques for converting dates from one calendar to another.[43]

Manuscript evidence for the spread and use of all this material in the twelfth century itself is sadly scanty. This is partly due to the rather poor survival rate of twelfth-century manuscripts, but it must also be acknowledged that library catalogues drawn up in the late twelfth and early thirteenth century show little trace of astrometeorology specifically. Of course, since this knowledge was transmitted within the wider astrological surveys increasingly linked to medical and astronomical knowledge, this also is not conclusive. Studies of manuscripts containing scientific texts have been equally tentative in their findings.[44] The fundamental studies of Thorndike were updated and extended by Jenks, who worked on astrometeorology specifically, and who found only five manuscripts or fragments datable to the twelfth century containing works relevant to his study. No fewer than three out of this tiny total were copies of the *Book of the Nine Judges*, demonstrating its rapid success as a one-volume survey of key fields and techniques but making it impossible to tell whether astrometeorology was valued above the other contents.[45]

---

[42] See R. Mercier, 'The Astronomical Tables of Abraham bar Hiyya', in S. Stern and C. Burnett, Eds., *Time, Astronomy and the Calendar in the Jewish Tradition*, Leiden and Boston, Brill, 2014, pp. 155–208.

[43] Töyrylä, p. 29.

[44] Pioneering work was done by L. Thorndike in a number of studies. See: 'The Latin Translations of the Astrological Tracts of Abraham Avenezra', *Isis*, 35:4, 1944, pp. 293–302; 'Daniel of Morley', *The English Historical Review*, 37: 148, 1922; and 'The Latin Translations of Astrological Works by Messehala', *Osiris*, 12:1956, pp. 49–72.

[45] S. Jenks, 'Astrometeorology in the Middle Ages', *Isis*, 7:2, 1983, pp. 185–210. The manuscripts containing the *Book of the Nine Judges* are: Dublin, Trinity College, MS. 368, ff. 43r–137r; Oxford, All Souls College, MS 332 (fragments 4 and 6); and Vienna, Osterreichische Nationalbibliothek, MS Vindobonensis 2428, ff. 1r–160v. The other manuscripts and texts are Erfurt, Amplonianische Handschriften-Sammlung, MS Ampl. Quarto 365, ff. 50r–52r (containing Hermann of Carinthia's *Liber imbrium*); and Rome, Vatican Library, MS 643, f 99r/v (an anonymous *De pluviis*).

The conclusions as to the position of astrometeorology in the rising universities of the second half of the twelfth century thus have to be tentative. On the one hand, it is clear that demand for weather-forecasting knowledge and techniques was sufficient for translators and teachers to produce specialist treatises in rapid succession and even in competition with one another. On the other hand it is not possible to trace the spread and use of these treatises, far less actual practice of astrometeorology, in western, Christian Europe before the thirteenth century. It is to that important period, and the institutions that provided the spaces within which astrometeorology could be studied, that the next chapter will turn.

As the previous chapter showed, demand for knowledge of astrometeorology grew across northern and western Europe in the twelfth century. This accompanied the production of numerous texts in Latin, offering a range of complex and increasingly sophisticated techniques for making actual weather forecasts, ranging in scope from one day to a whole year. Enough evidence also survives to show that ambitious rulers were very interested in both the prestige and the practical advantages offered by the new science. This helps to explain the fact that advanced training in astronomy and astrology was being made available across much of western Europe by the 1150s. It therefore comes as no surprise to find that scholars located in ecclesiastical centres were also very interested in this new knowledge, which was so closely related to their existing concerns with computus and the calendar. One significant example of this is provided by the apparently remote English diocese of Hereford, mentioned in the previous chapter.

Bishop Gilbert Foliot's patronage has already been described; his successor was William de Vere, who seems to have been brought up in the household of Henry I and his second wife, Adeliza.[1] William had been a canon of St Paul's, London, and later entered the service of Henry II; it may have been in this capacity that he visited the Holy Land.[2] He was appointed bishop of Hereford in 1186, and successfully combined his episcopal duties with further service to the king. Bishop William appointed scholars educated in the new Schools to be canons of Hereford Cathedral, and these included well-known figures such as Gerald of Wales and Robert Grosseteste. It was in the 1190s that the poet, Simon du Fresne, who was associated with the cathedral, wrote a poem

---

[1] Julia Barrow, 'Vere, William de (d. 1198)', Oxford Dictionary of National Biography, Oxford, Oxford University Press, October 2007, www.oxforddnb.com/view/article/95042 (accessed 24 November 2017).

[2] H.E. Mayer, 'Henry II of England and the Holy Land', *EHR*, 97, 1982, pp. 721–739.

celebrating the level of learning to be found in Hereford.[3] Simon claimed that the cathedral school contained experts not only in the Trivium but also in the Quadrivium, including those skilled with the astrolabe, planetary tables, the construction of lunar and solar calendars, the calculation of time and even the prediction of future events by the technique of geomancy. The latter involved the casting of 'figures', four of which are listed by name in the poem, which were interpreted in a manner related to astrological techniques. According to Simon, Hereford possessed an expert practitioner, who could answer individual questions and penetrate the secrets of the universe. This individual is not named, but may well be Roger of Hereford (d. 1198).[4]

Roger does not appear to have been a canon of Hereford, but could have been a master in the cathedral school or a scholar in the service of the bishop. If he is the 'Roger Infans' who witnessed charters for Hereford then his association with the staff of the bishop's household and court is strengthened. His astronomical expertise is suggested by his probable authorship of wide-ranging treatises on the main branches of the 'new' sciences of the stars. These demonstrate Roger's familiarity with works translated by John of Seville and Hermann of Carinthia, amongst others, and prove that he was sufficiently skilled to undertake weather forecasts by astrometeorological means. Indeed, he asserts that consultation of the stars can explain 'all natural change in the physical world' in a rational and mathematical way.[5] However, it appears that the readers and clients whom he envisaged were more interested in their personal futures and health than in weather forecasts. That Roger's writings were well received up to the fifteenth century is shown by the fact that some twenty-three manuscripts containing at least portions of his works are known.[6] They seem then to have fallen from favour, since no printed version was produced. Nevertheless, Roger's combination of wide-ranging experience, access to cutting-edge knowledge, and a favoured position in an episcopal court that was both remote and strategically important, is characteristic of this period. For this reason, his writings are worth attention.

---

[3] For the poem see R.W. Hunt, 'English Learning in the Late Twelfth Century', *Transactions of the Royal Historical Society*, 19, 1936, pp. 19–42 (at pp. 36–37).

[4] See C. Burnett, 'Hereford, Roger of (fl. 1179-1198)' *ODNB*, Oxford, Oxford University Press, 2004, www.oxforddnb.com/view/article/23955 (accessed 24 November 2017).

[5] For fuller discussion see R. French, 'Foretelling the Future: Arabic Astrology and English Medicine in the Late Twelfth Century', *Isis*, 87:3, 1996, pp. 453–480.

[6] N. Whyte, Roger of Hereford's *Liber de Astronomice iudicandi*, M.Phil Dissertation, Cambridge, University of Cambridge, 1991, pp. 55–56; and J. North, *Horoscopes and History*, London, Warburg Institute, 1986, at p. 39.

Perhaps especially helpful for aspiring students and practitioners were Roger's versions of the fundamental tables of the 'natures and times' of the planets, signs and houses, and of the degrees of strength and weakness conferred upon the planets as they passed through the signs and houses. Various subdivisions of signs, related to those found both in general works on astrology and in astrometeorological treatises, are set out. These tables seem to have formed Book One of Roger's survey of astrology, since they end with the statement that Book One is now finished. In several manuscripts these 'handy tables' were copied alone, without Roger's expositions of how to use them in analysing clients and providing answers to their questions. One example is Bodleian, MS Digby 149 (ff. 189–194), while MSS Digby 57, Digby 58, Laud 644, and Auct. F III 13 contain various selections from this material.[7] These tables appear mainly to be derived from sources being translated and taught in France in the middle of the twelfth century, which will be discussed in detail in the next chapter. An exception is the one headed *De virtutibus planetarum in signis,* which has been identified as being based directly on the tables of al-Khwarizmi.[8] The final section deals with the 'testimonies' accumulated by any planet when located in the various types of sign and house divisions set out in the individual tables, the 'friendships' and 'enmities' between the planets, and further means of gaining 'testimonies'. This idea of calculating and then adding up 'testimonies', as a quick and mathematical way of judging the relative levels of power exercised by the planets in a given formation, is an attractive means of making an astrological judgement more 'scientific'. It also, clearly, reduces both the scope and the need for individual judgement on the part of the practitioner. This idea was not lost on the compiler of a thirteenth-century treatise on astrometeorology, who may have been none other than the philosopher and scientist, Robert Grosseteste, who was a canon of Hereford before becoming bishop of Lincoln (in 1235).

The treatise in question is known as the *De impressionibus aeris* and it sets out a simplified method for making an astrometeorological forecast, related to the approach of Roger of Hereford.[9] Argument continues as to the date of this short work, and whether its espousal of astrometeorology is compatible with the condemnation of judicial astrology that Grosseteste included in his *Hexaemeron.* It is unhelpful that, while seventeen

---

[7] Whyte, pp. 55–56.   [8] Ibid, p. 34.

[9] For the text see L. Baur, Ed., *Die Philosophischen Werke des Robert Grosseteste, Bischofs von Lincoln,* Aschendorff, Munster, 1912, pp. 41–51. Translations of selected passages are given in R.C. Dales, *The Scientific Achievement of the Middle Ages,* Philadelphia, University of Pennsylvania Press, 1973, pp. 65–67.

manuscript copies have been identified, of which two are from the thirteenth century, the attribution to Grosseteste is found only in fourteenth-century copies.[10] However, whilst authorship remains unproven, the argument that acceptance of astrometeorology suggests acceptance of the whole of judicial astrology is not convincing. The experts delegated in thirteenth-century universities to separate acceptable parts of the new science of the stars from the unacceptable universally found astrometeorology to be unexceptionable, as will be discussed later in this chapter. Moreover, there is no reason to think that Grosseteste would come to a different conclusion. There is nothing in astrometeorology that contradicts the Church's teaching on human free will and individual responsibility. On a more purely scientific level, Grosseteste's critical comments concerning astrologers' false claims to greater accuracy than was actually possible in their calculation of planetary positions would not apply to the very simple calculations set out in the weather-forecasting treatise.[11] Indeed, in Part Five of his commentary on the Creation, Grosseteste goes at some length into the positive comments made by Church Fathers as to the powers of the planets as signs of forthcoming weather.[12] More will be said on the status of astrometeorology as a technique later; for the moment it is important to look at what this treatise actually says.

Its first section is very closely related to information set out in Ptolemy's *Quadripartitus*, although the material is almost certainly received via at least one intermediary, and there are significant differences in approach. Grosseteste's handling of the subdivisions of signs is significantly different from Ptolemy's, whilst his exposition of planetary aspects is very simplified. The treatise opens in a very straightforward manner, with little theory, and takes considerable care to provide simplifications and guides for beginners. It begins with the statement that the balance of atmospheric conditions on a given day can be judged by calculating the positions of the planets on that day and then taking into account the signs in which they are placed and the sectors of their orbits within which they are moving. The natures and powers of the signs and planets, and the

---

[10] The work was accepted by R. Southern in *Robert Grosseteste: The Growth of an English Mind in Medieval Europe*, Oxford, Clarendon Press, 1986, p. 107.

[11] The criticism is found in Part Five, chapter ix, of Grosseteste's *Hexaemeron*. A somewhat different conclusion on this question is found in E. Peters, *The Magician, the Witch and the Law*, Sussex, Harvester Press, 1978, pp. 85–86.

[12] Grosseteste, *Hexaemeron*, Ed. R. Dales and S. Gieben, Oxford, Oxford University Press for British Academy, 1982, Part Five, chapters vii and viii. For a translation of all the relevant passages see *Robert Grosseteste: On the Six Days of Creation*, Trans. C. Martin, Oxford, Oxford University Press for British Academy, 1996, pp. 164–168.

factors at play as the planets move through the signs, are then set out. The exposition appears to draw on Roger of Hereford's use of terms such as 'testimonies' when explaining how to judge the balance of powers amongst the planets in a specific configuration. Key facts are given without any attempt at theorising or explanation, and at points there is a slightly dismissive attitude to such an attempt. This is a set of practical instructions for novices who wish to be able to make weather forecasts on a scientific basis.

Ptolemy's model of planetary movements is adopted, and its central terms are briefly dealt with, in order to explain that planets can move backwards as well as forwards around their paths. A note of originality, or at least a concern to expound a complex point more fully, appears in the explanation of why planets can be further from the Earth at certain times than at others, even though their paths are circular. It is also explained that these varying distances determine their effective speeds, and that this in turn causes changes in their degree of power over the air surrounding the Earth. This is expounded through a detailed discussion of the geometrical effects of the concept that planets move around epicycles whilst also following their larger, circular paths around the Earth. The writing in this section is less clear than Grosseteste's usual Latin style, and the length of the digression is also odd in such a short treatise. However, the belief that this method of weather forecasting is solidly based in mathematics and science is effectively communicated.

With the necessary information in place, the treatise takes the unusual step of providing a fully worked example of how to make a weather forecast. The reader is expected to have access to appropriate planetary tables, and to be able to produce a full set of planetary positions for a chosen date. In this case the date selected is 15 April 1249. The preparation of a circular diagram has already been recommended. This should have eight concentric circles, and be divided into twelve sections, one for each sign of the zodiac. The diagram is used to produce an almost mechanical interpretation, since it facilitates the calculation of the number of testimonies (in other words the degree of power) to be allocated to each planet. Having placed each planet, calculated its testimonies, and balanced them against each other, the conclusion of this example is that the Sun and its qualities will dominate the weather on the chosen day, and that it will accordingly be fine and relatively hot, if slightly variable. It is possible that the text that survives is a revised version, since a comment on the accuracy of the forecast is incorporated into it. The instructions themselves create the impression that a forecast is actually being made, and this is echoed in the further prediction that July 1249 will be particularly hot. However, a note as to the actual weather on the chosen day is also given, and modestly records that the weather was as forecast.

Equally difficult to judge is the warning about the likely effects of the coming long drawn-out stay of Saturn in Capricorn. This is due to begin in 1255 and to last for five years, and the interpretation echoes the biblical warnings of coming years of famine. In other words, the weather will be unusually cold throughout this time, with long winters and poor summers. An impression is given that this is intended to be helpful to those responsible for making provision to deal with the shortages, just as Pharaoh was able to do in the biblical story. Sadly, the limitations of the manuscript evidence make it impossible to tell whether the apparent prediction is in fact an addition made with hindsight and intended to boost the credibility of the technique. However, this uncertainty does not alter the fact that this treatise presents an astrometeorology that is both stripped down to astronomical basics and of clear value to society. Such advance information would obviously be attractive to those running large estates or responsible for providing charity to the starving, and helps to explain the value placed on the possibility of making long-term weather forecasts. It is therefore especially interesting to see the mixture of enthusiasm and caution with which the complexities of forecasting are handled here.

Within the genres of theological and scientific writing, this practical treatise occupies a different place from the discussions of more classical meteorology that Grosseteste included in his *Hexaemeron*, but a comparison is worthwhile since it produces interesting evidence on the development of ideas in relation to the science of the stars more broadly. The exact details of the Creation, and the implications for the structures and workings of the universe, are handled at some length in the latter work, as would be expected. Here, as a work of scholarly theological commentary, there is careful acknowledgement of questions still debated, such as the nature of the matter from which the luminaries were made. Grosseteste knows Aristotle's view on this, but also sets out three other possible views. He is equally detailed and cautious on the relationship between the bodies of the luminaries and their light.[13] Yet, there is no doubt but that the planets provide both 'signs' and 'visible impressions' as to future 'qualities of the air and weather', which should be carefully observed and acted upon by the humans for whom God's providence has created them. Detailed criticisms of judicial astrology are also found here, and show clear knowledge of what is being criticised. The argument that

---

[13] *Hexaemeron*, Trans. Martin, pp. 161–162.

astrologers cannot read planetary positions with the precision they claim is an old one; but Grosseteste adds what sounds like a note from personal experience. He says 'this is clear to those who have worked hard with astronomical calculations and tables'.[14] Indeed, he echoes the criticisms of Ibn Ezra when he says in the same chapter that astronomers cannot be certain of the exact moment of the 'revolution' or turning of the year at the vernal equinox for any given location, although this is a key concept in their calculations. Nevertheless, he does not contradict the practical procedures set out in *De impressionibus aeris*. Moreover, the discussion of regional variations in climate also acknowledges the varying powers of planets through the portions of the year and sections of their orbits.[15] There appears to be no contradiction between the two works, and the view that it would be irresponsible to neglect astrometeorology is found in both, if to differing degrees.

This analysis of the views and expertise of Robert Grosseteste also helps to shed light upon the position that astrometeorology came to occupy in the universities during the thirteenth century. The acceptance of astrometeorology into the emerging curriculum was not necessarily a given, since it remained separate from the teaching of Aristotle's natural philosophy. Its presence as part of wide-ranging surveys of the new sciences of the stars was also potentially problematic, as the various forms of what came to be defined as judicial astrology were increasingly condemned. It may perhaps have been partly in order to separate astrometeorology from the suspect forms of judgement from the stars that extracts from these broad surveys were produced, presented as separate treatises on the entirely acceptable science of weather forecasting. Study of surviving evidence on university curricula suggests that, in both medicine specifically and natural philosophy more broadly, the basic knowledge required to calculate the positions of the planets for a chosen day and time appears to have been assumed. These more practical and instrument-based skills were part of the quadrivial subjects of astronomy and mathematics, which would have been studied before students progressed to medicine and other more specialised subjects. There were also ongoing disputes as to the overall acceptability of the new forms of scientific knowledge.[16] Within natural philosophy, Aristotle's *Meteorology*, for instance, was taught as part of the established corpus of Aristotle's scientific works at Oxford throughout the first half of the

---

[14] Part Five, chapter ix, p. 167.   [15] Ibid. pp. 174–175.

[16] See R. Lemay, 'The True Place of Astrology in Medieval Science and Philosophy', in P. Curry, Ed., *Astrology, Science and Society; Historical Essays*, Woodbridge, Boydell, 1987, pp. 57–73.

thirteenth century.[17] However, the 'Oxford' commentaries on this work do not cross-refer to the new knowledge on astronomy; and meanwhile in Paris all study of Aristotle's works on the physical sciences was banned in 1210 and again in 1215.[18] Nevertheless, it is clear that detailed teaching of astronomical and astrological theories and techniques was found in all major centres of learning by the middle of that century. This was especially important for medicine, but weather forecasting was increasingly present as an area of study.

Evidence for the acceptance of weather forecasting by means of the planets and stars comes from multiple sources. A general approval was given by Aquinas' extremely authoritative encyclopaedia on theological issues, the *Summa Theologiae*. Part One of this impressive work was completed by 1269, and one of the topics dealt with is the question of the powers of the stars over earthly things (Question 115). Aquinas sets out clearly the conclusion that the heavenly bodies can indeed cause physical effects in the terrestrial realm, and quotes St Augustine's statement that: 'Bodies of a grosser and inferior nature are ruled in a certain fashion by those of a more subtle and powerful nature'. Similarly, in the second part of Part Two of the *Summa,* the topic of divination is covered. Here, Aquinas' conclusion is that weather forecasting on the basis of the stars is not actually divination, since it uses knowledge drawn from previous observations and experience, and does not involve any invocation of demons, either explicit or implicit.

Roughly contemporary with Aquinas' great work, and almost equally influential in its own way, was a work attributed to Albertus Magnus. This eminent scholar and theologian, known in his own time as 'the universal doctor', taught in Paris from 1245 to 1248. The work in question is the *Speculum astronomiae* (or *Mirror of Astronomy*). This, as its title suggests, examines the ever-growing literature on astronomy and astrology in detail, and it had the very practical aim of separating the acceptable from the superstitious and unacceptable.[19] Its author or compiler lists and discusses a formidable array of titles, partly by making use of older surveys and booklists. The arguments put forward are in

---

[17] R. French, 'Teaching Meteorology in Thirteenth-Century Oxford: The Arabic Paraphrase', *Physis*, 36, 1999, n.s.fasc.1, pp. 99–129, at p. 100. More than one Latin version of this work existed; but as the thirteenth century advanced, the 'new' translation of William of Moerbeke was increasingly dominant. This latter version survives in at least 190 manuscripts. See P. Schoonheim, Ed. and Trans., *Aristotle's Meteorology in the Arabico-Latin Tradition*, Leiden and Boston and Cologne, Brill, 2000, p. xiv.

[18] French, 'Teaching Meteorology', p. 103.

[19] For discussion of the date and authorship of the work see P. Zambelli, *The Speculum Astronomiae and Its Enigma*, Dordrecht/Boston/London, Kluwer, 1992.

accordance both with the conclusions of Aquinas, mentioned above, and the comments made by Albertus Magnus himself in his detailed commentaries on the physical works of Aristotle.[20] The work is important for the account it gives of the state of knowledge on all branches of astronomy and astrology in Western Europe by the 1260s, and is worth a more detailed examination.

Its preface notes that anxiety is growing concerning books on the science of the stars, and that this is for two reasons. The first is that work on the stars is being caught up in broader concerns about new forms of scientific study; and the second is that works of necromancy are being passed off as dealing with astronomy and thus bringing the science into disrepute. Chapter One moves on logically to define astronomy, and observes that the Latin term *astronomia* covers two large but distinct areas of knowledge. The first of these concerns study of the structure of the heavens and the regular movements of the heavenly bodies; and the component parts of this field of study are set out in some detail.[21] This subject is declared to be 'a great wisdom' and to produce true knowledge. Chapter Two then proceeds to classify and list works falling within this area of true knowledge. These include planetary tables, and it is noted that fundamental work was done by Ptolemy (whose identity is discussed), but that this work is now outdated. The tables of Toledo are commended, and it is noted that many writers have produced tables for their cities, adapted to the correct location and to the Christian calendar. Examples specifically noted are those for Marseilles, London and Toulouse. Also of clear value are guides to the use and functions of the astrolabe. All these are necessary for what is called: 'a great and noble part of philosophy'.[22] Chapter Three moves on to the 'science of the judgements of the stars', which is commended as being a link between the study of the physical world and that of higher things. The acceptable and very valuable part of this subject is that which constitutes a 'middle science' and provides knowledge of the ways in which changes in the heavenly bodies bring about changes in earthly things. A detailed account of this knowledge is promised, and its value is not to be diminished by the sad fact that Latin culture has had to acquire it from other languages through the efforts of translators.

What follows in Chapters Four and Five is a clear definition and outline of the preliminary, 'factual' information on the signs, their natures and specific affiliations; the houses; the planets; and the interactions between all these factors produced as the planets move through

---

[20] Ibid, chapter seven, 'Astrology in Albert's Undisputed Works', pp. 61–74.
[21] Ibid., pp. 208–213.   [22] Ibid., 214–219; quotation pp. 218 and 219.

their orbits. An impressive range of technical terminology is included here, especially on matters to do with the subdivisions of signs and houses, and the aspects between planets. Commended works include Ptolemy's *Quadripartitus*, and the introductory portions of the surveys by Albumasar, Alchabitius and Sahl, as well as the first part of the *Book of the Nine Judges*.[23] Rather more complicated is the next topic, defined as the first part of the knowledge of how to make judgements from the stars. In other words this is mundane astrology, here, as often, called the study of (celestial) 'revolutions'. Further subdivisions follow, in accord with the topics discussed in detail in preceding chapters. Attention is first given to the topic of significant planetary conjunctions. Next comes the 'astrological new year', in other words the chart for the new or full Moon prior to the Sun's entry into Aries, and its significance for foreknowledge of major events, food prices, earthquakes, floods and disasters. The third area consists of knowledge of changes of season and weather, produced by the movements of the planets and their varying effects on the atmosphere – in other words, astrometeorology.[24] Considerable technical knowledge is assumed here, since both the twenty-eight mansions and the twelve 'posts' or 'gates' of the Moon are included, together with a rather idiosyncratic form of reference to the 'opening of the doors' (here rather confusingly the term 'gates' is again used). Works listed for this subject are al-Kindi's *De pluviis*; the treatise attributed to Jafar Indus, the *De imbribus*; the treatise beginning *Sapienties Indi*; part of Ptolemy's *Quadripartitus*; and part of the *Prima pars artis* of John of Seville.[25]

The central part of the *Speculum* moves on to deal with the more problematic portions of judicial astrology and then with the troubling proliferation of texts on astrological images and their magical uses. Chapter Twelve returns to the identification of works that are acceptable and even necessary for human well-being. First place here is given to astrometeorology, which is said to be based wholly on the scientific principle that things below are subject to those above, a principle actually established by the Creator.[26] This principle, maintained by God's will until the end of time, is further stated to have been recognised by Ptolemy and 'Albumasar'. Thus, the portion of the 'science of the stars', which concerns changing weather should be accepted and preserved, and this in turn necessitates the preservation of all the background information and skills which it requires. For the same reasons, whilst 'Albumasar's' theory that the planets have rational souls is to be condemned,

---

[23] Ibid, 222–227.   [24] This is reached at ibid, pp. 230–231.
[25] For discussion of the authorship of this text see chapter five above.
[26] Zambelli, pp. 250–251.

his basic teachings on astronomy and the effects of planetary movements are in accordance with both the acceptable parts of Aristotle's philosophy and with Christian belief.[27] Considerable space is given to the argument that much of 'Albumasar's' work is acceptable and should be exempt from condemnation, just as should the general work of 'Alcabitius'.

This emphatic endorsement of astrometeorology was significant, because the *Speculum astronomiae* was well received when first issued and continued to be cited into the sixteenth century.[28] The care taken to identify both separate treatises on this subject and relevant parts of broader works is doubly important: firstly for its recognition that astrometeorological knowledge was disseminated through both formats, and secondly for its concern that this material was not to be rejected simply because it travelled together with much less acceptable forms of applied astronomy. Nevertheless, the problem of the condemnations of superstitious and necromantic works, and particularly of the full and carefully researched condemnation of 1277, remains. The very care taken in the *Speculum astronomiae* to separate true science from error and things to be condemned shows how serious was the threat to the new branches of scientific knowledge. Specificity was needed, if the clearly valued science of astrometeorology was to be protected from the very general terminology used in the section of the condemnation of 1277 that covered works of magic. This declared that all 'books, rolls or pamphlets' (*libros, rotulos seu quaterniones*), which contained necromancy or instructed on divination and sorcery (*experimenta sortilegiorum, invocationes demonum*) or indeed anything that contradicted true faith and morality were to be included in the condemnation.[29] This may sound like a reference simply to ritual magic and outright necromancy, but it must be remembered that Aquinas and other commentators had greatly expanded the definition of demonic invocation. Both Aquinas and Bonaventure questioned whether contact with demons could produce true foreknowledge, and concluded that within major limits it could, but that in order to gain such information the querent knowingly or unknowingly contacted a demon. Moreover, repeated contact constituted a pact, and thus proved that the person concerned was a magician.[30]

Any deliberate attempt to gain knowledge of future events thus fell under suspicion of opening the enquirer up to temptation by demons.

---

[27] Ibid., 251–253.   [28] Ibid. p. 1.

[29] Peters, *The Magician, the Witch and the Law*, p. 91.

[30] Bonaventure 7.2.1.3.2; and 7.2.2.2 conclusion point 9, in Bonaventure, *Commentaria in Quatuor Libros Sententiarum Magistri Petri Lombardi*; in *Opera Omnia, Tomus 1*, Florence, Collegium S. Bonaventurae, 1885.

Far worse, any ongoing use of such techniques and of the information thus gained constituted a pact with the demon involved, even if the human had no such intention. If astrometeorology was to be saved from suspicion, then the *Speculum* provided the arguments and the evidence to do this. That the 'new' astronomy was established in scientific and social practice around the middle of the thirteenth century is demonstrated by its rising prominence in the growing genre of surveys or encyclopaedias of knowledge. However, the evidence suggests that this rise was not uncontested. An early leader in the field of surveys of acceptable knowledge was the very conservative work of Thomas of Cantimpré. This Flemish Dominican, who was taught by Albertus Magnus in Cologne, studied for some time also in Paris and was aware of new developments in thought. Thomas' work on *The Nature of Things* was composed ca. 1230–1245, and its conservatism may be due to the fact that it was intended to provide a work of reference for those preaching to the laity. Its final version is made up of twenty books, and books 16 to 20 deal with cosmology, the planets, and the atmosphere. The popularity of the work is shown by the fact that versions of it have been identified in at least 160 manuscripts.[31] Book Eighteen has the interesting title of *De passionibus aeris*, but this, like the preceding discussions of cosmology and geography, includes nothing of the new science. Its concerns are with the traditional meteorological topics of thunder, lightning, falling stars, winds, clouds and rainbows.[32] It would appear that awareness of the knowledge opened up by the new branches of astronomy was to be restricted to trained experts.

More up to date, and more willing to disseminate the new science, is the work of Vincent of Beauvais. Vincent was another Dominican, but his work reached a rather different audience from Thomas'. In the 1240s Vincent and the early parts of his encyclopaedia came to the attention of the king of France, Louis IX, and he then spent a considerable period of time based in the royal abbey of Royaumont. Vincent's great *Speculum maius* had four main parts, one of which was his *Speculum naturale*. There is no complete modern edition of this, but several early modern versions are available via the Europeana website.[33] The most relevant

---

[31] See R. McKeon, 'The Organisations of Sciences and the Relations of Cultures in the Twelfth and Thirteenth Centuries', in Z. McKeon and W. Swenson, Eds., *Culture, Education and the Arts: Selected Writings of Richard McKeon, Vol. 2*, Chicago and London, University of Chicago Press, 2005, pp. 121–154.

[32] Thomas Cantimpratensis, *Liber de Natura Rerum*, Vol. 1, Text, Ed. H. Boese, Berlin/New York, De Gruyter, 1973, pp. 396–402.

[33] www.europeana.eu/portal/en/record/9200129/BibliographicResource_3000004610078.html (accessed 24 June 2019).

part is Book 16, which deals with works of God on the fourth day of Creation, and thus with the luminaries, the signs (of the zodiac), the times (as calculated by computists), and related matters. Following in the footsteps of the *Speculum astronomiae* various authorities on the origins and powers of the stars are cited here, and the views of Albumasar and Aristotle are discussed in detail in chapters 18 and 19. Chapters 23–31 deal with the names, properties and orbits of the planets, including 'modern' information on cycles and retrograde movements. Chapters 34–39 deal with the zodiac signs, their positions and their subdivisions, and 40–42 give the powers of the planets in the various signs. Chapters 64–70 discuss the seasons of the year, and this shift into seasons and times leads the way into the rest of the book, which deals essentially with topics included in ecclesiastical computus. A cautious attitude is suggested, since the fundamental theory that the stars and planets have power over terrestrial things is espoused, but within limits. Understanding of astronomical basics, including the movements and properties of the planets, is presented as a central part of modern, scientific knowledge and even the relatively technical topic of the modulation of planetary powers caused by passage through subdivisions of signs is covered. However, whilst this leads directly into discussion of the seasons, no instructions for astrometeorology are included. The reader who wished to acquire such a practical application of this knowledge would need to consult a specialist (or undertake further study).

Given the enormous importance of the weather, long-term forecasts were of considerable economic and political value. The problem with them was not a theological one, as has been seen, but rather a practical one. Weather conditions are notoriously fast-changing and hard to predict with accuracy, and the making of forecasts involved complex analyses of the ongoing interactions of a wide range of complex factors. Astrometeorological judgements were at least as complex as medical judgements, and despite the attempted simplification by Grosseteste they remained just as dependent upon the skills and experience of the forecaster. The close relationship between the science of the stars and that of medicine has already been stressed, and it remained the case in the thirteenth century that any physician able to make 'modern' prognoses in relation to illness would also be able to make weather forecasts. Moreover, rulers in the Mediterranean regions of Europe were increasingly confident enough to employ an astrologer as a recognised member of their court. A pioneer in this, as in much else, was the Emperor Frederick II, who was for several years the patron and employer of Michael Scot. Indeed, it has been argued that Scot was one of the leading contributors to the intellectual achievements of Frederick's court.[34] Scot's early career remains vague, but he is recorded as having accompanied the archbishop of Toledo to the Fourth Lateran Council in 1215, something that attests to his status in the hierarchy of the Church as well as his scholarly credentials and milieu. During his time in the service of the archbishop he seems to have translated up-to-date works of Arabic astronomy and science, particularly that of 'Alpetragius'. This was the *De motibus celorum* (or *On the Movements of the Heavens*) of Scot's older contemporary, al-Bitruji, and it helped Scot to gain a reputation as a leading practitioner of astronomy and astrology.[35]

Scot's most important work is his *Liber introductorius*, which was intended, as its name suggests, to explain the new science in terms that a beginner could follow. Its exact date of composition is not recorded, but a strong case has been made for ca. 1230.[36] The preface of the work includes an outline of its planned structure and coverage, which is very helpful since the final portion of the work has either been lost or was never completed.[37] Even so, the text as it survives contains nearly 450,000 words. The planned structure was for the main section of this compendious work to have four parts, covering between them the 'secrets of the philosophers concerning things both heavenly and terrestrial and of the whole art of astronomy'. This suggests that mundane astrology, with astrometeorology within it, would be included as was usual in such surveys. The basic concepts and information were provided in the first section, which included an illustrated star catalogue, with descriptions of all the constellations, together with an exposition of planetary positions and influences, and another of the mansions of the Moon. These elements were more popular than the full *Liber introductorius*, with more than twenty copies of the catalogue known to survive.[38] It appears that Scot's version of astrometeorology, assuming that it existed, has been lost along with the majority of the fourth part of his survey.[39] This is unfortunate, since Scot's knowledge of recent Arabic

---

[34] C.H. Haskins, *Studies in the History of Medieval Science*, 2nd ed., Cambridge, Harvard University Press, 1927, p. 272.

[35] For a brief summary see G.M. Edwards, 'The Two Redactions of Michael Scot's *Liber Introductorius*', *Traditio*, 41, 1985, pp. 329–340.

[36] Ibid.

[37] A useful extract is printed by Edwards in 'The Two Redactions', p. 330, N.7. The full text of the preface is given in his thesis, which is available at: http://digitallibrary.usc.edu/cdm/ref/collection/p15799coll36/id/111855 (accessed 13 November 2017).

[38] 'The Two Redactions', pp. 331–332.

[39] No complete, printed edition of the work exists. However, published summaries make no mention of astrometeorology, despite Scot's Aristotelian interest in classical meteorology and expertise in Islamicate astrology. See also C.H. Haskins: 'Michael

astronomy and of Aristotle's natural philosophy was extensive, and his discussion (for instance) of the rainbow showed a readiness to include analysis of challenging observations within his expositions of theory.[40]

Michael Scot's contemporary, Guido Bonatti, seems to have spent all of his long career in Italy, and at least by his own account to have made a very positive contribution to the ongoing power struggles in the region of Florence. Bonatti seems to have been interested in the affairs of Frederick II although, unlike Scot, he does not appear to have been in the actual service of the emperor. Bonatti's chief patrons included Guido da Montefeltro (1223–1298), ruler of Urbino, who was believed to consult the astrologer on most important matters, including military ones. Like other leading astrologers concerned to improve their careers and reputations, Bonatti decided to record his astrological expertise in the form of an encyclopaedic survey of the subject, covering all the main branches of the subject. In contrast to the mixed fate of Scot's work, Bonatti's survives complete in both manuscript and printed forms, and was actually printed several times.[41] As this suggests, the work is more succinct, and the chapters stick more directly to traditional, practical matters, in contrast to Scot's interesting but highly theoretical discussions of several issues only indirectly linked to the practice of astrology. Nevertheless, both the early editor and the printers experienced some confusion as to the exact number and composition of the treatises that make up the work. A helpful guide is provided by the Prologue, included in the Ratdolt edition of 1491 and apparently written by Bonatti himself. This is addressed to his nephew, simply named as 'Bonatti', and states that the complete book consists of six parts: Introductory; on Interrogations; on Elections; on Revolutions of years (and conjunctions); on Nativities; and on Rains.[42] However, manuscript copies give a different view. For instance, the beautifully illuminated copy made for presentation to King Henry VII of England (now British Library MS Arundel 66) gives the

Scot', *Isis*, IV, 1922; and 'Science at the Court of the Emperor Frederick II', *American Historical Review*, XXVII, 4, 1922, pp. 669–694.

[40] For the argument that Scot's four-fold rainbow was based on actual observation, see T.C. Scott, 'Michael Scot and the Four Rainbows', *Transversal; International Journal for the Historiography of Science*, 2, 2017, pp. 204–225.

[41] The text was edited by Johannes Angelus and printed in Augsburg, 1491, by Erhard Ratdolt; also in Venice by Penzio, 1506; and in Basel, 1550, by Jakob Kundig. The Ratdolt edition is accessible from the website of the Bayerische Staatsbibliothek: https://bildsuche.digitale-sammlungen.de/index.html?c=viewer&lv=1&bandnummer=bsb00025600 (accessed 24 June 2019); for the Basel version see http://hardenberg.jalb.de/display_page.php?elementId=5363 (accessed 14 December 2017).

[42] For a translation of this Prologue see Guido Bonatti *Liber Astronomiae (Part 1)*, Trans. R. Zoller, Ed. R. Hand, Berkeleye Springs, Project Hindsight and Golden Hind Press, 1994, pp. iii–v.

work the title *Decem tractatus astronomiae (Ten Treatises on Astronomy)* but states in the prologue that it has seven parts. In this version the section on Nativities is given greater prominence, while *De pluviis et ymbribus* (the portion on weather forecasting) is listed as part seven (f. 53).[43] From this it seems that, even though the treatise on astrometeorology sometimes appears to be an addition at the end of the volume, it was in fact a planned part of the work.

The fundamental information on the signs, planets, houses and conjunctions is set out in the early parts, and is drawn upon as the reader works through the following topics in turn. An attractive aspect of the work is its provision of tables and guides on technical matters, and this is found in the outline of astrometeorology also. After a general opening, chapters are given on signs for when rain will or will not fall, general methods of forecasting rain, the wet and dry mansions of the Moon, methods of predicting future weather conditions more broadly and a table of the mansions of the Moon. This is followed by instructions for predicting the actual times of rains and winds, and then guidance on when Saturn is likely to prevent rain. The technicalities of 'lunar posts' and 'openings of the doors' are here simplified to helpful expositions of the effects to be expected when the Moon is in aspect with each of the other planets. The resulting treatise is still detailed, but is genuinely more useful for the less experienced than earlier works on technical astrometeorology. However, this very brevity and practicality has a somewhat contradictory effect. On the one hand, astrometeorology is made accessible to a wider audience, but on the other it appears of less interest to Bonatti himself than the detailed coverage of Elections and Nativities.

Evidence of the geographical spread of this updated, slightly more explanatory and practical, version of scientific astrometeorology is perhaps provided by the slightly later compilation traditionally attributed to 'Leopold of Austria'. The work has the title of *Compilation of the Science of the Stars,* and is made up of ten books. Both the identity of its compiler and the actual works which were summarised and excerpted raise problems. 'Leopold' has generally been identified as Leopold I of Austria (1292–1326) even though his actual identity is handled very cautiously in the earliest printed edition. This was issued by Ratdolt, in Augsburg, 1489, in a beautifully illustrated and hand-coloured version.[44] Its preface

---

[43] On this manuscript see J. Fronska, 'The Royal Image and Diplomacy: Henry VII's *Book of Astrology* (British Library, Arundel MS. 66)', *eBLJournal*, 2014, Article 7. The star catalogue in this manuscript has some unusual features, discussed by Fronska at p. 4; however, the main text is standard.

[44] For an example see: http://diglib.hab.de/wdb.php?distype=img&dir=inkunabeln%2F14-astron (accessed 24 June 2019).

makes a spirited argument in support of the powers granted by God to the heavenly bodies, whilst acknowledging that false claimants to the status of scientific expert are bringing the subject into some disrepute. Long study, it asserts, has gone into making this selection of reliable, scientific texts – and within them, astrometeorology is placed unusually high in the sequence, constituting the sixth book. Unfortunately, no information on 'Leopold' is given, other than that he is a 'son of Austria' (*filius Austrie*). Equally, the reader is told in so many words not to seek for the names of individual authors. The implication is that everything in the volume can be accepted as tested and trustworthy, and thus needs no further introduction. The treatise on astrometeorology adopts the same air of confidence, and informs the reader in its opening section that the editor has read many volumes of the works of philosophers on the subject of weather forecasting, and has taken from them all that is needed.

In the customary fashion, the text opens with key points on the signs and the stars in each of them, before moving on to the planets, their intrinsic qualities, and the effects on them of each of the signs as well as of aspects between them. The main section provides 'the rules set out by the philosophers for forecasting the weather'. As with Bonatti's work, the text is succinct and practical, and again includes a list of the mansions of the Moon, with their levels of humidity or dryness. The main technique expounded is that of forecasting weather for each quarter of the year by drawing up a chart for the new or full Moon preceding each solstice or equinox. Thus, 'at the Sun's entry into Aries, if Saturn is in a wet [sign or mansion] this indicates wet weather' although it is noted that 'Saturn mainly signifies cloudy and cold weather'. If the chart is dominated by Saturn with Venus, Mercury and the Moon, there will be a great quantity of rain; and even more if they are in watery signs. Most significant for this forecast will be whether any of the planets are situated close together and at the boundary between Capricorn and Aquarius, or whether they are in aspect with one another in Aries and Cancer or Leo. Even so, Jupiter always brings temperate weather, and winds 'from the left'.

As will be seen this is familiar territory both in the fundamental data being provided and in the clear effort to produce unassailable certainty through removing much of the need for complex and potentially unsupported judgements. Nevertheless, more skill is assumed than in the very simple approach taken by Grosseteste's treatise. It is unfortunate that the date of this compilation cannot be established with certainty. Enough has been said to show that, at least in the case of its astrometeorology, it was based on traditional materials and could certainly have been put together in the late thirteenth century. Moreover, one of its texts does contain one date, which is 1271. The deliberate vagueness as to its editor/compiler is unhelpful, and no manuscript earlier than the fourteenth century has been found; but at least its first three books had been translated into French by 1324. This is shown by the fact that the translation survives in a manuscript that belonged to Mary of Luxembourg, the second wife of Charles IV of France, and 1324 is the date of Mary's death.[45]

Taken together, the evidence provided by the works of Michael Scot, Guido Bonatti and Leopold of Austria demonstrates a widespread interest in all branches of the science of the stars in thirteenth-century Europe. Edited versions, produced by experts and practising astronomer/astrologers, were being copied for both scholars and powerful patrons; and within all this, astrometeorology had an assured place. As has been shown, even severe critics of judicial astrology found weather forecasting an eminently scientific, and socially useful, branch of knowledge. It escaped the repeated condemnations and bans of the thirteenth century, and found its way into several of the encyclopaedias of the time as well as into the genres of literature intended to advise and counsel kings and rulers. Leading practitioners appear to have been concentrated in the lands comprising the Empire, but it is hardly surprising that both texts and teachers can be traced in France and England also. If numbers of surviving manuscripts can be taken as indicators then readers of astrometeorology in the thirteenth century were somewhat conservative in their choices; but, as the next chapter will show, numbers of copies of treatises on weather forecasting, like copies of scientific works in general, rose sharply in the following century.[46] It is in this world of expanding scientific knowledge, further stimulated by the arrival of the printing press, that the final development of medieval astrometeorology took place.

---

[45] This is Paris, Bib. Nat., Ms Fr. 613. See Leopold of Austria, *Li compilacions de le science des estoiles, Books I-III*, Ed. F.J. Carmody, Berkeley and Los Angeles, University of California Press, 1947.

[46] Jenks found only 42 thirteenth-century copies of the astrometeorological works that he studied, as compared with 144 from the fourteenth century and 172 from the fifteenth century. See 'Astrometeorology in the Middle Ages', *Isis*, 74, 2, 1983, p. 188.

7   Astrometeorology and Mechanisation

The previous two chapters have shown that by the end of the thirteenth century astrometeorology had found its place both in universities and in the courts of the powerful (secular and ecclesiastical). As part of this process it had also been officially cleared of the demonic and heretical associations taking ominous shape around judicial astrology and its claims to foretell the future. This, naturally, did not exempt it from the ridicule that accompanies any claim that something as changeable as the weather can be forecast with anything like genuine reliability. However, this problem was counterbalanced by the obvious advantages that fore-warning of coming weather conditions offered to almost everyone in society, from farmers and fishermen through estate managers and mer-chants to generals and rulers. If that were not enough, the close alliance between the science of the stars and that of medicine created further arenas within which astrometeorological forecasts were highly desirable.

However, by the same token, weather forecasting in the new manner was no longer cutting-edge science by the beginning of the fourteenth century. The surveys and treatises produced in the thirteenth century have themselves been seen to introduce little that was new in the way of either concepts or practical procedures. Instead, the key developments were, on the one hand, a drive to make the process of forecasting more streamlined, and on the other the provision of updated and scientifically calculated planetary tables and star catalogues. The success of wide-ranging, technical outlines of astronomy and astrology issued under the names of famous practitioners, like that of Guido Bonatti, demonstrated that the idea of the highly skilled expert continued to have power. Indeed Bonatti, like his predecessors in both the Islamicate and the Latin worlds, made frequent reference to his own experience and skill, and the benefits they could bring. However, the posthumous reputations of Michael Scot and Bonatti himself – which were glamorous but very negative – show the dangers of this strategy. It may be partly for this reason, as well as the fact that what had been a radically new science was now widely accepted, that a new attitude to the relationship between the heavenly bodies and the

sublunary world began to gain ground. This was expressed in the assertion, overt or implied, that the links between the two were as regular and
predictable, if complex, as the movements of the celestial bodies themselves. All that was therefore needed to analyse the workings of these
links was technical expertise; and nothing supernatural or demonic was
involved.

Growing confidence in relation to the broad patterns of these movements, and to the view that they obeyed rules that are both constant and
intelligible, is demonstrated by the drive to replicate them in mechanical
form. The clearest evidence of this drive is the widespread determination
to produce mechanical models of the cosmos whose moving parts
would accurately reproduce not only the orbits of the planets but also
the units of time marked out by movements along those orbits – in other
words, mechanical clocks. Clockmaking was a recognised trade, at least
in Cologne, by 1183, and trade was good enough for that city to have
a street of clockmakers by 1220.[1] Further impetus towards innovation
came in 1232 when the Emperor Frederick II received from the Sultan
of Damascus an astronomical clock. This had 'images' of the Sun and
Moon that moved mechanically around models of their courses and
thus 'infallibly' indicated the hours of both day and night.[2] Its value
was estimated at the impressive figure of more than 20,000 marks,
but the chronicler sounds still more impressed by its scientific accuracy.
This might have been disputed by a writer known as Robert the
Englishman, who reported in the late thirteenth century that clockmakers
were attempting to build a 'wheel or disc', which could exactly model
the rotation of the equinoctial circle, but had not quite succeeded.[3] The
problems appear to have been overcome during the first half of the
fourteenth century, when large, public, mechanical clocks began to
appear across Europe. This has been claimed as 'one of the great turning
points of history'.[4]

It must be noted that the development of increasingly accurate mechanical clocks, acclaimed as providing a reliable model of celestial movements and timings, could not and did not stand alone. Closely associated

---

[1] E. Volckmann, *Alte Gewerbe und Gewerbegassen*, Wurzburg, Memminger, 1921, p. 129.

[2] *Chronica regia Coloniensis, continuatio IV*, ed. G. Waitz in *MGH, Scriptores rerum Germanicarum, xii*, Hannover, MGH Institute, 1880, p. 263.

[3] Cited in L. White, Jr., *Medieval Technology and Social Change*, Oxford, Oxford University Press, 1962, p. 122. See also L. Thorndike, 'Robertus Anglicus', *Isis*, 34, 1943, pp. 467–469. Details of authorship and date have been debated but do not affect this point.

[4] J. North, *God's Clockmaker; Richard of Wallingford and the Invention of Time*, London, Continuum, 2005, p. xv.

with it were advances in adapting planetary tables for new locations and times, and equally impressive was the development of *equatoria* that provided working (if schematic) models of celestial orbits and positions. The latter were composed of discs bearing graduated scales, which simulated the movements of the planets. These were still scarce, but could provide a more user-friendly, visual equivalent to planetary tables.[5] An innovative and well-documented version was produced by Richard of Wallingford, the astronomer and abbot of St Albans, in 1327. This could be used to calculate the positions of all the planets and also, unlike most such instruments, produced data for eclipses.

Evidence of the level of demand amongst scholars for accurate and updated planetary tables is given, for instance, by the speed with which the revised, regional set known as 'English tables' (*tabulae Anglicanae*) spread. These are datable to 1348 and were probably produced in Oxford. They appear already in a fourteenth-century manuscript from Prague, and further updates were still in use in the fifteenth century. In Italy they were translated into Hebrew, and were referred to by Pico della Mirandola in his *Disputations against Astrology*.[6] Their (modest) success may have been partly due to their relative simplicity in use, although it came at the price of limited scope. Far more widely copied, if more complex to use, was the body of planetary tables and accompanying materials known collectively as the Alfonsine Tables. These survive in hundreds of manuscripts from the middle of the fourteenth century onwards, and have been the subject of considerable research and dispute.[7] They update the Tables of Toledo that dominated in the twelfth century, and draw (not always consistently) upon both Ptolemy's own tables and those of al-Khwarizmi.

In principle the Alfonsine Tables make it possible for users to calculate positions for all the planets, based on Ptolemaic models of mean motions, and adapted to a range of calendars and dating eras as well as locations. One subset within the Tables provides the fundamental data for daily readings for each planet, with basic values given for up to 60 days (depending on the complexity of the planet's movement). Another subset offers mean planetary positions for the meridian of Toledo across a

---

[5] For an overview see J. North, 'The Quadrivium', in H. de Ridder-Symoens, Ed., *Universities in the Middle Ages* (Vol. 1 of W. Ruëgg, Ed., *A History of the University in Europe*), Cambridge, Cambridge University Press, 1992, pp. 337–358.

[6] Ibid.

[7] For an edition and full analysis see J. Chabas and B. Goldstein, *The Alfonsine Tables of Toledo, Archimedes*, VIII, Dordrect and Boston and London, Kluwer, 2003. The authors make an important case for regarding the Tables as genuinely the product of Alfonso's Toledo, despite surviving only in later 'editions'.

sequence of dates, with accompanying tables that make it possible to recalculate the dates into those for other calendars. A popular addition was a star catalogue based on Ptolemy's, but with data updated to the time of Alfonso (1252) and with Latin transcriptions of Arabic names for major stars. In 'luxury editions' this could be illustrated with images linked to those in classical works of astronomy, although these were not scientifically necessary.[8] This complex body of materials, despite being copied under the generic title of 'Alfonsine Tables', was in fact edited and transmitted in varying forms, and with differing sets of explanations and instructions. By far the most popular of the latter were those identified with Paris and datable to the 1320s, which were aimed primarily at users in northern Europe who were mainly concerned with the Julian calendar. Even so, while these tables undoubtedly constituted a serious body of basically reliable astronomical knowledge, they were fraught with difficulties for the novice. Since the tables were themselves fundamental for the spread of scientifically based astrometeorology it is important to pursue this point and its consequences.

Recognition of the difficulties experienced by those whose training was based in the more traditional 'arts' curriculum comes already from the work of one of the Paris-based commentators and interpreters of the Tables. This is John of Saxony, who was trained in Paris by one John de Lineriis in the 1320s. John de Lineriis himself was clearly an expert in the construction and use of the Tables, since he sent a set of 'canons' (notes and instructions) to Robert of Florence (also known as Robert the Lombard) when the latter was dean of Glasgow (ca. 1320) as well as compiling a longer set, in three sections, in 1322. By 1327 John of Saxony himself had become expert enough to compose his own canons for the Tables.[9] It was John of Saxony who worked hardest to produce materials that would enable other scholars to use the Alfonsine Tables. A basic textbook on the science of the stars, in the form of a commentary on the highly regarded *Isagogue* of 'Alcabitius' came first, in 1330–1331.

---

[8] This practice continued in later centuries and with further revisions of the tables. An example is provided by B.L. Arundel MS 66, a 'Book of Astrology' compiled for King Henry VII of England, which has updated tables on folios 1 to 32 and an illustrated star catalogue on folios 33 to 47. The longitudes for the stars have been updated to 1440 and a colophon claims this was done at Oxford and by the astrologers of Duke Humphrey of Gloucester. See: J. Fronska, 'The Royal Image and Diplomacy: Henry VII's *Book of Astrology* (British Library, Arundel MS 66), *eBLJ*, 2014, article 7; and H. Carey, 'Henry VII's Book of Astrology and the Tudor Renaissance', *Renaissance Quarterly* lxv, 2012, pp. 661–710. Digitised images are at: www.bl.uk/catalogues/illuminatedmanuscripts/record.asp?MSID=8695&CollID=20&NStart=66 (accessed 24 June 2019).

[9] On both scholars and their works see L. Thorndike, *History of Magic and Experimental Science, Vol. III*, New York, Columbia University Press, 1934, pp. 254–266.

Testimony to the success of this work is provided by the fact that it was issued in print no less than nine times in Venice alone, between 1485 and the end of the sixteenth century. Excerpts occur in other works, and parts of it were translated into French. John took the step of introducing material from the Alfonsine Tables into his commentary, to show how they supplemented Alcabitius' text. He also strongly recommended the making of direct observations, using the growing range of astronomical instruments for the purpose. In a later work he moved on to produce a detailed guide to the Tables, working systematically through the canons and providing worked examples for Paris in 1355.[10] Here he noted that many masters and scholars of Paris were abandoning the attempt to study astronomy because they found the Tables too hard to use, and it may have been for this reason that he also drew up an *Almanach scilicet temporale* (effectively a set of lists of ready calculated planetary positions) for 1336 to 1380, for the meridian of Paris. Armed with a copy of this 'almanac' would-be forecasters did not need to make independent calculations – as long as they were working in a region whose coordinates were not too far removed from those of Paris. This innovative and labour-saving device clearly met a need, and it was widely copied beyond the actual period covered. Thus, while John of Saxony did not compose or edit a treatise specifically on astrometeorology, he provided all the basic materials needed for 'modern' work in the field. His own knowledge of the subject is demonstrated, for instance, by his comment that he, like Ibn Ezra earlier, had found that the Moon's entry into a watery sign (under certain conditions) was a reliable predictor of rain.[11]

Another fourteenth-century expert on astronomy and its applications, whose work demonstrates the range of issues arising at the time, was Firminus de Bellavalle, who lived through much of this century.[12] For at least part of his career he was a canon of Amiens; but his main fame was as a recognised expert on *computus* and on the ever-growing discrepancy between the Church's calendar and the actual positions of the planets and of the luminaries in particular.[13] It was in this capacity that he was summoned to Avignon to advise the papal court, and his skill with the Alfonsine Tables was central to this consultation. However, his most popular work was his treatise on astrometeorology (ca. 1340), another

---

[10] Translations of extracts from John's 'Rules' or canons, with extracts from his 'edition' of the Tables, are given in E. Grant, Ed., *A Source Book in Medieval Science*, Cambridge, Harvard University Press, 1974, pp. 465–488.

[11] Thorndike, Vol. III, pp. 264–265.   [12] For a survey of his work see ibid., pp. 269–277.

[13] For further information see C.P. Nothaft, *Scandalous Error: Calendar Reform and Calendrical Astronomy in Medieval Europe*, Oxford, Oxford University Press, 2018, pp. 207–208; and 228–233.

text on this subject selected for an early printed edition.[14] His handling of the material was divided into seven parts, covering the standard topics, and drawing, as was customary, on a range of sources. It opens with an account of the qualities of the important divisions of the heavens, the stars, the seasons and the main territorial and climatic zones on Earth. With the basics established it moves on to selected portions of mundane astrology, and covers the making of large-scale weather forecasts from great conjunctions, eclipses, and charts for the 'revolutions of the year'. Next comes the making of general forecasts from data at new and full Moons. Fourth is the making of detailed forecasts for specific locations, bringing together information and procedures from the foregoing sections. Fifth is the still more technical issue of the making of forecasts that include analysis of planetary interactions, starting with the aspects of the Moon before moving on to those involving other planets and groups of planets. Sixth is the topic that was given considerably more importance in the original sources, that of the prediction of rains. Finally, and testimony to the inclusiveness and ambition of the work, is a coverage of weather signs, many of them going back to the classical texts discussed in the opening chapters of this book.

Analysis of the text has shown that Firminus drew upon all the established authorities, and made particular use of al-Kindi, Abu Ma'shar and Ptolemy.[15] Like his thirteenth-century predecessors he also gave a table setting out the twelve zodiac signs and their significant divisions. He helpfully explains that these are based on the star positions given by Ptolemy, which are 'now' out of date. However, although such issues were closely related to the technicalities involved in updating aspects of the calendar and thus fell within his expertise, he does not take it upon himself to change Ptolemy's figures. His book would thus, despite its attempts at clear and comprehensive handling of key technical issues, need to be accompanied by skilled use of tables or by the making of careful observations if it were to be accurately used in practice. That it was intended for consultation by would-be weather forecasters is further shown by its inclusion, again following its forerunners, of a table of the mansions of the Moon, with Latin versions of their names as well as transliterations of Arabic. These were fundamental in full astrometeorological forecasts, as has been seen. Equally so were the powers of the

---

[14] It was printed in 1485 and again in 1539; ibid., p. 271. Nine manuscripts have been identified; see Jenks, 'Astrometeorology', p. 188. A copy of the Ratdolt edition, printed in Venice, 1485, and now in the Biblioteca Nazionale Centrale, Florence, is at: https://archive.org/details/ita-bnc-in1–00001030-001 (accessed 24 June 2019).

[15] Thorndike, p. 273.

planets and the effects that each of them had when situated in each zodiac sign, something else that is succinctly covered here. Less established as part of treatises on weather forecasting specifically, but linked (as has been seen) to use of the Alfonsine Tables, were the tables of fixed stars. Indeed, Firminus not only used the Tables but drew upon a set updated to 1338, as well as showing knowledge of the work of John of Saxony.[16] Thus Firminus gave a thoughtful account of the key topics and procedures of astrometeorology, drawing upon the surveys of the previous century as well as upon the classics of the subject, and updating the whole through use of recent versions of the famous Alfonsine Tables. John of Saxony and Firminus de Bellavalle may be said to exemplify ongoing and expert work to produce modernised versions of astronomical tools and astrometeorological textbooks, updated to take account of increasing mathematical and technological expertise. However the widening popularity of the subject is shown by the fact that other writers continued to produce works that enjoyed at least a modest circulation.

A case in point is the anonymous author/editor of the text known as *Exafrenon*.[17] This is accepted as probably English in origin, and as necessarily being composed before John of Eschenden discussed it in his own, innovative *Summa* of astrology in the 1340s.[18] Eschenden, also known as John of Ashenden, appears in the records of Merton College, Oxford, from 1337 to 1355. He is referred to as *magister* or Master, although his degrees and qualifications are not recorded.[19] At one point John of Eschenden refers to the *Exafrenon* as being by Grosseteste, although he is inconsistent on this; and his uncertainty is hardly surprising since the part of the work that deals directly with the making of forecasts is based heavily on the treatise ascribed to Grosseteste. The *Exafrenon* would have been mainly of interest to users in England, since it incorporates tables for the meridian of London centred on the year 1296 (though going back to 1175 and on to 1416). A fourteenth-century focus is provided by reference to Oxford Tables, which are probably those dated to 1310. The 'editor' works to combine an account of the basics of mundane astrology, which were not covered by Grosseteste, with a

---

[16] Ibid., p. 275.

[17] Ibid., pp. 120–126. The earliest surviving manuscript appears to be BL, Royal Ms. 12 C XVIII (fourteenth century). Bodleian MSS Digby 67, 180 and 194 are all fifteenth century; and in Digby 67 the work appears in Middle English translation.

[18] J.D. North accepted it as an early work of Richard of Wallingford, and published it as such in *Richard of Wallingford: An Edition of His Writings with Introductions, English Translation and Commentary*, Vol. 1, Oxford, Clarendon, 1976, pp. 183–243. He discussed it further in *God's Clockmaker*, p. 329.

[19] See K. Snedegar, 'Ashenden, John', *Oxford Dictionary of National Biography*, 2004 https://doi.org/10.1093/ref:odnb/39190 (accessed 24 June 2019).

version of the latter's explanation of planetary orbits, how these affect the powers of the planets as they move, and how specific types of forecast may be made. Technical matters such as the calculation of the ascendant, and its importance for setting out major components of a chart (the divisions known as 'houses') are also included. A readership amongst students of astronomy is suggested by the comment that a forecaster needs access to, and skill with, tables, canons, and an almanac in addition to these basic instructions.

Richard of Wallingford may have produced this work; its unusual combination of Abu Ma'shar and Grosseteste into a brief beginner's guide might fit his known aims. North's demonstration that an undoubted work of Richard's repeats the instructions for setting out astrological houses is strong evidence, although not conclusive since *Exafrenon* could have borrowed this material as well as that of Grosseteste. Some demand for this knowledge amongst those who were happier reading Middle English than Latin is suggested by the survival of a translation of the work in two fifteenth-century manuscripts.[20] It must be admitted however that the copy now included in Bodleian MS Digby 67 was once owned by John Reynham of Merton College, Oxford, who was not an amateur in this field, and who gave a significant collection of books to Merton at his death in 1376. One of these is now Ms 188 in the Merton collection, and carries an inscription on its first folio, added at Merton, which praises Reynham's scholarship as well as describing him as a member of its community of scholars.[21] Moreover, most of the other booklets bound together in Digby 67 are in Latin.[22] Clearly therefore, the treatise was mainly read by those with an existing background in the subject matter, even if they were attracted by its promise of clear exposition of basic matters. Its broader significance comes from the evidence it provides that there was an ongoing demand for 'new' surveys of, and guides to, astrometeorology.

Equally complex, although very different, is the treatise on meteorology and weather-prediction drawn up under the conservative title of 'On Weather' (*De impressionibus aeris*) by Robert of York, who was also known as Perscrutator, in 1325.[23] Almost nothing is known of the career

---

[20] These are now Cambridge, Trinity College, Ms. O.5.26 and Oxford, Bodleian, Ms. Digby 67.

[21] R. Thomson, *A Descriptive Catalogue of the Medieval Manuscripts of Merton College, Oxford*, Cambridge, Brewer, 2009, pp. 138–139.

[22] For an account of the Cambridge manuscript see J. Fitzgerald, 'A Middle English Treatise on Comets in Cambridge, Trinity College MS O. 5. 26', *ANQ: A Quarterly Journal of Short Articles, Notes and Reviews*, 21:1, 2008, pp. 11–22.

[23] Thorndike, Vol. III, pp. 108–117.

of this natural philosopher, who gives his name as Robert and his location as York in his own text. The treatise on weather forecasting appears to have been his most popular work, although he also wrote on alchemy. The nickname Perscrutator is recorded as early as the fourteenth century, and clearly acknowledges the depth and thoroughness of the reading that lay behind Robert's work. Despite the traditional title given to the astrometeorological treatise it is in fact an idiosyncratic piece of work. It enjoyed some success, and was known to John of Eschenden who commented favourably upon it.[24]

The author makes repeated claims to originality and to having used reason and his own observations rather than depending simply upon established authorities. From the latter he claims to have taken only 'tables and rules' – a statement that suggests that he himself was not a practising astronomer, but rather someone who believed that he could bring a new approach to this expanding but still rather technical and challenging subject. The key novelty is that he brought together many of the fundamental topics of classical meteorology, which were at this time separately (and carefully) studied in relation to Aristotle's controversial works on natural philosophy, with the newer and more technically astronomical field of astrometeorology. His treatise starts with a novel, and potentially controversial, exposition on the elements and their 'movers', which builds into a demonstration that there must be seven of these latter. It is scarcely surprising that these seven 'movers' are none other than the planets. With this established, the stars, the belt of the zodiac and the natures and divisions of all these celestial zones and bodies, are added into the scheme. This provides the basis for an explanatory account of the 'exaltations' of the planets in specified signs and divisions.

Despite its novel introduction, the main account of the workings of the heavens is firmly based upon the well-known, scientific principle that what is above affects and influences what is below in established ways that can be analysed and therefore predicted by human reason. It is thus possible for the author to build to a triumphant finale in which his eight Conclusions are offered. These revert to tradition in that Conclusion 1 provides rules for forecasting rain; although 2 moves on to frost, hail and snow, and 3 covers thunderstorms, thus narrowing coverage of astrometeorological topics. From there, attention moves to the 'classical' meteorological issues of earthquakes (4), comets (here unusually defined as 'stars produced in the air'), winds (6), and tides (7). Finally, conclusion 8 deals with the forecasting of plagues and pestilences. As this

[24] Ibid.

interest in a topic traditionally covered by mundane astrology suggests, Robert of York does accept the astrological 'rules' on great conjunctions and their effects on health and harvests as well as on weather. The author's combination of erudition and individuality is clear, but his very refusal to situate his work within established subject boundaries would necessarily limit its attractiveness to scholars. It is possibly for this reason that the treatise was never printed, though it continued to circulate to some degree in manuscript and was known because of John of Eschenden's enthusiasm for it.[25]

A more successful attempt to reconcile astrometeorology, and indeed mundane astrology more generally, with persistent and growing theological criticisms was made by John of Eschenden himself. His ambitious contribution, given the title *Summa iudicialis de accidentibus mundi* (roughly, 'A *summa* on mundane astrology') was completed in Oxford in 1348.[26] Its preface states that it is a 'compilation of the statements of the astrologers concerning the prognostication of world-events'. The validity, usefulness and virtues of the science of the stars, as expounded by the established authorities, are strongly asserted, whilst the arguments of attackers are rejected. The detailed contents list that follows shows that it is divided into sections listed as treatises. Treatise One deals, as usual, with fundamental questions and procedures, while Treatise Two moves on to specific questions. Here, astrometeorology accounts for the first seven of the twelve subsections, or Distinctions. First on the list is the prediction of heating of the air, through study of factors such as conjunctions, eclipses and charts for the key points of each year. Next, logically, comes forecasting of cold weather, and then calm, dry, moderate weather. The subject that dominated the early treatises, that of rain, comes only in the fourth Distinction, and is followed by snow, winds and storms, and thunder and lightning. The rest of the Treatise moves on to natural disasters, plagues, harvests, wars and other traditional concerns. For a practising or would-be astrologer who desired a quick overview of authoritative methods of making forecasts, backed up by informed comment, the attraction of this work is obvious.

That Eschenden was established as a successful practitioner of mundane astrology, chiefly using the conjunction theories of Abu Ma'shar, is shown by the survival of predictions that he made on the bases of

---

[25] Ibid.

[26] John's name is given in various different versions. It seems best to use that preferred by Thorndike, who has given the fullest account of John's works in Vol. III of his *History*, pp. 325–346. North prefers the form Ashenden; see for instance 'Astrology and the Fortunes of Churches' in his *Stars, Minds and Fate: Essays in Ancient and Medieval Cosmology*, London and Ronceverte, Hambledon, 1989, pp. 59–89.

conjunctions and eclipses occurring in 1345, 1349, 1357 and 1365. In his *Summa* he claimed to have predicted in 1345 the coming of the great plague of 1348, although the prognostication actually covered all the usual topics of such predictions. It appears, however, that John of Eschenden was a theorist rather than an expert in actual astronomical calculation, if the evidence of a manuscript in the Bodleian Library, now Digby 176, can be trusted. This is a collection of fourteenth-century material, which was given to Merton College, Oxford, by William Reed, the bishop of Chichester, who had been a Fellow of Merton. Its first text is headed 'Rules for the forecasting of coming weather, by Master William de Merle' (a later hand has added 'of Merton').[27] This is followed by careful observations on the weather, from 1337 to the start of 1344. On folios 9 and 13 are texts relating to eclipses, with the note that in each case the astronomical calculation itself was made by William Reed while the consequent prediction was drawn up by Eschenden. This has led to doubt as to Eschenden's ability to use the Tables.[28]

Eschenden's judgement on the conjunctions and eclipses of 1357 was that they would produce serious and long drawn-out disease to humans and animals for eight years and six months, bringing many deaths. He also predicted many wars and political upheavals, as well as prolonged cold and wet weather, with violent winds as well as rain, hail and snow. Autumn weather would be especially badly affected. All this would bring famine caused by damage to crops and disease caused by corruption of the air, thus adding to the death toll. The benign influence of Jupiter would lessen the effects at first, but when Mercury rose to dominance then its turbulent effects on the air would lead to breathing difficulties, destructive disputes and terrible winds. In the final part of the eight years Saturn would be the dominant force, and so meteorological, medical and political effects would all become worse still. Eschenden's further analysis of the great conjunction of 1365 added the depressing news that amongst its chief effects would be great downpours of rain, causing major destruction in at least one country.

Even if John of Eschenden was not confident in actual calculations using the Alfonsine Tables, he could clearly claim success for his prognostication, and this may well have increased respect for his expertise. He was also explicit in rejecting the main branches of judicial astrology as both innately despicable and also less socially useful than prediction of largescale events. As part of his case for the utility, theological

[27] Thorndike, Vol. III, p. 141, n. 1.
[28] North, 'The Alfonsine Tables in England', in his *Stars, Minds and Fate,* pp. 327–359, at p. 348.

acceptability, and intellectual coherence, of mundane astrology, he also gave significant support to Abu Ma'shar's theories as to the relationship between celestial configurations and major historical events. This too is presented in the first part of the *Summa,* and takes the form of a demonstration that the key theories were compatible with the chronological materials provided by medieval world histories. Here the chronological tables within the Alfonsine Tables were drawn upon, and John was able to conclude, for instance, that the calculation made by the Tables' compilers that there had been 3,101 years and 318 days between the Flood and the birth of Christ was a triumph of exact, modern science. The rest of this first part moves on from theory and methodological argument to set out Eschenden's preferred versions of the usual basic materials and concepts. As has been seen, this was an expected part of an astrologer's demonstration of personal expertise as well as an attraction for those seeking to identify best practice in this complex field. The complete *Summa* is, as both medieval and modern readers have noted, very long.[29] Interestingly, Eschenden, despite the academic title given to his work, writes as a practising astrologer and even counsels others as to the lifestyle practitioners should follow, and the types of questions that they should and should not work to answer. He repeats the views of the *Speculum astronomiae* as to the damage done to scientific astronomy by the false claims of both judicial astrologers and magicians, and like the *Speculum* again he asserts the established truth that 'impressions of the air', like heat and cold, all come from the celestial bodies.

Eschenden's expertise was further recognised through commissions to draw up astrometeorological forecasts. One example of the latter is known to survive. This detailed weather forecast is found in only two manuscripts (now Bodleian, Ashmole Mss. 192 and 393). It is addressed to someone both 'most dear' and 'most reverend', although it seems that it was requested through a mutual friend.[30] The forecast covers the years 1368–1374, a period when, according to Eschenden's previous calculations, the effects of the conjunctions of 1357 and 1365 would still be felt. It opens with five charts of the heavens, the first three of which all set out planetary positions, including conjunctions, for dates in the crucial year of 1365. The first is for 1 August of that year, when Saturn, Jupiter and Mars would all be in conjunction in the final division (Face) of Libra. The second is for 17 August in the same year; and the third sets out the details of a great conjunction in October of the same fateful year, when

[29] Thorndike notes that its prolixity and repetitions have led to his decision not to read it all (p. 330); North calculates its length as ca. 375,000 words (p. 71).
[30] Thorndike, p. 343; and Ashmole 192, I, 4, f.12r.

(as noted by many commentators at the time) all the planets except Mars would be together in the rather ominous sign of Scorpio. These conjunctions of 1365 laid down the conditions still expected to prevail in the opening years of the forecast. The final two charts provide data for two dates in 1369, whose conjunctions would inflect the ongoing consequences of 1365. On these bases Eschenden forecasts a prolonged period of disturbed weather, with severe consequences. The first years would see excessive rains leading to floods, while the last three years would be marked by prolonged drought. Specific forecasts are given for many months within the period. For instance, in late October and all of November 1372, unusually cold weather would add to the growing problems. It is clear that all those who could should take measures to prepare for the coming crop failures, food shortages and consequent high prices.

There is little doubt that such forecasts were made with serious intent, and were treated seriously by recipients. The amount of specialised work involved in making the calculations was considerable, and required skills in relatively advanced mathematics that were still scarce in fourteenth-century Europe. Interest in checking forecasts against actual weather is also demonstrated in surviving manuscripts from Oxford, Wurzburg and (probably) Basel. The earliest example is found in Ms Digby 176, as noted above, where weather conditions from January 1337 to January 1344 are set out. The manuscript itself consists of a set of originally separate booklets, apparently acquired from various sources by Reed and assembled together for him, but rebound in the seventeenth century. Its contents list is medieval, and attributes both the 'Rules for weather forecasting' and the following *Consideraciones temperiei pro 7 annis Christi* ('Notes on weather for 7 years') to William Merle. Merle has been identified as rector of Driby, Lincolnshire and the notes on weather relate primarily to part of that county, although with references to observations made in Oxford and in the town of Lincoln.[31] The records occupy folios 4r to 8v of the manuscript, and are copied out in more than one hand. They include detailed comments on how specific crops were affected by the weather conditions noted, and on the places in which various observations were made. They appear to sum up what may originally have been more detailed notes, and focus on weather events that might be

---

[31] For facsimiles of the weather records, with accompanying translation, see W. Merle, Ed. G.J. Symons, *Merle's MS. Consideraciones temperiei pro 7 annis Per Magistrum Willelmum Merle, Socium Domus de Merton: The earliest known journal of the weather: kept by the Rev. William Merle, Rector of Driby, Lincolnshire, 1337–1344*, London, 1891 (printed for Symons by Stanford, London).

considered excessive or unseasonal. An earthquake and a comet are also recorded.

The observations have no explanatory introduction or dedication, and their preservation and copying are difficult to interpret. They are rather misleadingly headed on f4r 'Weather conditions at Oxford for seven years'. It is possible that Merle recorded them in order to test his own rules for forecasting, and that Reed was interested in them for the same reason. No other copy of them has been found, but the acceptance of Merle's work by both Reed himself and the scholars of Merton may lie behind the fact that five other versions of Merle's 'Rules' for weather forecasting are known.[32] The inference seems to be that Merle's forecasts and observations were found to be sufficiently in agreement with one another to give support to his work. This interest in support from observation may be linked to the fact that, in the long version of Merle's 'Rules' found in Ms. Digby 147, the author cites as his authorities the classical writers on meteorology – Aristotle, Virgil and Pliny – together with Ptolemy's *Quadripartitus*. Thus Merle appears to be linking his work to the classical authorities, and their reliance upon directly observed 'signs' of coming weather, rather than the potentially contentious, Islamicate science of astrometeorology. Further evidence of this is that he makes unusually little reference to the Arabic authors whose work was relied upon by other writers in this field. Indeed, his level of reliance on weather signs of classical types is rather surprising at this date. Equally unusual is the fact that, despite its title, the full version of the treatise deals with ongoing effects of past weather conditions as well as with straightforward predictions.[33] However, this approach was apparently not what 'modern' readers wanted, since most versions of the 'Rules' give extracts specifically on forecasting, rather than the full text.

Much more mainstream in approach was the work of one Eyno of Würzburg, who is known only from this one, meteorological treatise.[34] This is longer than even the full version of Merle's text, and starts as was customary with key information concerning celestial phenomena and the central categories to be applied when interpreting the interactions between the heavenly bodies and earthly weather. These included both brief outlines of the long-established climatic zones of the Earth, and points on deciding which terrestrial locations were most likely to be affected by phenomena occurring in specific sections of the zodiac.

---

[32] These are in: Oxford, Bodleian, Mss. Digby 97 and 147; Oxford, Corpus Christi College, Ms. 293 A IV; Berlin, Staatsbibliothek, Ms. Lat. 2^0 192; and Boston, Francis Countway Library of Medicine, Ms De Ricci 20.

[33] See Thorndike, Vol. III, pp. 143–144.   [34] Ibid., pp. 145–146.

A certain amount of more classical, meteorological information is also given, within the discussions of phenomena such as snow, hail and thunderstorms. This study seems to have been less successful than Merle's, with only one complete copy being known.[35] The notes of actual weather in this case are added into the text as proof of the reliability of the forecasting methods which Eyno brings together. They cover the years 1331–1355, although without the continuous, monthly summaries given by William Merle. Indeed, the two forecasters would presumably have disagreed, since Eyno is confident that his long-term observations have shown the efficacy of established, astrometeorological forecasting. He uses phrases emphasising personal record-keeping and objective observation, and states that he has put down in his treatise things that he has 'proved' for himself. Eyno is, however, like William Merle in paying special attention to weather that goes beyond the norm. He records rains which caused floods and damage to bridges and crops, together with storms, winds and the consequent changes in prices of commodities such as grain. Eyno's combination of theoretical expertise and objective testing was sufficient for him to venture and record his own weather forecasts on certain occasions. For instance he notes with some emphasis that he successfully forecast snow on three separate occasions in the winter of 1341.

More closely related to the approach of Eyno of Würzburg than that of William Merle are the contents of a composite manuscript now in Basel University Library. The volume once belonged to the Dominicans of Basel, although the location of the author is not recorded.[36] The contents of this manuscript are not exclusively astrometeorological, and it also contains a copy of John of Seville's translation of the textbook of 'Alcabitius'. This is dated to 1355, although other parts of the manuscript date from the late fourteenth and early fifteenth centuries. Also in the opening sections of the volume are a commentary on the *Centiloquium* believed to be by Ptolemy, a treatise on mundane astrology (concentrating on annual revolutions), and short extracts on other aspects of

---

[35] This is now Nuremberg, Stadtbibliothek Cod. Cent V 64, part 1.

[36] The manuscript is Basel, Universitätsbibliothek, Ms. F. III. 8. A digital facsimile is available at: www.e-codices.unifr.ch/en/list/one/ubb/F-III-0008 (accessed 24 June 2019).

For discussion and English paraphrases of the records see L. Thorndike, 'A Weather Record for 1399–1406 AD', *Isis*, 32, 1940, pp. 304–323; and 'A daily Weather Record from the Years 1399 to 1401', *Isis*, 57, 1966, pp. 90–99. The later article is followed on pp. 99–101 by a 'Climatological Analysis of the Basel Weather Manuscript' by R. Frederick, H. Landsberg, and W. Lenke. Their analysis leads to the suggestion that the weather recorded fits with a location in west-central Europe, and perhaps with Besançon in particular.

mundane astrology, and especially on astrometeorology. The latter include an extract from the *Summa* of John of Eschenden. The manuscript overall contains an impressive collection of materials on the science of the stars, and opens with fundamental texts on teachings attributed to Ptolemy and Alcabitius. These are followed by extracts taken from works attributed to Zael, Albumazar, Messehalla and Alkindi, as well as anonymous pieces, some of which are astrometeorological. On folio 92r is the heading 'Notes and excerpts on predicting storms according to the planets' (*De tempestate e planetis cognoscenda notae et excerpta*), and the promised extracts continue to folio 103r, with more on folios 105r–110r. The intervening folios 103r–104v contain 'Observations on weather/storms 1399–1401 (from personal experience)'. Folios 110v–115r contain further personal observations on weather; with folios 116r–222v then giving daily notes on weather.

The astrometeorological details for 31 August 1399 (on fl16r) open, in accordance with scientific procedure, with a chart for the conjunction in force on that day. The heading (which may have been added later) states that this depicts the conjunction that preceded the entrance of the Sun into Libra. This was thus the conjunction that fell closest to the Autumn equinox, giving it particular importance in both mundane astrology generally and astrometeorology in particular. The manuscript gives a strong impression of being the work of a group or series of scholars, since the personal experiences are recorded in another different hand. They are also in the past tense (like those of William Merle) adding to the impression of careful, empirical testing of the theoretical material. Indeed, there are suggestions that the compilers were alert to correlations between the planetary conditions and prevailing weather, especially in relation to times of marked change. In the first year, 31 August 1399 to 31 August 1400, several such correlations appear to have happened. A note in the centre of the chart for 31 August 1399 points out that the period dominated by the conjunction was marked by wet weather, although some days were dry. The note after the end of the technical analysis of the conjunction states that 31 August itself was cloudy, with rain lasting three hours during daytime, and strong wind and rain in the night. For the next day, 1 September, the column of astronomical data gives positions in Virgo for the Sun, the Moon, Mercury and Jupiter, with Saturn in Sagittarius, Mars in Scorpio and Venus in Libra. The commentary points out that the Moon was moving away from the conjunction and towards Venus, and that both the Moon and Jupiter had quartile (negative) aspects with Saturn but sextile (positive) aspects with Mars. This combination would suggest tension between competing patterns of weather, in relation to both rainfall and temperature. The note on actual weather says that the day was cloudy, with rain, while the night was also cloudy, with cold air but apparently no rain. This is compatible with the planetary data, though no comment is given.

More explicit are the weather entries for 8 October 1399 and 15 March, 24 March, 7 April, 6 June, 3 August and 11 August 1400. The first of these records that the day was pleasant and healthful, with both cloud and sunshine; but that about vespers rain arrived together with a strong West wind and continued through the night. After this comes a note that it was about vespers on this day that Mercury moved into Scorpio (a Water sign). The 15 March saw fair, warm weather by day, although clouds gathered in the afternoon. Rain then fell after sunset. A note here points out that the Moon was in the ascendant and in aspect with the position it would hold when it was full. On 24 March there was heavy rain, and a note that the Moon was again in a significant relation to its position when full. The 7 April was cloudy, with short intervals of sunshine and a strong West wind. Confidence in astrometeorological procedures was perhaps growing, since there is a note that this correlates with the Moon moving away from conjunction with Jupiter, and towards Mercury, from an Air sign. The 6 June saw a rapid change in the weather, from cloudy and wet with a West wind, to dry, hot and rather still, with light and low East wind. The comment here is a rather brief observation that the Moon was 'Oriental' (in other words on the ascendant). Finally, the 3 August saw a heavy thunderstorm, which began a week of disturbed weather. On 11 August is the record that the weather became fair and warm, and that there was a change in the air. The additional note points out that Mercury, having been retrograde, began to move directly (forwards) again. If this early section records careful observation and possible identification of the most significant factors for local weather, that process might lie behind the change which becomes clear in the later sections of this weather almanac. Here the data on planetary positions and movements are accompanied only by brief entries on weather. The latter are so schematic that they may be tentative predictions rather than records.

Thus, late medieval weather forecasting seems to have found itself in a slightly contradictory position. On the one hand, there was broad agreement on the basic principles of astrometeorology, and it is clear that they were also perceived as in accordance with the achievements of current science. Yet on the other hand its practice remained both a matter for those with expensive, technical skills and the focus of ongoing concerns as to where it merged into unacceptable and 'superstitious' forms of astrological enquiry. Surviving, late medieval manuscripts of both treatises and Tables continue to come overwhelmingly from scholarly and professional sources. Rather surprisingly, texts on astrometeorology never occur in the same volumes as treatises on farming and estate management.[37] Those who needed or wanted weather forecasts going beyond traditional observations of weather signs would therefore have to consult professionals and to pay for their services. An analysis of surviving late medieval manuscripts containing the most popular astrometeorological texts has found that the majority of them appear to have been made by or for practising astrologers and physicians (fifty-three out of seventy-three volumes). The majority of the rest were the property of monastic communities.[38] The same study found that the most popular authority in both the fourteenth and fifteenth centuries was al-Kindi, with a total of fifty-two known copies of the two treatises that circulated under his name. Next in popularity was the work attributed to Robert Grosseteste, with thirty known copies. Overall, the long-established texts retained their status despite the appearance of newer versions of the material.[39] Of the later writers, the most popular was the work of John of Eschenden (nineteen copies) while that of John of York (*Perscrutator*) has ten copies, and Firminus of Bellavalle's has nine. The fact that Eschenden's work was chosen for early issue in printed form (by Bolanus and Santritter in Venice, 1489) provides further testimony as to its popularity.[40]

Whilst the surviving manuscripts that bring together astrometeorological theory with actual records of weather are few, their very existence is highly significant. Weather forecasting was clearly taken seriously, and was apparently being studied both theoretically and practically at least in England, the Empire and (possibly) France. Moreover, the close association between the science of the stars and medicine meant that any fully trained physician would be able to draw up predictions based upon the rules of mundane astrology, if not fully detailed astrometeorology. But how acceptable was this? Once again the evidence appears contradictory. On the one hand even critics of judicial or superstitious astrology, such as Nicole Oresme in fourteenth-century Paris, continued to abide by the conclusions of the *Speculum astronomiae* and to accept that the celestial bodies affected the natural world on Earth. He described the accurate calculation of the positions of the stars and movements of the planets as potentially a 'great and excellent science'; although he insisted that it was flawed in practice by lack of the requisite accuracy in calculation.

---

[37] Jenks, 'Astrometeorology', p. 195.   [38] Ibid., p. 198.   [39] Ibid.
[40] The copy in the Bibliothèque Nationale, Paris, is available in digital reproduction: http://gallica.bnf.fr/ark:/12148/bpt6k59654r/f2.image (accessed 24 June 2019).

A practical problem of increasing significance, which gave weight to Oresme's criticism, was the failure to deal with the growing tension between classic texts based on Ptolemy's works and the actual, contemporary positions of the stars, which were by then several degrees away from Ptolemy's figures. This was due to no fault of Ptolemy's, but to the same phenomenon of precession which was causing related problems with the calendar. Skilled astronomers could make the requisite calculations and adjustments, and incorporate them into updated editions of the Alfonsine Tables; but this in itself could cause confusion when the Tables were read alongside treatises that still gave the original figures. Still worse confusion resulted when some texts had been silently updated and revised at earlier periods, so that students could find themselves attempting to reconcile apparently contradictory data. It is thus entirely possible that Oresme was correct when he stated that positions given by 'the ancients' were still used by some astrologers, even though the stars 'are not now in the position they were in then'.[41] Similarly, Oresme accepted that predicting world events from great conjunctions, predicting forthcoming weather, and predicting the state of bodily humours and health, were all possible and potentially valuable. However, he also asserted that they could not be accurate in detail, and that weather forecasting in particular was undermined by the practical problems he had described. Moreover, as far as he could see, the detailed rules set out in astrometeorological works were not given any clear basis. This is rather a harsh judgement, given the guarantees of extensive personal observation and experimentation that most authoritative writers on the subject proffered, as has been noted. Nevertheless, for Oresme, the resulting forecasts are in fact worthless, and the practical experience of sailors and farmers is to be preferred. He is silent as to classical meteorology and weather signs, which he appears to place in a different category.

Despite his reputation and his royal patrons, however, Oresme (and his followers) failed to discredit the astrologers who produced ever-increasing numbers of annual predictions, giving both outlines of coming world events and prognostications of weather for the coming year, based on the interpretation of great conjunctions, annual revolutions, eclipses and the appearance of comets. The achievements of astrologers in the

---

[41] For the translation see Grant, *Source Book in Medieval Science*, pp. 488–494, at p. 489. For discussion see G. Copeland, *Nicole Oresme and the Astrologers*, Cambridge, Harvard University Press, 1952. Interesting points are also made in K. Bales, 'Nicole Oresme and Medieval Social Science', *American Journal of Economics and Social Science*, 42, 1983, pp. 101–111.

fourteenth and fifteenth centuries are celebrated in growing detail by the renowned, professional astrologer, Simon de Phares, in his *Recueil des Plus Celebres Astrologues*, written 1494–1498.[42] The work is addressed to King Charles VIII of France, and opens with a long defence of astrology that also makes numerous criticisms of the ignorance of the attackers. The key points are that these attackers are failing to distinguish between science and superstition, and that the destruction of astrology would be a great, practical loss to the kingdom. To back up his points, he promises a list of all the great astrologers, from the beginning of the world, and the tables, rules and instruments they gave the world. It seems to be mundane astrology that he most wishes to defend (or perhaps sees as most defensible) since he promises also to outline the successful predictions of great events made by astrologers. These will be the predictions and prognostications made on the basis of revolutions of years, great conjunctions, comets, and other unusual stars, eclipses, and 'other types of evidence'. 'Nativities', in other words horoscopes for individuals, are slipped in here; but attention rapidly moves back to broader issues. The work is also intended to show that astrologers have done service by predicting such things as political crises, wars, famines, plagues, times of great cold or heat, deluges, earthquakes and storms.[43] Simon de Phares delivers much of what he promises, in increasing (if sometimes imaginative) detail as he approaches his own time. The final section of his book covers the period from the late fourteenth century to his own lifetime, and gives the names of some 152 'great astrologers', many of whom were also physicians, clerics or royal advisers, whose predictions he has heard of or actually read. All made predictions and forecasts of the types promised, or else made scientific advances in astronomical techniques. Knowledge of their published predictions was clearly facilitated by the arrival of printing, and indeed comments are given on the printed editions of the predictions.[44]

The fact that Simon de Phares was able to provide information on the valuable achievements of so many astrologers serves as witness to two key developments at the end of the medieval period. The first is the rise in the number of universities, and of associated teaching positions in astronomy and medicine, which provided training and support for many of those named by de Phares. Highly qualified practitioners in these subjects also had expertise in mundane astrology and astrometeorology; and holders

---

[42] Simon de Phares, *Le Recueil des Plus Celebres Astrologues*, Ed. J-P Boudet, Tome I, Paris, Champion, 1997. The work survives in what may be at least partially an autograph manuscript, now Paris, B.N.F., fr. 1357.
[43] Ibid., pp. 38–39.   [44] Ibid., pp. 530–604.

of university chairs seem to have been expected to read their prognostications and forecasts for the coming period to selected audiences. Such audiences were still small, but nevertheless this would make forecasts available both in greater numbers and to more people. The second, even more radical in its impact, was the arrival in northern and western Europe of printing with movable type. The next chapter will examine this in detail; but it is sufficient to say at this point that one of the most effective ways for entrepreneurial printers to boost their incomes was to publish copies of the annual prognostications and forecasts of respected practitioners. Mention of their qualifications and patrons served as support for rival publications, in a market that expanded rapidly both for forecasters and their readers.

8   Weather Forecasting and the Impact of Print

The previous chapter showed that the fourteenth century saw impressive developments in the science of the stars (as well as in associated fields such as clockmaking and instrument making). However, the very advances that produced marvellous mechanical clocks and increasingly precise astronomical tables meant that astrologers' claims to calculate accurate planetary positions could no longer be dismissed as fantasy. For mundane astrology more generally and for astrometeorology specifically this was not a direct threat, since these forms of astrology were acceptable and socially useful. Nevertheless, it was an inconvenient fact that anyone who could perform astrometeorological calculations could also draw up horoscopes for other applications, including the forbidden ones. Moreover, levels of anxiety about sorcery and necromancy were growing, as inquisitors discovered worrying numbers of practitioners across Europe. Neither astrometeorology nor medicine was perceived to depend upon magic, or to involve contact with demons. Nevertheless, as in the thirteenth century, practitioners of the forbidden arts continued to claim that their rituals were merely applied versions of the science of the stars. All those working in the field therefore had to be prepared for intense scrutiny, even as demand for high levels of scientific expertise continued to grow. The rising numbers of universities across Europe, and the founding of chairs in astronomy and medicine, provided a productive response to both pressures. The holders of the chairs increasingly showed their value to local society in general, as well as to powerful individual patrons, by issuing annual forecasts as to probable trends in crops, prices, threats to human health, political stability and, underlying all of these, weather. These annual prognostications became almost as much a requirement for ambitious city-governors as public clocks, and they dominate the story of weather forecasting in the fifteenth century alongside the more traditional picture of royal and aristocratic patronage.

Competition for the most qualified experts is shown by the frequency with which they moved from one centre to another as their reputations grew. Moreover, their powers were both exploited and promoted by pioneers in another, even newer technology of the time – that of the printing press. As the developments to be discussed in this chapter will show, astrometeorology and printing were close allies almost from the first arrival of printing in Europe, although this relationship has been little examined. The expansion of university study of astronomy and astrology across northern Europe, following Charles V's sponsorship of a chair in Paris in 1379, is shown by the fact that the newly founded University of Louvain (approved by Pope Martin V in 1425) sought prominent practitioners from its beginning.[1] John of Gmunden, who died in 1442, was the first professor of astronomy at the prestigious university of Vienna, and he was succeeded by Georg Peurbach.[2] Peurbach himself had studied in France, Germany, and Italy, and had established such a reputation that he had been employed as court astrologer to both Ladislaus V of Hungary and the Emperor Frederick III. In 1459 the University of Krakow followed the fashion, founding a chair in astrology.[3] Astrology and astronomy were being taught at Erfurt already by 1359, when John of Stendhal, who was based in Magdeburg, wrote a textbook for the Erfurt students, although it is not clear that Erfurt had a professor in the subject. The textbook was John's commentary on Al-Qabisi's introduction to astrology.[4] Similar evidence relates to the teaching of astrology at Bologna in 1405 and at Padua in the late fifteenth century.[5] At Ingolstadt, astronomy was being taught by ca. 1470, when Johann Engel arrived there.[6] Martin Polich of Mellerstadt taught at both Leipzig and Wittenberg before becoming physician to Frederick the Wise of Saxony in 1482.[7] He then issued annual prognostications for

---

[1] See R. Lemay, 'The Teaching of Astronomy in Medieval Universities, Principally at Paris in the Fourteenth Century', *Manuscripta*, 20, 1976, pp. 197–217, at 200–201; and S. Vanden Broecke, *The Limits of Influence; Pico, Louvain and the Crisis of Renaissance Astrology*, Leiden, Brill, 2003, p. 29. For the scale of teaching at Paris see also: E. Poulle, 'Les astronomes parisiens au XIVe siècle et l'astronomie alphonsine' in *Histoire littéraire de la France publiée par l'Académie des Inscriptions et Belles-Lettres*, Tome 43, Fasc. 1, Paris, 2005, pp. 1–54; and D. Jacquart, 'Médecine et astrologie à Paris dans la première moitié du XIVe siècle', in G.F. Vescovini and F. Barocelli, Eds., *Filosofia, scienza e astrologia nel Trecento europeo*, Padua, Poligrafo, 1992, pp. 121–134.

[2] J. North, *Cosmos: An Illustrated History of Astronomy and Cosmology*, p. 269.

[3] R. Lemay, 'The Late Medieval Astrological School at Cracow and the Copernican System', *Studia Copernicana*, 19, 1978, pp. 337–354.

[4] C. Burnett, 'Al-Qabisi's Introduction to Astrology: from Courtly Entertainment to University Textbook', in R. Fontaine et al., Eds., *Studies in the History of Culture and Science; A tribute to Gad Freudenthal*, Leiden, Brill, 2011, pp. 43–69, at p. 49.

[5] Ibid. See also M. Shank, 'Academic Consulting in Fifteenth-Century Vienna: The Case of Astrology', in E. Sylla and M. McVaugh, Eds., *Texts and Contexts in Ancient and Medieval Science. Studies on the Occasion of John E. Murdoch's Seventieth Birthday*, Leiden, Brill, 1997, pp. 245–270.

[6] Thorndike, *History*, Vol. 5, p. 344.   [7] Ibid., p. 455.

1483–1490, with that for 1489 addressed to the Emperor Frederick III. In the Iberian Peninsula, a chair in astronomy and astrology was established at Salamanca ca. 1460, and its first incumbent was Nicholaus Polonius.[8]

As early as 1405, annual predictions based on revolutions of the year and great conjunctions were issued in versions that survive by Henry Andrea of Gislingen, Blasius of Parma and Melletus de Russis of Forli. Another one, for 1406 by Roger de Saint Simon of Poitiers, is also known.[9] Master Peter of Monte Alciano, of Pavia, produced prognostications that were clearly in demand. Those for the years 1419, 1421, 1430, 1448 all survive, and copies reached the Palatinate as well as (probably) France and England.[10] Evidence of study of weather forecasting in particular is provided by the work of Niccolo de Comitibus, a Paduan aristocrat, who wrote ca. 1466 a work on mundane astrology that paid special attention to astrometeorology. The work notes that especially critical attention is given to weather forecasts, since people check whether or not they are correct. It also asserts that earlier writers did not make the techniques of prediction entirely clear. Niccolo therefore sets out what he identifies as the most important factors, giving a simplified account of conjunctions, and a list of the sixteen chief winds. The following six chapters, the heart of the work, are all devoted to astrometeorology, while chapter seven caters for those not skilled in astrology by giving traditional signs of coming weather, prefaced by some personal observations.[11]

The career of Joannes Vesalius, great-grandfather of the more famous Andreas Vesalius (author of the *De humani corporis fabrica*) illustrates the growing range of consumers and patrons of these predictions and forecasts. This Vesalius studied at Cologne and Pavia before coming to the new University of Louvain in 1429. By 1455 he had advanced to being one of the most important physicians in Brussels and was also being consulted and paid by Duke Philip the Good of Burgundy.[12] Already in 1430 the council of Louvain commissioned from him an almanac and prognostication for 1431, which he duly read in the University. This was required to include forecasts of 'things that will happen in the following year'. It was presumably successful, since others are recorded for 1439 and 1440, and he was commissioned to produce later almanacs

---

[8] See J. Chabás and B. Goldstein, *Astronomy in the Iberian Peninsula; Abraham Zacut and the Transition from Manuscript to Print*, Transactions of the American Philosophical Society, Volume 90, Part 2, Philadelphia, 2000, p. 4.

[9] Thorndike, *History*, Vol. 4, pp. 88–89.   [10] Ibid., p. 92.   [11] Ibid., pp. 250–254.

[12] Vanden Broecke, *Limits of Influence*, p. 31.

for the duke. The level of demand for such annual forecasts is shown by the arrival in Louvain of its first printer, Jan van Westfalen, in the 1470s, and the fact that he began almost immediately to publish annual prognostications of this type.[13] Here again the renown achieved by one individual is made clear, as is the demand for his prognostications amongst rulers, scholars, and civic authorities. There is equally striking evidence of astrometeorological expertise, and of the issuing of annual prognostications, in Krakov even before the establishment of the university chair. This is provided by Ms. 764 in the Jagiellonian Library, which contains a full prediction for 1451, which has been attributed to Martin Bylica.[14] Bylica himself was one of the most famous astrologers and physicians at the court of Matthias Corvinus (King of Hungary 1458–1490) and studied at Krakov before entering Corvinus' service. The prediction in Ms 764 covers the standard categories, including forecasts of the weather for each month.

In England, university-level production of such prognostications is less clear. However, that prognostications and forecasts were drawn up for private consumption by powerful patrons is suggested by the work of John Dunstaple.[15] Unusually, Dunstaple was a musician and artist as well as being skilled in astronomy and astrology, and his combination of talents secured him employment in the households of the duke of Bedford; Joanna of Navarre, the widowed queen of England; and Joanna's stepson Humphrey, the duke of Gloucester. His range of knowledge is displayed in a manuscript now I 3 18 in Emmanuel College, Cambridge, which has a collection of texts on mundane and judicial astrology, as well as a short treatise 'on rains' (*de pluviis*). Further materials dealing with chiromancy, physiognomy and the method for drawing up an almanac are also included. The name of Dunstaple is given in two places, most prominently in the inscription on the opening page that names him as the compiler and scribe of the volume.

Related to the ongoing work in both astronomy and mundane astrology, and apparently another field for academic and civic competition, was the compilation of comprehensive and updated tables of planetary and stellar positions. These drew upon the Alphonsine corpus, but demonstrated the skill and mastery of advanced instrumentation and calculation achieved by their compilers. They also provided ready-

---

[13] Ibid., p. 36.

[14] See S.C. Rowell, 'The Jagiellonians and the Stars: Dynasty-Sponsored Astrology in the Fifteenth Century', *Lithuanian Historical Studies*, 7, 2002, pp. 23–42, at p. 29.

[15] On Dunstaple's career see H. Carey, 'Judicial astrology in theory and practice in later medieval Europe', *Studies in the History and Philosophy of Biological and Medical Sciences*, 41, 2010, pp. 90–98.

calculated data for use by those less able to make the requisite calculations, and thus provided material for would-be forecasters. An example is provided by late fifteenth-century Bologna, where one university master was required to compile an annual 'tacuinus' or almanac. This was to show the sign positions, in degrees and minutes, for each planet on each day of the coming year. It was also to show the aspects of the planets to the Moon and to one another on the same basis. Finally it was to give the dates of Sundays and all major feasts, including the moveable feasts of Easter and all those dependent upon it. His colleague was then to use all this material to produce his judgement for the year to come.[16]

In fact Bologna was, if anything, rather late in this field. A forerunner was Abraham Zacut, a Jewish astronomer in Salamanca, who was forced into exile in 1492. Zacut therefore published his *Perpetual Almanac (Almanach Perpetuum)* in Portugal, in 1496, although he had carried out most of his calculations in Salamanca.[17] As was customary, the work gives a set of canons or rules for use, followed by tables. The latter are extensive, with full sets for each of the planets, including the Sun and Moon, calculated at intervals of one to ten days, in order to cover the whole of each planet's perceived course, including retrogrades. In the case of Mercury this necessitated calculations covering no less than 125 years, while the tables for the Moon give data for 11,325 consecutive days (covering some 31 years).[18] Zacut worked from the Alphonsine Tables, but made recalculations and updates of his own. Like the masters of Bologna, he also gave tables of ascendants, and further added data on planetary houses. These are calculated for each month, starting at the astrological starting point of March. Further help for other astrologers was given in the form of exact configurations for the first six astrological houses, at noon on stated dates, for the meridian of Salamanca.[19] With all this, horoscopes could be worked out by later users with only relatively basic adjustments.

Most celebrated of all such works was that of Johann Müller, better known as Regiomontanus, the successor to Peurbach. Peurbach himself had completed eclipse tables for Vienna in the 1450s, and is best known for undertaking a revision and edition of the Latin version of Ptolemy's *Almagest*. Regiomontanus completed the latter work after Peurbach's death, as well as producing an impressively full *Calendar* and *Ephemerides*. These were seized upon and printed soon after their production, by Ratdolt, the publisher of many astronomical and astrological works. Indeed, Ratdolt's first publication in Venice was Regiomontanus'

---

[16] Rowell, p. 32.   [17] See Chabás and Goldstein, *Astronomy in the Iberian Peninsula*, p. 2.
[18] Ibid., pp. 2–3.   [19] Ibid., pp. 95–100.

Calendar, issued in 1476, and followed in 1481 by the *Ephemerides.*[20] Both were reissued many times, and in rival editions, although Ratdolt's are impressive for their clarity and accuracy of layout.[21] The two works between them established a gold standard for the calculation and clear presentation of large quantities of astronomical data. In printed form the *Ephemerides* alone run to well over 600 pages, and their appeal for would-be practitioners of astrometeorology (as well as other applied forms of astronomy) is obvious.

They open with a useful 'Table of Regions' providing times to be applied when recalculating for various cities and regions, and then a short preface with basic rules and explanations. As had become standard, the approved numerical values for the 'dignities' or powers of each planet in each sign are given, together with tables giving the established symbols for each planet, sign, and aspect. Another introductory table relates to lunar mansions. After these comes a set of rules for deriving prognostications from the data, which opens with the encouraging promise that it covers the key points very briefly. The first paragraphs do indeed give brief notes on the usual basics, and to these is added useful information on the major stars, their locations and their powers. With the fundamentals established, the first set of specific instructions relates to the important matter of making weather forecasts. Rather unusually, no comment is made here as to the sources of the information, so that the impression is created that these rules and dicta are those tried and tested by Regiomontanus himself. The reader is first instructed in the basic characteristics of the four seasons of the year, and then reminded that the natures of the signs, as given earlier, must always be taken into consideration. Then come statements on the effects upon the seasons of planetary aspects involving signs of the same elemental triplicity. For instance, if planets are in aspect or conjunction in fire signs this signifies excessive heat and drought when it happens in summer; but in winter it will temper the cold, wet nature of the season. This section concludes with the guiding principle that the powers of the planets in the signs involved, as well as the aspects between them, must be considered. A final point is that the powers and natures of the fixed stars (which have also been set out above) should never be discounted.

---

[20] Thorndike, *History,* Vol. 5, pp. 340–342.

[21] A digital copy of Ratdolt's version of Regiomontanus' *Ephemerides 1484-1506* is hosted online by the Europeana website. The work belongs to the University of Vienna: www.europeana.eu/portal/en/record/9200209/o_225215.html (accessed 24 June 2019). A rival edition, also produced in Venice, but in 1498, can be viewed via the Gallica website at: http://gallica.bnf.fr/ark:/12148/bpt6k596433/f1.image (accessed 25 June 2019).

Next, and filling some two printed columns, come specific points concerning the effects of individual planets when in aspect with one another. These start as was customary with Saturn. Comments on the effects of the signs in which the planets involved are placed, and especially on the elemental qualities (fiery, earthy, etc.) of these signs, are also given. Thus, a major conjunction of Saturn with Jupiter in a fire sign will bring drought, while in a water sign it will bring deluges and floods. Conjunctions of Saturn with any other planet will have related (if weaker) effects. Similarly, an opposition, square or sextile aspect between Saturn and Jupiter will bring great disturbance of the atmosphere, with destructive rains, winds and hail both before and after the occurrence of the aspect itself, when they take place in watery signs. These same aspects will have related effects when they occur in air signs, as the atmosphere will undergo great changes. The concept of the 'opening of the doors', which played an important role in the weather forecasting treatises translated in the twelfth century, also appears here, in the form of a very abbreviated set of notes on specific combinations of planets and aspects. These are addressed to a reader already familiar with the calculations and procedures involved. After these expositions of major aspects of Saturn (mostly involving Jupiter) come shorter notes on Saturn's interactions with Mars, the Sun, Venus and Mercury. For instance, Saturn in conjunction with Mars in a water sign will cause thunderstorms and hail for three days before and after the aspect, whilst a square or opposition between these two very frequently generates lightning flashes and tempests.

As would be expected, considerable space is devoted to the effects of the Moon, which is dealt with last and fills more than one column of this introductory text. Here special attention is given to aspects occurring from New Moon to Full Moon, as well as to specific signs. For instance, an opposition of the Moon and Jupiter in Aries (fire) and Scorpio (water) will spread white clouds across the sky, while the same aspect with Mars will add thunder and lightning. If the Moon subsequently moves towards Mercury there will be an 'opening of the door' of the winds. Equally, an opposition or square of the Moon at this time with Jupiter will loose the winds. This concludes the presentation of key points on weather forecasting, and the next section (of four columns) deals with the choice of the best days for beginning tasks. More detailed guidance on the timing of medical and agricultural activities is dealt with in the space of just one column. Perhaps to satisfy traditionalists, or for reasons of completeness, an outline of 'Weather forecasting according to al-Kindi' is next given. This opens with the effects of Saturn in Aries, and with the familiar words *Saturnus in ariete*. Here the focus is on the signs, and the effects of each planet in each sign, under specified conditions. Thus the final entry covers Mercury in Pisces. Still further help in the application of the detailed information is then provided in the forms of a circular diagram showing the signs and their aspects to one another, and a square one showing the houses and their positions.

The ephemeris itself follows. This combines tables of planetary positions with calendar information for each year, in a highly user-friendly manner. Each year is dealt with in turn, and each opens with standard calendar information in the form of the Golden Number, Sunday (or dominical) letter (or letters in the case of leap years) and ready-calculated dates of moveable feasts. The latter already sets this work apart from the perpetual calendars that accompanied works on computus, but something more unusual is to come. This comprises lists of planetary retrogrades (periods of apparent backward movement) that will occur during the year, and tables and diagrams of eclipses. Then come monthly calendar pages, similar in presentation to those of the perpetual calendars. Here, however, there is no reference to the dating system of the Roman calendar, which numbered the days of each month in relation to nones, ides and kalends. In this consciously modern work the days are simply numbered consecutively. Each month is given an opening of the book. The left-hand page, divided into nine vertical columns, has a line for each day. The first column gives major feasts, with the dominical letter also on the appropriate lines. Then come columns for the planets, in the order Sun, Moon, Saturn, Jupiter, Mars, Venus and Mercury. The right column covers 'Caput draconis', the Moon's ascending node (the user is left to calculate the opposite, descending node). Each column gives the position of the relevant planet on a daily basis, in degrees and minutes, with the appropriate symbol inserted whenever there is a move into a different sign. On the facing page, again on a daily basis, are the planetary aspects. The first six columns deal with the aspects of the Moon to each of the other planets; the final column gives the aspects of the Sun and other planets to one another. It is thus possible at a glance, for instance, to see when major conjunctions will take place, and very little effort is needed to relate them to eclipses. In other words, Regiomontanus has provided all that is needed for the compilation of yearly almanacs and prognostications, and Ratdolt and his competitors were making it available in printed editions. This publication included all that the first of the two masters of astronomy and astrology at Bologna was to cover in his annual 'tacuinus', and more besides, and made it available to anyone who could afford to buy the book. The latter point perhaps helps to explain the issuing of multiple versions of the work, of varying print quality, since the price of the Ratdolt edition would be beyond the means of many would-be purchasers.

Whether regionally based astrologers were amongst the owners of Regiomontanus' work cannot be known for certain, but it seems highly likely that they were. Simon de Phares was certainly well aware of the achievement involved, and described 'Johannes de Monte Regio' as an excellent astrologer, the most skilled the world had seen for 100 years, for whose services Italians and Germans competed.[22] His chief publications are listed in laudatory terms, and de Phares is known to have possessed a copy of the *Calendar*.[23] Moreover, the evidence given by de Phares concerning levels of demand for prognostications in the late fifteenth century, both printed and private, is striking. For instance, de Phares writes of a Master Jehan Anthoine who composed a marvellously accurate prognostication based on the revolution of the year for 1472, addressed to the duke of Savoy.[24] Considerably more information is given concerning Master Conrad Heingarter, with whom de Phares studied for three years. Heingarter is stated to have produced a series of predictions for Jean de Bourbon, as well as working for King Louis XI ca. 1469.[25] Master Hugues de Beauregard, of Bourges, produced a series of prognostications in the 1490s based on revolutions of the year.[26] Paul of Middlebourg, a master of Padua and physician to the duke of Urbino, is listed as having composed a prognostication covering twenty years that achieved a considerable reputation; while Jehan Lichtenberger, astrologer to the Emperor Frederick III, issued another series of prognostications, including one for forty years. This was printed, as de Phares says, and appeared first in Strasbourg in 1488.[27] Another expert mentioned by de Phares is Antonius de Camera, who issued yearly predictions in the 1460s for patrons including Piero de Medici and King Matthias (Corvinus) of Hungary.[28]

In France itself the first printed almanacs and prognostications were issued in Paris in the 1490s, although the production of these works for the French market rapidly spread to Antwerp and Geneva.[29] Already by 1475 printing businesses had spread from Mainz through the Rhineland

---

[22] On de Phares himself, see chapter seven above.
[23] De Phares, Ed. Boudet, pp. 587–588 and 590–591.   [24] Ibid., p. 583.
[25] Ibid., pp. 586–587.   [26] Ibid., p. 592.
[27] Ibid., pp. 593–594. See further D. Kurze, 'Popular Astrology and Prophecy in the fifteenth and sixteenth Centuries: Johannes Lichtenberger', in P. Zambelli, Ed., *Astrologi hallucinati; Stars and the End of the World in Luther's Time*, Berlin and New York, de Gruyter, 1986, pp. 177–193.
[28] Thorndike, *History*, Vol. 4, pp. 438–440.
[29] W. Eamon, 'Astrology and Society', in B. Dooley, Ed., *Companion to Astrology in the Renaissance*, Leiden/Boston, Brill, 2014, pp. 141–192. See also T. Charmasson,

and into Italy (where there were at least fifteen), Paris, Lyons and Seville. By 1480 at least 110 towns across Europe have been calculated to have presses. Most German cities had them, the number in France had risen to five, and Caxton had set up shop in London in 1476.[30] The preeminence of Venice is clear by the 1480s. Further evidence of the close relationship between astrology and printing is provided by the career of Johannes Engel, whose time at Ingolstadt has already been mentioned. He had studied in Vienna under Regiomontanus in 1468 before moving to Ingolstadt, and was in Augsburg by 1489, where he acted as an editor for Ratdolt until 1491. He compiled yearly prognostications from 1484, printed in both Latin and German, using his own versions of the Alphonsine tables. His 1488 *Opus astrolabii plani in tabulis* delivers the promised tables of astronomical and astrological data, together with no fewer than 360 charts and sample horoscopes, and is a very impressive piece of printing. He also edited for Ratdolt a collection of the treatises attributed to Abu Ma'shar on the great conjunctions, very important for mundane astrology, which was printed first in 1489. Finally, his version of fully calculated *Ephemerides* covered 1494–1500, and was printed in Vienna by Winterburger, the city's first printer, as was his *Almanach novum* that went up to 1510.[31]

Another pioneer of printed almanacs and prognostications, although not of full ephemerides, was Johannes Laet. He collaborated with Joannes de Westfalia, the first printer in Louvain, to issue printed prognostications from 1475 until 1485.[32] This enterprise was so successful that Laet was followed by his son, Gaspard, who produced prognostications in French as well as Latin from 1496. All this is recorded by de Phares, who laments the poor quality of the French translations.[33] A major centre of production for these early almanacs and prognostications was Antwerp, from where they could be exported into surrounding regions, including both France and England. However, it rapidly faced competition from Rouen, where examples were issued in 1509 and 1517, at least, by Guillaume d'Amours.[34] These almanacs varied considerably in size and detail, but those of Gaspard Laet may

---

'L'établissement d'un almanach medical pour l'année 1437', in *Comptes-rendus du 99e Congrès national des sociétés savant, Section des sciences, Fasc. V*, Paris, 1976, pp. 217–234.

[30] The pioneering study is that of L. Febvre and H-J Martin, translated by D. Gerard as *The Coming of the Book*, London, Verso, 1984. For the figures quoted see pp. 167–186.

[31] See J. Hamel, 'Engel, Johannes' in T. Hockey et al., Eds., *Biographical Encyclopedia of Astronomers*, New York, Springer, 2014, p. 339.

[32] Vanden Broecke, p. 37.   [33] De Phares, Ed. Boudet, p. 598.

[34] A copy of his *Prenostication nouvelle lan mille cinq cens XVIII composee sur le climat de France* is held by the Wellcome Institute, London, as EPB/B283/B.

be taken as representative. His prognostication for 1497 was drawn up in Louvain and printed in Paris, in French, by Le Caron. It has not only the promised prognostication but also a one-page 'almanach' for the year.[35] The latter is basic, and focused on giving dates for new and full Moons, with the days in each month best for the main forms of medical treatment. However the prognostication, dedicated to the eminent patron, the aristocratic bishop of Liège, gives special attention to weather forecasts. These come first, and are arranged by season starting with winter. Spring will begin when the Sun enters the first degree of Aries, which is stated to take place almost one hour after noon on 10 March. Laet notes that this is also the 'revolution of the year'. Rather ominously, Saturn will be on the ascendant, with Jupiter in the same sign, and Venus in aspect with Saturn. Cautiously, Laet states that his interpretation follows the doctrines of 'Albumasar', Ptolemy and Ibn Ezra, and it is their work that leads to the forecast that Spring will begin windy and cloudy. The negative placing of Mercury leads to a further suggestion, attributed to Ibn Ezra, that there is a danger of strong winds, thunder storms and even tempests.

The earliest prognostication known to have been printed in England was that issued by Wynkyn de Worde in 1497 for 1498. It was rapidly followed by Pynson's almanac for 1500, which was probably pirated and translated from one composed by Jasper or Gaspard Laet.[36] In fifteenth- and sixteenth-century England, however, the term prognostication could be applied to medical prognoses and guides as well as to broader applications of mundane astrology. An example of the types of materials produced in the period is provided by one surviving copy of Caxton's *Myrrour of the World*.[37] This has sixteen folios of manuscript material in a sixteenth-century hand added at the end. These include a table of the planets ruling the hours each day, as calculated by the astronomer and astrologer John Somer ca. 1367. Somer himself had been commissioned to draw up a 'kalendarium' for Joan, Princess of Wales, in 1380, before receiving royal grants from Richard II and Henry IV; his fame in late medieval England is demonstrated by the fact that he was one of the astronomers recommended by Chaucer in the introductory section of his

---

[35] A digital version is available at Les Bibliothèques Virtuelles Humanistes: www.bvh.univ-tours.fr/Consult/consult.asp?numtable=B452346101_C2095&numfiche=234&mode=3&ecran=0&offset=0 (accessed 25 June 2019).

[36] H.S. Bennett, *English Books and Readers, 1475 to 1557*, Cambridge, University Press, second edition, 1969, p. 119.

[37] Now New York, Pierpont Morgan Library, 776.

Treatise on the Astrolabe.[38] Folios 6r to 11v of the additions to Morgan 776 contain further relevant materials, including a short text on prognostication by thunder, and more sophisticated astrological tables and charts. Amongst these, on folio 10v, are weather prognostications.[39] The compiler of this collection of materials seems to have been most interested in medical applications, but clearly made or studied weather forecasts as well.

Overall, whilst there is a considerable amount of evidence concerning astrologer-physicians working both in the courts of the English elite and in cities like London, none is recorded as having compiled or published a prognostication concentrating on forecasting the weather.[40] The absence of locally calculated almanacs and prognostications in England may be related to the scarcity of printers, and the economics of distributing large quantities of printed materials, rather than a lack of interest or skill in the forecasting of weather. It is well known that the majority of the almanac prognostications purchased in England until the middle of the sixteenth century were imported, and were predominantly the work of the Laet family.[41] Since water transport was the cheapest means of carrying heavy goods, carriage across the Channel added little to the price of the almanacs themselves, and it would appear that the reading public in England were able to read prognostications in French or Latin.

Evidence of English readiness to engage in do-it-yourself prognostication and weather forecasting is provided by the success of Leonard Digges' *Prognostication of right good effect fructfully augmented, contayninge playne, briefe, pleasant, chosen rules, to iudge the wether for euer, by the sunne, moone, sterres, cometes, raynbowe, thunder, cloudes, with other extraordinarie tokens, not omitting the aspectes of planetes, with a brefe iudgemente for euer, of*

---

[38] For Somer's work see *The Kalendarium of John Somer*, Ed. L. Mooney, Athens, Georgia, University of Georgia Press, 1998.

[39] C.F. Bühler, 'Sixteenth-Century Prognostications: Libri Impressi cum Notis Manuscriptis – Part II', in *Isis*, 33, 5, 1942, pp. 609–620.

[40] See H. Carey, *Courting Disaster*; and S. Page, 'Richard Trewythian and the Uses of Astrology in Late Medieval England', *Journal of the Warburg and Courtauld Institutes*, 64, 2001, pp. 193–228.

[41] See: L. Kassell, 'Almanacs and Prognostications', in J. Raymond, Ed., *The Oxford History of Popular Print Culture; Volume One: Cheap Print in Britain and Ireland to 1660*, Oxford University Press, 2011, pp. 432–445; and B. Capp, 'The Potter Almanacs', *eBLJ*, 2004, article 4. The classic work on the subject remains Capp's *English almanacs, 1500–1800; astrology and the popular press*, Ithaca, New York, Cornell University Press, 1979. The most recent survey is that of S. Kusukawa, 'Incunables and Sixteenth-Century Books', chapter 4 of A. Hunter, Ed., *Thornton and Tully's Scientific Books, Libraries and Collectors*, 4th edition, London and New York, Routledge, 2016.

plentie, lacke, sickenes, death, vvarres &c.[42] This was first issued in 1553, and proved such a success that it was revised and reissued in 1555. It was further updated and reissued numerous times, including by Digges' son. As the title shows, it promised to make it possible for skilled amateurs to produce their own prognostications, paying special attention to the forecasting of weather. Digges himself was a member of a wealthy family, educated at Oxford and a member of Lincoln's Inn, who wrote on several scientific topics as well as issuing at least one annual almanac for Kent in 1556. He was convicted of high treason after taking part in Wyatt's rebellion against Queen Mary's marriage in 1554. Although he was not executed for this crime, he was financially ruined; but the success of his *Prognostication* was great enough that it did much to restore his fortunes.[43]

The need to address an audience of non-specialists helps to explain why its opening sections concentrate on rules for weather forecasting from direct observation of the Sun, Moon and the appearance of the heavens. Brief versions of the long-established Aristotelian information are given here, with special attention to discussions of comets and eclipses. Throughout, Digges diplays his learning by citing classical writers such as Pliny alongside medieval authorities on astrology, whilst always communicating his own expertise and observation. This comes across, for instance, in the rather technical coverage of the aspects of the Moon, and the effects of its placing in each zodiac sign. To ensure that everyone could follow these guidelines, this section is followed in turn by tables for calculating the sign position of the Moon. The old links between such study of the Moon, its position in relation to the Sun, and the ecclesiastical science of computus are maintained by Digges, who devotes the next eight chapters to topics within this field. Considerable space, with impressive attention to appropriate scientific instruments, is also given to means of telling the time both by day and at night, before the construction of an accurate calendar is reached in chapter 21. This is then followed by basic calendar tables for each month. What Digges promises to make possible is for the user of the book to produce calculations and forecasts whenever they wish, rather than having to wait for the turn of each year and to purchase readymade forecasts. The more technical astrometeorological procedures outlined would require consultation of an almanac or ephemeris, which is not

---

[42] An edition of the 1555 version is available online at: https://quod.lib.umich.edu/e/eebo/A17556.0001.001?view=toc (accessed 25 June 2019).
[43] See S. Johnston, 'Digges, Leonard', ODNB, 2004, https://doi.org/10.1093/ref:odnb/7637 (accessed 4 January 2019).

provided; but anyone able to acquire and use the scientific instruments carefully described and specified by Digges would also be able to purchase and use such a publication. A further attraction is that, interspersed with the astrometeorological material, are sections on topics such as star risings and animal behaviour going all the way back to Pliny, whose authority is occasionally invoked.

How, then, was the mid-sixteenth-century user of Digges' work to 'judge the weather'? First, it is explained that key days are the three days after a new Moon, the three days before a full Moon, and the middle day of any phase. For longer-term judgements, the Moon's sign when it enters each phase must also be known, since the element associated with the relevant sign will influence the weather until the next turning point, within the general conditions associated with the prevailing season. Both Regiomontanus and Guido Bonatti are boldly cited as authorities for this. More specific forecasts using a combination of the Sun's sign and that of the Moon are then outlined. For instance, while the Sun is in Aquarius (late winter) there are three combinations that signify rain. These are the new Moon occurring in Aquarius, the new Moon in Sagittarius, or the full Moon in Leo. In early spring, when the Sun is in Pisces and Aries, a new or full Moon in Virgo, Libra or Sagittarius will bring rain, while disturbed and changeable weather is forecast if the Moon is in Aquarius or Pisces at the key points. It might be expected that similar 'judgements' would be given for the Sun in each zodiac sign, but this is not the case. Attention is focused on the transition from winter to spring and on the autumn, with particular interest in the forecasting of rain and storms.

Most of the forecasts covered so far require only knowledge of the positions of the Sun and Moon, which can be calculated from tables given in the book itself, but the later sections are for the astronomically expert. Full-blown astrometeorology is reached with the sections giving outcomes based on aspects between all the planets, where exact calculations of planetary positions are assumed (no instruction on how to make these calculations is offered). Digges appears to assume that anyone prepared to tackle this section would be in possession of a full ephemeris, and would know how to adjust it for their own location. The interest of these sections for the modern reader comes from the light they cast on how at least one maker of weather forecasts proceeded. As usual, he moves from the more general factors to the more specific. Thus, the first topic is that of aspects between the outer planets, and the effects produced by the signs involved. For instance, an opposition, square or sextile aspect between Saturn and Jupiter when at least one is in a water sign will cause disturbances of the air, and lead to strong winds, thunder and hailstorms. A conjunction, square, or opposition between Saturn and Mars, especially in summer, will have a related, though milder, effect. It is tempting to think that the effects of the Little Ice Age on the English weather were already being felt, since of the forty-five aspects covered the great majority portend storms, rain, cloud and cold, whilst only five signify good weather or heat. The power wielded by the outer planets is demonstrated by the fact that discussion of their most important aspects is followed up by an exposition of the attention to be paid to the direction of movement of the planets, as well as to the point of aspect itself. If either planet will be strengthened or weakened by entering into aspect with another planet, or into another sign, or into a position close to that of the Sun, this must be taken into account. For a full forecast, the position in relation to the powerful, fixed stars must be considered, as must the sign (and any planets) on the ascendant. An account is also given of the Mansions of the Moon, though Digges pays less attention to these than did many astrometeorologists.

After these technicalities, and the layers of detailed information that they add into the total to be considered, it is dismaying to come to still further, detailed sections on planetary aspects, this time covering all the planets except the Moon. At this point the faint-hearted might reflect that one penny was a small price to pay to have all this work done for a full year. However, the indefatigable Digges presses on, and even adds the information that, whilst the most powerful aspects are the conjunction, opposition and square, not only the sextile but also the trine can be taken into account. The same applies to the separate section on aspects of the Moon, where the prognosticator needs to know not only the positions on the chosen day but also whether the Moon is moving away from another planet, and if so what other planet is involved. For example, any aspect of the Moon with Saturn, in a water sign, is a predictor of cold, cloudy weather, but if the Moon (which moves very much faster than Saturn) is moving out of the aspect and towards the Sun then the weather will worsen further. The final technicality to be taken into account is similarly complex. This is the interpretation of the multilayered interactions between key planets, their sign positions, and their relationships to the rays of the Sun at dawn and dusk. For this topic, all twelve signs, and each planet within each one, are dealt with in turn. A reader who applied this technique in addition to all that has gone before would be entitled to feel that they had undertaken a complex piece of scientific analysis; whether they made their results public would presumably depend upon their level of confidence.

It appears that Digges was successful in addressing interested amateurs whilst displaying his mastery of technical astronomy and astrometeorology, since his work sold very well over a long period. He also seems to have identified a gap in the market, since those who wanted weather forecasts would find little of use in the standard works intended for practitioners of astrological medicine. It was tactful for him to avoid giving attention to the making of prognostications on political events, since he wrote during a period of considerable political and religious turmoil in England that had significantly affected his own career. How many of his readers actually succeeded in producing their own forecasts cannot be known, but almost everyone would be capable of calculating the position of the Sun and the phase and position of the Moon. In combination with the knowledge of the elements associated with the signs occupied by each, and the characteristics of the season, this would produce a satisfactorily scientific forecast over the medium to long term, especially if the annual risings of stars were also considered. For shorter term forecasts, the additional information provided by observation of clouds, the behaviour of birds, and the sky's appearance at dawn and sunset would add further detail. The insight into just what was involved in making a full, astrometeorological forecast might have been of interest as an example of the wonders of modern science, even for those who did not embark on the task themselves.

Digges' exposition of both a simplified form of astrometeorology and a highly technical one raises the question of just what level of detail could be expected at different price points in the growing market for printed, ready-calculated astrometeorological works. It is frequently stated by book historians that by the second half of the sixteenth century, at the latest, the annual almanacs and prognostications were selling in sufficient numbers to make a major contribution to the profits of the printing houses. It is also obvious that considerably more detail could be expected from a pamphlet covering thirty-two octavo pages than from one broadsheet. Sadly, despite the large numbers originally produced, the fact that almanacs were by nature and definition ephemeral has meant that few of them survive complete from this early period. Nevertheless, examination of surviving examples produced across Europe and in a range of languages shows that the format and contents were surprisingly uniform by the late sixteenth century. In each case the purchaser acquired a highly portable compendium of useful data. These apparently trivial publications made it possible for individuals to organise and plan their activities across the year in a way that blended religious and scientific parameters with more personal considerations. Central to most of these concerns was the perennial question of what the weather would be like, and the compilers of almanacs continued to offer impressively detailed, if notoriously unreliable, forecasts.

To take just one example, Buckminster's *Almanacke and Prognostication* for 1598, issued for London but declared to apply to the whole of England, offered a 'daily disposition of the weather', as a major component of its prognosticatory section.[44] No comment or explanation of the procedures involved is given, but the topics considered are in accordance with astrometeorological norms. The section opens with details of the eclipses of the year, and the explanation that, in combination with other factors, they forecast heavy cloud and very wet weather accompanied by strong winds and storms, which will have negative effects on both humans and animals throughout the year. The winter quarter, which began in December 1597, will be markedly stormy and changeable, with high winds causing damage to ships and buildings. Depressingly, spring will bring little relief, since it will be unseasonably cold and wet, with rain, hail and storms causing further problems. The summer will achieve only moderate heat, and that only in the early part of the season, since changeable weather and storms will return in August, bringing gales and thunderstorms. After all this it will not be surprising that the bad news continued into the autumn, when the storms and changeable weather would, if anything, worsen.

The promised daily forecasts are set out in monthly sections linked, as might be expected, to the phases of the Moon. In April, for instance, the reader will already have been informed by the calendar section that Spring began on March the tenth, and that the Sun would enter the earth sign of Taurus on April the eleventh. The depressing overall prediction for the season has already been given. Now we learn that the first and second days of the month will see 'fayre fresh wether', but this will end when the Moon reaches its first quarter at twenty-three minutes past two in the afternoon of the third day, in the watery sign of Cancer. The weather that day will be mixed, whilst the fourth will be overcast and cloudy, and the fifth and sixth cold and raw. Things change again from the full Moon on the eleventh of April, in the airy sign of Libra. The weather that day will be fair, and remain clear on the twelfth. Sadly, the thirteenth and fourteenth will see a return to cloudy weather, while the fifteenth and sixteenth will be wet and windy. The Moon was to enter its last quarter on the morning of the 18th in the air sign of Aquarius, and the forecast is for the weather to be slightly less wet, but with the following days affected by wind and thunderstorms. Fortunately

---

[44] This almanac has been published in facsimile as 'Shakespeare Association Facsimiles, No. 8', *An Almanack and Prognostication for the Year 1598, made by Thomas Buckminster, 1598* (sic), Intro. E. Bosanquet, Oxford, Oxford University Press for the Shakespeare Association, London, 1935.

the month would end better, as the new Moon in the earth sign of Taurus would see in 'very seasonable wether'.

At this point it is clear that the well-known scientific and technological advances of the sixteenth century had the effect of popularising astro-meteorology rather than challenging it. This chapter has traced the late medieval rise of two key elements which underlay this early modern triumph of astrometeorology. These are: the establishment of astronomy and mundane astrology as prestigious, and socially useful, subjects within the growing number of European universities; and the spread of printing houses, which could make good profits from the sale of astro-meteorological treatises and prognostications. The popularity of the annual almanacs as a desirable product of this modern science is impres-sively demonstrated, as noted above, by their appearance across all of Europe in the sixteenth century, at a range of price levels. Their testi-mony as to the dominance of astrometeorology in the making of weather forecasts throughout this period makes them worth further attention here. Public awareness of the genre, as well as disappointment with the frequent inaccuracy of the weather forecasts, are demonstrated by refer-ences to almanacs and forecasters in both literature and drama. Amongst the most famous commentators are Rabelais and Shakespeare, the former highly critical of the exploitative qualities that he perceived in the prognostication sections of the almanacs, and the latter merely depicting almanacs and their data being consulted by a wide range of characters in both comedies and history plays.

Rabelais' attitude to the almanacs and their prognostications was surprisingly harsh, but his belief in their wide popularity is entirely borne out. A survey of the data brought together in the Universal Short Title Catalogue provides immediate evidence of this, since the heading 'almanac' brings up 522 publications produced between 1460 and 1600, to which 'almanach' adds a further 529 titles for the same period.[45] Even this is clearly only a small sample of what once existed, however. Hoogendoorn's recent, monumental compilation of data concerning the publication of scientific works in the Low Countries devotes a section to 'Calendars, Almanacs and Prognostications', issued between ca. 1470 and 1700. No fewer than 1400 works are included for the Low Countries alone, and even this list is introduced with the melancholy reflection that a full listing is not possible.[46] Clearly, annual almanacs were very popular in the Low Countries, as they were across the Holy Roman Empire in the

---

[45] This is online at: https://ustc.ac.uk/index.php/search (accessed 4 January 2019).
[46] K. Hoogendoorn, *Bibliography of the Exact Sciences in the Low Countries from ca1470 to the Golden Age (1700)*, Leiden and Boston, Brill, 2018, p. 1173.

same period, to judge from the data provided by the USTC. Here, Augsburg emerges as an early leader in the field, rapidly followed by Nuremberg, Strasbourg and Antwerp. Exact information on the financial rewards reaped by the publishers of almanacs is still harder to find, but a study of the records of the Duchy of Brabant is suggestive. These show that the printer Claes de Greve appealed to the ruling council of the duchy in 1512, and that his complaint focused on an almanac compiled by the celebrated Jasper Laet. De Greve had the rights to this almanac, and was in the process of printing it when he discovered that a rival, Henrik Bosbas, was rushing out a cheaper, pirated edition. The almanac was clearly lucrative, since de Greve successfully sued Bosbas in Antwerp and was paid compensation, but Bosbas still stated that he was going to repeat the procedure in coming years. De Greve then went to the council of the duchy, and paid for two successive privileges, protecting his rights for a total of twelve years.[47]

The international popularity of almanacs is further shown not only by the spread of Laet almanacs across many parts of Europe but also by surviving records of booksellers. Of course, many almanacs were sold at fairs by peddlers who kept no detailed records, but snapshots of almanac sales in England are available. One is provided by the 'day book' of John Dorne for 1520. Dorne was a Dutch bookseller based in Oxford, and he sold at least forty items listed as almanacs or prognostications in January alone, with one of them identified as the work of Jasper Laet.[48] By 1588 one bookseller in Cambridge stocked 234 almanacs, and hundreds of thousands of almanacs were being printed in England.[49] In the early seventeenth century the Stationers' Company was granted a monopoly on the printing of almanacs in England, and this was so lucrative that the company fought tenaciously (and sometimes expensively) to protect it.

Study of early modern almanacs is now growing, with attention focused on the medical knowledge that they transmitted and on the evidence they provide as to popular literacy and popular culture. However, study of their meteorological contents has been, as noted above, slight. Indeed, one study of sixteenth-century German almanacs produced the observation that their 'astrological and meteorological details'

---

[47] E. Armstrong, *Before Copyright: The French Book-Privilege System 1498-1526*, Cambridge, Cambridge University Press, 1990, pp. 15–16.

[48] Ibid., p. 16 (note 2).

[49] R. Simmons, 'ABCs, almanacs, ballads, chapbooks, popular piety and textbooks', in J. Barnard, D. McKenzie and M. Bell, Eds., *The Cambridge History of the Book in Britain; Volume 4, 1557–1695*, p. 508.

were 'incredibly tedious'.[50] It is therefore worth stressing that these publications, produced to carefully calculated standards and price points, were sought after by users of all social levels as well as all European countries. They certainly reached social classes that most printed publications did not, but this does not mean that they were aimed primarily at that market. They continued to be both produced and consulted by highly educated professionals. It is also clear that access to astrometeorological weather forecasts was an important part of daily life by the later sixteenth century. The very existence of rival publications naturally helped to support the critics, who needed only to observe that it was not possible that almanacs offering contrasting forecasts could all be correct. Nevertheless, it is important to note that these criticisms expressed disappointment at the unreliability of the individual forecasts, rather than an outright rejection of their scientific basis. The influence of the planets on all physical aspects of human life was still accepted, and remained central to the study and practice of the more theoretical forms of medicine. Problems of reliability were therefore attributed to fallible practitioners, not to astrometeorology itself.

Thus the story of medieval meteorology emerges as one that encompasses the dramatic rise and prolonged success of a new science. This history, as has been seen, spanned no less than five centuries in Latin Europe alone, despite the late arrival of the science in that region. What is more, this version of meteorology triumphantly survived such challenges as the acceptance that the Aristotelian and Ptolemaic, Earth-centred, model of the universe was mistaken. This does not mean that the almanacs show no effects from the changes in scientific ideas that took hold in the sixteenth and seventeenth century. It is noticeable that the meteorological 'authorities' named undergo a significant change. In the late fifteenth century, Ptolemy, Albumasar and Haly Abenragel were all authorities frequently cited in European almanacs, with Aristotle coming a very poor fourth. Some fifty years later the names of those now rejected as 'Turks' had all but disappeared, whilst Ptolemy retained his popularity and Aristotle began to appear considerably more frequently, in line with the increasing prestige of classical Greek authors. Nevertheless, this shift in the authorities cited was not accompanied by any major change in the types of forecast made, or in the procedures being taught and used, as has been seen in the case studies presented above. This leads to an apparently paradoxical conclusion – namely, that the very medieval

---

[50] R. Barnes, 'Hope and Despair in Sixteenth-Century German Almanacs', in H. Guggisberg and G. Krodel, Eds., *The Reformation in Germany and Europe: Interpretations and Issues,* a special issue of *Archiv für Reformationsgeschichte,* 1993, pp. 440–461.

science of astrometeorology reached the height of its popularity and acceptance at a time acclaimed as one of scientific revolution. However, the paradox is something of an optical illusion, since the new scientific models were self-consciously based on ancient antecedents, and even the acceptance of a heliocentric universe did not challenge the belief that the celestial bodies affected the Earth, its atmosphere, and its weather. Indeed, the lingering death of astrometeorology was to span the seventeenth century and even reach into the eighteenth century, a phenomenon that the Conclusion to this book will examine.

Conclusion
The Afterlife of Medieval Meteorology

This conclusion will attempt to provide a brief outline of the extraordinarily slow demise of astrometeorology, which lingered on into the nineteenth century. A key factor, already noted, was that the fundamental concepts, adopted from Islamicate sources in the twelfth century, remained unchallenged throughout the early modern period. These centred on the belief that atmospheric changes, driven by planetary influences, created meteorological effects and thus caused changes in the weather. It was only in the eighteenth century that the system was rejected, even by more advanced thinkers. The fact that astrometeorology was not finally discredited until the nineteenth century probably related to the absence of any equally satisfying model with which to replace it. As late as 1834, one P. Murphy produced, in London, what was effectively an updated version of astrometeorological ideas. In this work, overt astrology was stripped out and replaced by enthusiastic claims as to the electrical influences generated by the planets. It was entitled *The Anatomy of the Seasons, Weather Guide Book, and Perpetual Companion to the Almanac*, and was optimistically dedicated to King William IV. Murphy aimed to prove that the concept of electrical-magnetism provided the key to drawing up a 'modern' model of the ways in which the heavenly bodies drove meteorological phenomena. His Preface argued that: 'the first grand division of meteorology appertains to the seasons; and its second to the weather'. Furthermore, whilst the seasons are accepted as being determined by regular astronomical phenomena, Murphy goes on to make the strikingly familiar assertion that 'the lunar action' is 'the chief guide to the ordinary variations and change of the weather'. Moreover, the effects of the Moon itself on 'the atmosphere' are 'in great part regulated throughout the year by the existing action at the time in the annual circle'. If astrometeorology itself was dead by 1834, then this book was clearly a descendant, and it made equally impressive claims to offer an accurate understanding of how weather worked and thus how it could be predicted.

194

Murphy supported his claims to modernity and rigorous scientific accuracy by the time-honoured means of ridiculing the almanacs. In his first chapter he quoted an article in the *Penny Magazine* of June 1832, which noted that human beings' ongoing dependence upon the weather continued to make them willing to trust in almanacs and prognostications. The author lamented that 'the prognostications of the same vain science that are published every year on the subject of the weather, continue to be not only bought but believed, almost as much as they were in the darkest ages, by hundreds of thousands, even in our own comparatively enlightened England. *Moore's almanac still sells a quarter of a million of copies*' (sic).[1] Murphy's book may not have enjoyed the success he hoped for, but both he and the contributor to the *Penny Magazine* were certain of the ongoing and powerful desire for an accurate means of forecasting the weather. Underlying this desire is the fact that, throughout the eighteenth century, would-be weather forecasters who rejected 'astronomical' models found themselves forced to revert to observation of traditional weather signs. They tended simply to add locally transmitted information to the time-honoured lists passed down from classical antiquity. Rather more startlingly, weather-related 'prognostics', already old in the early middle ages, were dusted off and represented as tried and tested 'wisdom'. Most popular was the doctrine that observing the occurrence of sunshine and/or wind over the twelve days of Christmas would provide forecasts of weather for the coming twelve months.[2]

It is perhaps equally surprising that the body of new astronomical observations, calculations and instruments, which grew rapidly from the sixteenth century, did not bring about any complete rejection of astrometeorology. Instead, astronomers and mathematicians put problems with forecasting down to the complexity of the variables to be factored in. Their favoured answer to the problem was one first seen in the fourteenth century, as discussed in Chapter Seven. This was the acquisition of data via empirical observation, in the form of daily records of the weather. If these could be accumulated in sufficient quantity, and from wide-ranging locations, then the information thus produced could

---

[1] P. Murphy, *The Anatomy of the Seasons, Weather Guide Book, and Perpetual Companion to the Almanac*, London, J. Bailliere & Co., 1834, p. 4.

[2] See for example *The Newest, Best and Very-Much Esteemed Book of Knowledge* (Anon), frequently published up to 1764. This opens with 'Infallible Signs of Rainy Weather from the Observation of Divers Animals'. On p. 68 of the 1764 edition (London, Wilde) comes the 'Prognostication for ever' supposedly 'after the doctrine of Albertus, Alkind, Haly and Ptolomy', which predicts the weather simply from the conditions observed on Christmas Eve and Christmas Day.

be used to increase the accuracy with which planetary interrelationships and mutual influences were interpreted for any given location.

This line of thought can be seen very strongly in the writings of Tycho Brahe (1546–1601). Already in 1564 he had tried out the method of forecasting the weather by making observations on the twelve days of Christmas.[3] His treatise on the star that appeared in the constellation of Cassiopeia in 1572, and that he proved to be new, is striking in asserting the triumph of mathematics and observation over long-established doctrine; it is equally striking in its support for astrometeorology. It propounded a *diaria metheorologica* based on his own calculations and observations, and supported the publication of daily astrometeorological forecasts as well as other interpretations of the material.[4] He acknowledged the difficulty in making the weather forecasts accurate, due to current lack of full understanding of the factors involved, and was one of the first to recommend the widespread keeping of daily weather records, in order to strengthen weather forecasting. He seems to have been confident that it was possible to modernise astrometeorology, just as he was also driving forward work on astronomical tables and instruments.[5]

Johannes Kepler (1571–1630) the student and successor of Tycho Brahe, took much the same stance in relation to astrometeorology. He himself made daily records of the weather, in each of the cities in which he lived between 1593 and 1624. His published *Ephemerides* and *Calendars* included both the observations and his weather forecasts, respectively. In these he placed emphasis on the geometrical relationships between the planets (the aspects) as observed from Earth, and paid less attention to the zodiac signs and houses than was traditional, but in effect his methods of forecasting were a streamlined version of the long-established ones. It is thus hardly surprising that those working in both astronomy and astrology elsewhere followed in these influential footsteps.

One who deserves special mention is John Goad (1616–1687) whose *Astro-Meteorologica, or Aphorisms and Discourses on the Bodies Celestial ...*, a long work first published in London in 1686, popularised the term astrometeorology itself. Goad was not a professional astronomer but a

---

[3] 'Tycho Brahe and Weather Prediction', c. Adam Mosley and the Department of History and Philosophy of Science of the University of Cambridge, 1999; at: www.sites .hps.cam.ac.uk/starry/tychoweather.html (accessed March 2018).

[4] For a modern edition see: Tycho Brahe, *De Nova Stella, 1573*, Ed. Regia Societas Scientiarium Danica, 1901.

[5] For a digitised copy of the work see: www.sdu.dk/da/bibliotek/materialer/om +samlingerne/herlufsholm/brahe/de+nova+stella This is a copy belonging to Roskilde Kloster, digitised by the University of Southern Denmark (accessed March 2018).

scholar, vicar and schoolmaster with a deep interest in the study of how the planets affect both weather and human health. As recommended by Brahe and Kepler, Goad combined his theoretical and mathematical work in mundane astrology with keeping a detailed weather diary. He stated in *Astro-Meteorologica* that it was based on records kept over thirty years; and Bodleian, MS Ashmole 367 contains the observations made in London, 1677–1679. The introductory address to the reader identifies the book as an ambitious work of natural philosophy, intended to increase understanding of the workings of the heavens in relation to the Earth. However, the 'epistle' to James II promises advances in understanding of winds, earthquakes and storms at sea, with consequent advantages for shipping. The practical gains offered to readers of the book are made still more explicit by the title page of the second edition (1699), which claims that Goad 'constantly presented Charles II, and several persons of quality of this nation, with a month's prediction of the weather beforehand, to his great credit and reputation; ... and has now left the method thereof at large. The like not extant in any language.'[6] So far from destroying astrometeorology, the new discoveries being made in astronomy, and the interest they were generating, seem to have increased confidence that even something as complex as the weather was on the verge of being fully understood and rendered accurately predictable.

Sadly, it must be acknowledged that any such hope was very slow to be realised. Increasing numbers of weather records were indeed kept across Europe in the seventeenth and eighteenth centuries, which are of great value to historians of weather.[7] It is tempting to speculate that this was a response to the ongoing extremes of weather, and consequent hardships, caused by the Little Ice Age, although in fact it clearly had multiple causes. Cultural historians have focused upon the self-conscious modernity of the 'Age of Enlightenment'; and Golinski has made a powerful case for seeing the eighteenth century as the time in which anxiety about climate change first appeared. Still more striking is the argument that this was when the British first formulated the concept of a 'national climate' closely linked to their much-vaunted national character.[8] Nevertheless, it

---

[6] A copy belonging to the Bavarian State Library has been digitised and is available at: https://books.google.co.uk/books?id=PrhRAAAAcAAJ&printsec=frontcover&source=gbs_ge_summary_r&cad=0#v=onepage&q&f=false (accessed March 2018).

[7] C. Pfister et al., 'Daily Weather Observations in Sixteenth-Century Europe', *Climatic Change*, 43,1, 1999, pp. 111–150, presents and analyses data from thirty-two weather diaries from central Europe; for discussion of British diaries and record-keeping from the seventeenth and eighteenth centuries see J. Golinski, *British Weather and the Climate of Enlightenment*, Chicago and London, University of Chicago Press, 2007.

[8] Golinski, *British Weather*, but see especially pp. 3–4.

is not easy, given the evidence presented in the chapters of this book, to accept the assertion that it was only in Britain, ca. 1700, that 'observers for the first time devoted attention to recording the weather on a daily basis'.[9] In fact it is surprisingly difficult to find any clear link between the making of these weather records and the gradual rejection of astrometeorology. They may well have built up evidence that weather patterns were so localised and variable as to defy any attempt at prediction – but that pessimistic conclusion was generally avoided. Instead, the increasing scorn heaped upon the whole practice of astrology, as something used by the unscrupulous to defraud the credulous, appears to have undermined astrometeorology as well, as in the article quoted by Murphy in the 1830s.

A survey of eighteenth-century, English almanacs provides a case study of responses to the growing attacks. In 1709, astrometeorological weather forecasts were still a central element of such almanacs, even if they were of varying detail and length. The most ambitious, and also most traditional, was *Astrologus Britannicus*, which provided a full ephemeris, as well as a table of lunar aspects for each day, and weather forecasts for each day of each month under the heading 'Mutual Aspects &'. At the other extreme perhaps were the almanacs issued under the names of Gadbury and Dove, which gave very brief weather forecasts, reduced to such basics as: 'frost', 'cold', 'rain' or 'pleasant for the season'. Both are representative of the increasing emphasis on predictions of large-scale upheavals in politics or health, and of natural disasters, rather than on weather forecasts. Dove actually has sections on: 'How to judge what weather will follow...' by observing the Sun at its rising and setting (C3v); 'How weather is foreknown by the Moon' (C4); and 'of the Judgment of the Weather by the Stars' (ibid.), all of which expound traditional weather signs based on direct observation. *Angelus Britannicus* is similarly sparing of astrometeorological material, although the compiler does give some brief comments on the prediction of weather in his 'judgement' for the autumn quarter. Belief in the combination of astrometeorology and individual observation is however espoused in *Merlinus Liberatus*, issued under the name of Partridge. Brief daily forecasts are given in the first section, as usual; the novelty comes in the 'Judgment on the Four Quarters of the Year' and especially in the Autumnal Quarter (C5). This includes the statement that: 'I have observed that when the square or opposition between Saturn and Jupiter happen in the Summer, it generally produces a wet season; which, if

---

[9] Ibid., p. xii.

rightly understood might be improved into something of use and advantage'. The author has himself been keeping records, since he discusses details of the wet summers of 1648, 1672, 1673, 1692 and 1708 as evidence. He concludes: 'Those that have journals of the weather by them may make further observations on these rays and influences; for if it holds generally, it can be no injury to truth'.

By the middle of the century *Merlinus Liberatus* for 1750 was still published under the name of Partridge, and still had a column for 'Aspects and Weather' in its first section, with brief and rather general weather forecasts. However, its astrological analysis for the year made no mention of weather, and political events dominated the almanac overall. *Speculum Anni Redivivum* was issued for 1753 by Henry Season, described as a licensed physician and student in the astral sciences, and celebrated as the author of eighteen previous almanacs. Season reduces the space for astrological information, and his weather forecasts are intermittent and laconic. January, for instance, is given only four forecasts, of which that for the 20th to 24th is simply 'weather indifferent for the season'. A long essay runs through the right-hand column of the openings for each month, in which Season offers his recommendations for a healthy lifestyle and animadverts against licentiousness and excess. The Judgement for the year takes on a defensive tone, demonstrating that the author is very aware of criticism of astrology; but does offer some comments on the weather under the section for Autumn. Here, a prediction of 'much cold rain near the beginning of the quarter' leads Season into a spirited counterattack upon an unnamed sceptic who had 'ignorantly bespattered all predicters of the weather with all the splenetic reproaches his idle malice could suggest to him' (C5). This attacker had called all weather forecasters 'adepts in delusion', a charge that is refuted by appeal to Goad's successes. Reliable almanac compilers and forecasters are named as Gadbury, Sharp and Wing (as well as the author himself) though it must be admitted that the bar is set rather low. The case made by Season is: 'Suppose Mr Sharp, myself, or Mr Wing, predict the weather but eleven times right out of twenty, yet still we should have the advantage of truth on our side'. It is clear that the claims made by earlier astrometeorologists were being challenged on the basis of evidence supplied by the daily observations that they themselves had recommended. As Season puts it: 'Judgement on the weather is a very abstruse point; such a variety of impediments may metamorphose the state of the air, especially in our island, that no man can name, neither would any man of reason presume to demand, every time it rains, on what spot of ground the rain will fall'.

Proof that belief in the possibility of an empirically verified astrometeorology died very slowly is provided by the successful career of Henry Andrews, who took over the editorship of *Vox Stellarum* in the 1780s.[10] From 1793 he included an annual address to the reader, similar to Season's comments on lifestyle and health, but here headed 'Meteorological Observations'. This was continued into the nineteenth century. *Vox Stellarum* for 1804 was published under the established name of Francis Moore. However, Andrews' interests are reflected on the cover, in the fact that it advertises not only the usual 'judgements' or 'observations' on the weather itself but also information on 'weather glasses'. The address to the 'Courteous Reader' stresses that the pages for each month show, at the top, the quantity of rain that fell in the same month during the previous year (1802, since the almanac was drawn up, as usual, in the year preceding the one it actually described). The figure given is, as the author states with pride, that measured by the Royal Society at their premises in London, and is exact, since it excludes any loss by absorption or evaporation. Thus, the predictions of rain, snow and other forms of precipitation stand beside the scientific record for 1802. Andrews has the modesty to say that he does not expect all his forecasts to be correct, but is equally bold enough to say that he has proved by checking his performance in previous years that the greatest part of them are likely to be so. He still recommends that 'Journals of the weather should be kept in different parts of the kingdom, and published from year to year' in order to 'bring Meteorology to greater perfection' (p. 7).

This appeal to an early version of citizen science is echoed in the section on 'Meteorological Observations Relating to the Weather in 1802' (pp. 42–43). Here, Andrews is happily able to record that, while the year was marked by drought, the heavy rainfall of July and early August was followed by a fine harvest time, just as his 'Rules and Maxims' (published in the almanac for 1803) would predict. This leads into a further recommendation for action, aimed specially at farmers. What is surprising, however, is that the 'Rules and Maxims' were related to the use of weather glasses and barometers, and that further details are here given of how to interpret the behaviour of the mercury in barometers and to relate it to changes in wind direction. Such instruments were beyond the means of many purchasers of almanacs, but Andrews urges all farmers to equip themselves with good weather glasses and to read them in accordance with his guidance. He even says that, without such an instrument, nobody could have been able to make a confident forecast

---

[10] J. Mori, 'Popular Science in Eighteenth-Century Almanacs: The Career of Henry Andrews of Royston, 1780–1820', *History of Science*, 54,1, 2016, pp. 19–44.

of the timely change in the weather in late summer of 1802. By the time *Vox Stellarum* for 1821 (the last of Andrews' issues) was published, the recruitment of citizen scientists to the cause of accurate meteorology had been further advanced by the greater availability of the new instruments. As the author says under 'Monthly Observations' for March (p. 7): 'If my readers will get a good barometer, with a thermometer in the same case, and record their observations daily ... they will soon find, that what I predict as to these matters, rests upon principles not to be disputed'. The 'Meteorological Observations' for 1819 (pp. 40–42) draw not only upon measurements of rainfall made in London but also upon 'correct journals' kept in Hertfordshire and in the region of Perth and Dundee, which correlate the weather records with the behaviour of the barometer and thermometer, just as Andrews had requested. Thus, it is still the case that only the expert is able to calculate correctly the balance between empirical observation and astrological theory, and thus make long-term predictions with any confidence. Yet it is also possible to inculcate all who can afford to buy the necessary equipment into the ranks of amateur meteorologists, able to deduce short-term forecasts from their reading of these instruments, under learned guidance.

Thus, by the end of the first quarter of the nineteenth century, the belief that accurate recording of the weather would increase the accuracy of astrometeorological forecasting had in fact been promulgated for some 300 years. This had produced, as has been seen, a potentially enormous quantity of detailed information, but over the same period, the underpinning theory of astrometeorology had gradually been rejected. Without such an overarching theory, and also without universal rules for using the new technology (particularly the barometer) it took a considerable time for a new method of weather forecasting to gain credence. Famously, it was Robert FitzRoy (1805–1865) who coined the term 'weather forecast' for the brief summaries he issued to *The Times* from 1861. FitzRoy is perhaps best-known as the captain of *HMS Beagle* who took Charles Darwin on his epoch-making voyage in the 1830s. After his retirement from active service in the navy in 1850, FitzRoy was elected to the Royal Society in 1851, and was put in charge of collecting data on weather at sea in 1854. His weather forecasts made use not only of a network of trained observers and of more accurate interpretation of data from instruments, but also, and crucially, of new technology for the rapid transmission of all this information.

With the publication of FitzRoy's seminal work *The Weather Book: A Treatise of Practical Meteorology* in 1862, a new age in the history of meteorology may be said to begin. The coining of the phrase 'practical meteorology' in the title encourages confidence that this is something that will work. The language of the preface is even bolder. FitzRoy declares: 'The means actually requisite to enable any person of fair abilities and average education to become practically 'weather-wise' are much more readily attainable than has been often supposed. With a barometer, two or three thermometers, some brief instructions, and an attentive observation, not of instruments only, but the sky and atmosphere, one may utilise Meteorology'.[11] Even though FitzRoy himself stated firmly that there was as yet no clear, agreed basis for understanding or modelling the weather, it is possible to argue that this sentence defines a new approach to scientific weather forecasting.

At this point it may be considered safe to declare the lingering death of astrometeorology finally over. It had, at last, been replaced by a system that combined satisfyingly 'modern' techniques with greater (if shorter-term) predictive accuracy. Nevertheless, it is the argument of this book that the distinctively medieval science of astrometeorology fully deserves to be awarded a place within the histories of meteorology, climate science, and weather forecasting. It has been shown that it was the medieval meteorologists, of both the Islamicate and the Latin worlds, who laid down the conceptual and terminological parameters within which discussion of the weather and its phenomena was conducted for over 500 years. Still more importantly, it was these early scientists, enthusiastic in their construction of an all-encompassing, working model of the universe, who dared to assert that accurate, daily forecasts of the weather were a real possibility. Their methods may no longer be accepted, but that belief remains as strong as ever, and is now enshrined as a part of daily news bulletins across the world.

[11] A copy of the second edition (1863), held at the Widener Library, has been digitised by Harvard University, and is available at: https://iiif.lib.harvard.edu/manifests/view/drs:7663678$1i (accessed March 2018). The quotation is from the opening of chapter 1, p. 1.

Bibliography

Unpublished Primary Sources

Anon, *Exafrenon*, in London, British Library, Ms Royal 12 C XVIII.
John of Eschenden/Ashenden, *Summa iudicialis de accentibus mundi*, in Cambridge, Trinity College, Ms O 5 26.
William de Merle, *De futura temperie aeris pronosticanda*, in Oxford, Bodleian Library, Ms Digby 97.

Early Printed Primary Sources

Guillaume d'Amours, *Prenostication nouvelle lan mille cinq cens XVIII composee sur le climat de France* (held by the Wellcome Institute, London, as EPB/B283/B).
Caxton, William, *Mirrour (Myrrour) of the World*, 1490 (with manuscript additions), in New York, Pierpont Morgan Library, PML 776/ChL 1770.

Digitised Primary Sources

Manuscripts

Basel, Universitätsbibliothek, Ms F. III. 8, a fourteenth-century astrological and astrometeorological collection, at: www.e-codices.unifr.ch/en/list/one/ubb/F-III-0008
Cambridge, Trinity College, Ms R. 17. 1, the Eadwine Psalter, at: http://trinsites-pub.trin.cam.ac.uk/james/viewpage.php?index=1229
Einsiedeln Ms 266, pp. 177–224: at: www.ecodices.unifr.ch/de/sbe/0266/177/0/Sequence-998.
London, British Library, Ms Arundel 66, 'Henry VII's *Book of Astrology*', at: www.bl.uk/catalogues/illuminatedmanuscripts/record.asp?MSID=8695&CollID=20&NStart=66
BL, Mss Cotton Titus D XXVI and XXVII at: www.bl.uk/manuscripts/FullDisplay.aspx?ref=Cotton_MS_Titus_D_XXVI
and: www.bl.uk/manuscripts/FullDisplay.aspx?ref=Cotton_MS_Titus_D_XXVII

Oxford, St John's College, Ms 17, ed. F. Wallis, on the Calendar and the Cloister website: http://digital.library.mcgill.ca/ms-17/

Printed Works

Abû Ma'shar, *Flores astrologiae*, printed Johannes Baptista Sessa, Venice, 1488 or 1506. Available via the website of the Warburg Institute, London, at: warburg.sas.ac.uk/pdf/fah820b2342376.pdf;
the Ratdolt edition of 1488, *Flores Albumasaris*, is available at the website of the Biblioteca Digital Real Academia de la Historia, at http://bibliotecadigital.rah.es/dgbrah/es/consulta/registro.cmd?id=44564
Brahe, Tycho, *De Nova stella*, 1573, is digitised at: www.sdu.dk/da/bibliotek/materialer/om+samlingerne/herlufsholm/brahe/de+nova+stella (This is a copy belonging to Roskilde Kloster)
Digges, Leonard, *Prognostication of right good effect fructfully augmented, containinge playne, briefe, pleasant, chosen rules, to iudge the wether for euer ...,* second edition, 1555, is available online at: https://quod.lib.umich.edu/e/eebo/A17556.0001.001?view=toc
Firminus de Bellavalle, *Pronosticon in mutations aeris*, printed by Ratdolt, Venice, 1485, is available at: https://archive.org/details/ita-bnc-in1-00001030-001
FitzRoy, Robert, *The Weather Book: A Treatise of Practical Meteorology*, 2nd ed., 1863, is at: https://iiif.lib.harvard.edu/manifests/view/drs:7663678$1i
Gaspard (Jaspard) Laet, *Prenostication de Louvain* for 1497, Paris, 1496, is available at Les Bibliothèques Virtuelles Humanistes: www.bvh.univ-tours.fr/Consult/consult.asp?numtable=B452346101_C2095&numfiche=234&mode=3&ecran=0&offset=0
Goad, John, *Astro-Meteorologica, or Aphorisms and Discourses on the Bodies Celestial...*, London, 1686 available at: https://books.google.co.uk/books?id=PrhRAAAAcAAJ&printsec=frontcover&source=gbs_ge_summary_r&cad=0#v=onepage&q&f=false
Guido Bonatti, *Liber Astronomiae*, the edition by Ratdolt, Augsburg, 1491 is available at the website of the Bayerische Staatsbibliothek: https://bildsuche.digitale-sammlungen.de/index.html?c=viewer&lv=1&bandnummer=bsb00025600
Hugo of Santalla(?), *The Book of the Nine Judges, (liber novem iudicum)* printed Peter Leichtenstein, Venice, 1509. Available via the website of the Warburg, at: https://warburg.sas.ac.uk/pdf/fah765nj.pdf
John of Eschenden/Ashenden, as printed by Bolanus and Santritter, Venice, 1489, is available at the website of the Bibliothèque Nationale, Paris: http://gallica.bnf.fr/ark:/12148/bpt6k59654r/f2.image
John Somer, *The Kalendarium of John Somer*, ed. L. Mooney, Athens, Georgia, University of Georgia Press, 1998.

'Leopold of Austria', *Scientia astrorum*, in the edition by Ratdolt, Augsburg, 1489, is available at: http://diglib.hab.de/wdb.php?distype=img&dir=inku nabeln%2F14-astron

Ptolemy, *Tetrabiblos*, trans. Plato of Tivoli c1133, printed in 1533 by Johannes Hervagius of Basel. Available via the website of the Warburg Institute, London, at: https://warburg.sas.ac.uk/pdf/fah750pto.pdf

Regiomontanus, *Ephemerides 1484-1506*, in Ratdolt's Venice edition of 1481 is available via the Europeana website: www.europeana.eu/portal/en/record/9200209/o_225215.html

The rival edition, of 1498, can be viewed via the Gallica website at: http://gallica.bnf.fr/ark:/12148/bpt6k596433/f1.image

Vincent of Beauvais, *Speculum naturale,* printed Venice, 1494; available at: http://alfama.sim.ucm.es/dioscorides/consulta_libro.asp?ref=X531445908 &idioma=0

Published Primary Sources

Abbo of Fleury, Ed. R. Thomson 'Two Astronomical Treatises of Abbo of Fleury' in J. North and J. Roche, Eds., *The Light of Nature (International Archives of the History of Ideas, 110)*, Dordrecht, Nijhoff/Springer, 1985, pp. 113–133.

Ed. M. Lapidge and P. Baker, 'More Acrostic Verse by Abbo of Fleury', *Journal of Medieval Latin*, 7, 1997, pp. 1–27.

Abraham Ibn Ezra, *The Book of Reasons (a Parallel Hebrew-English Critical Edition of the Two Versions of the Text)*, Ed. and Trans. S. Sela, Leiden and Boston, Brill, 2007.

The Book of the World, in *Abraham ibn Ezra's Sefer Haolam (Book of the World); Abraham Ibn Ezra's Astrological Writings, Volume 2*, Ed. and Trans. S. Sela, Leiden and Boston, Brill, 2009.

Abu Ma'Shar, *De magnis coniunctionibus*, Ed. K. Yamamoto and C. Burnett, *Abû Ma'sar on Historical Astrology. The Book of Religions and Dynasties (On the Great Conjunctions)*, Leiden/Boston/Köln, Brill, 2 vols., 2000.

Adelard of Bath, *Conversations with His Nephew: On the Same and the Different, Questions on Natural Science, and On Birds*, Ed. & Trans. C. Burnett, Cambridge, Cambridge University Press, 1998.

Aelfric, *Lives of Saints*, Ed. W. Skeat, Early English Text Society, 76, London, 1881

Catholic Homilies; The First Series: Text, Ed. P. Clemoes, Oxford, Oxford University Press for the Early English Text Society, Supplementary Series, 17, 1997.

De Temporibus Anni, Ed. M. Blake, Cambridge, D.S. Brewer, 2009.

Agobard of Lyons, *Liber contra insulsam vulgi opinionem de grandine et tonitruis*, in *Agobardi Lugdunensis Opera Omnia*, Ed. L. Van Acker, *(C.C.C.M.,* Vol. 52) Turnhout, Brepols, 1981, pp. 3–15.

Al-Farghānī, *Rudimenta astronomica*, trans. John of Seville 1135, Ed. F. Carmody, *Differentie scientie astrorum*, Berkeley, University of California Press, 1943.

Al-Khwarizmi, *Tables (Latin version)*, Ed. H. Suter, Trans. and Ed. O. Neugebauer, *The Astronomical Tables of al-Khwarizmi*, Copenhagen, Munksgaard for Danske videnskabernes selskab Historisk-filosofiske skrifter, 4, 2, 1962.

Al-Kindi, Ed. G. Bos and C. Burnett, *Scientific Weather Forecasting in the Middle Ages: the Writings of al-Kindi*, London and New York, Kegan Paul International, 2000.

Al-Majrīṭī, Maslama, Eds., P. Kunitzsch and R. Lorch, *Maslama's Notes on Ptolemy's Planisphaerium and Related Texts*. Munich, Bayerischen Akademie der Wissenschaften, 1994.

Anon, *Chronica regia Coloniensis, continuatio IV*, ed. G. Waitz in *MGH, Scriptores rerum Germanicarum, xii*, Hannover, 1880.

Anon, Ed. D. Anlezark, *The Newest, Best and Very-Much Esteemed Book of Knowledge*, last edition, London, A. Wilde, 1764.

Ed. J. Chabas and B. Goldstein, *The Alfonsine Tables of Toledo, Archimedes*, VIII, Kluwer, Dordrecht/Boston/London, Kluwer, 2003.

The Old English Dialogues of Solomon and Saturn. New ed, Woodbridge, Boydell and Brewer, 2009.

Aratus, *Phaenomena*, Trans. A. Poochigian, Baltimore, Johns Hopkins University Press, 2010; and A. Mair and G. Mair, Trans., *Callimachus, Lycophron, Aratus*, Loeb Classical Library, Cambridge, Harvard University Press, 1921.

Aristotle, *Meteorologica*, trans. E. Webster, in *The Works of Aristotle Translated Into English*, Oxford, Clarendon Press, 1923.

Augustine, *The City of God against the Pagans, Books VIII-XI*, Ed. J. Henderson, Trans. D. Wiesen, Loeb Classical Library, Cambridge, Harvard University Press, 1968.

De Doctrina Christiana, Ed. and Trans. R. Green, Oxford, Clarendon, 1995.

St Augustine: On Genesis, Ed. J.E. Rotelle, O.C.A., Trans. E. Hill, O.P., New York, New City Press, 2002.

Baudri of Bourgeuil, Ed. and Trans. M. Otter, 'Baudri of Bourgueil, "To Countess Adela"', *Journal of Medieval Latin*, 11, 2001, pp. 60–141.

Bede, *On Genesis*, Trans. C. Kendall, Liverpool, Liverpool University Press, 2008.

Historia ecclesiastica gentis Anglorum, Ed. and Trans. B. Colgrave and R. Mynors, Oxford, Oxford University Press, 1969; revised edn. 1991.

The Reckoning of Time, Trans. F. Wallis, Liverpool, Liverpool University Press, 1988, and 2nd edition, 2004.

On the Nature of Things and *on Times*, Trans. C. Kendall and F. Wallis, Liverpool, Liverpool University Press, 2010.

Historia abbatum, Ed. and Trans. C. Grocock and I. Wood, in Bede, *The Abbots of Wearmouth and Jarrow*, Oxford, Oxford University Press, 2013.

Bonaventure, *Commentaria in Quatuor Libros Sententiarum Magistri Petri Lombardi*, in *Opera Omnia*, Collegium S. Bonaventurae, 1885, iv vols.

Boretius, A., Ed., *Capitularia regum Francorum*, Vol. 1, *Monumenta Germaniae Historica, Leges*, sect. 2, Vol. 1, Hannover, 1883.

Borst, A., Ed., *Die karolingische Kalendarreform; Schriften zur Komputistik im Frankenreich von 721 bis 818; Monumenta Germaniae Historica, Schriften zur Geistesgeschichte des Mittelalters, XXI*, 3 vols., Hannover, 2006.

Brahe, Tycho, *De Nova Stella, 1573*, Ed. and pub. Regia Societas Scientiarium Danica, (Hauniae) 1901.

Buckminster, Thomas, *An Almanack and Prognostication for the Year 1598, made by Thomas Buckminster, 1598* (sic), facsimile: 'Shakespeare Association Facsimiles, No. 8', Intro. E. Bosanquet, London, Oxford University Press for the Shakespeare Association, 1935.

Byrhtferth of Ramsey, *Byrhtferth's Enchiridion*, Ed. M. Lapidge and P. Baker, Oxford, Oxford University Press for E.E.T.S., Supplementary Series, 15, 1995.

The Lives of St Oswald and St Ecgwine, Ed. and Trans. M. Lapidge, Oxford, Clarendon, 2009.

Calcidius, *On Plato's Timaeus*, Ed. and Trans. J. Magee, Cambridge, Harvard University Press for Dumbarton Oaks Medieval Library, 2016.

Chaucer, Geoffrey, *Treatise on the Astrolabe*, in S. Eisner, Ed., *A Variorum Edition of the Works of Geoffrey Chaucer*, Vol. 6, *The Prose Treatises*, Pt. 1, Norman, University of Oklahoma Press, 2002.

Daniel of Morley, Ed. K. Sudhoff, 'Daniels von Morley *Liber de naturis inferiorum et superiorum* nach der Handschrift. Cod. Arundel 377 des Britisches Museums zum Abdruck gebracht', *Archiv für die Geschichte der Naturwissenschaften und der Technik, Band 8*, 1917.

Philosophia, Ed. G. Maurach, *Mittellateinisches Jahrbuch* 14, 1979, pp. 204–55.

Dorotheus of Sidon, *Dorothei Sidonii Carmen Astrologicum*, Ed. D. Pingree, Leipzig, Teubner, 1976.

Eusebius, *Life of Constantine*, trans. T. Cushing, in P. Schaff and H. Wace, Eds., *Nicene and Post-Nicene Fathers*, 2nd series, 1, New York, Christian Literature Publishing Company, 1890.

Firmicus Maternus, *Matheseos Libri VIII, Ancient Astrology Theory and Practice*, Trans. J. Rhys Bram, New Jersey, Noyes, New Jersey, 1976.

FitzRoy, R., *The Weather Book; a Treatise of Practical Meteorology*, London, 1862.

Geoffrey of Monmouth, *Historia regum Britanniae (History of the Kings of Britain)*, Ed. Reeve, M., Trans. Wright, N., Woodbridge, Boydell, 2007.

Gerland, *Computus*, Ed. Lohr, *Der Computus Gerlandi; Edition, Übersetzung und Erläuterungen*, Stuttgart, Steiner, 2013.

Goad, John, *Astro-Meteorologica, or Aphorisms and Discourses on the Bodies Celestial...*, London, 1686.

Guido Bonatti *Liber Astronomiae (Part 1)*, Trans. R. Zoller, Ed. R. Hand, Berkeley Springs, Project Hindsight and Golden Hind Press, 1994.

Günzel, Ed., *Aelfwine's Prayerbook: B.L. Cotton Titus D. xxvi+xxvii*, Woodbridge, Boydell and Brewer for the Henry Bradshaw Society, 108, 1993.

Helperic, *Liber de computo*, in Migne, Ed., *Patrologia Latina*, vol. 137, cols. 17–29.

Hermannus Contractus (of Reichenau), *De mensura astrolabii* Ed. R. Gunther in *The Astrolabes of the World*, Vol. 2, Oxford, Oxford University Press, 1932, pp. 404–408.

De mense lunari, Ed. A. Borst, 'Ein Forschungsbericht Hermanns des Lahmen', *Deutsches Institut für Erforschung des Mittelalters*, 40, 1984, pp. 379–477, at 474–477.

Hugo of Santalla(?), *The Book of the Nine Judges*, Ed. and Trans. B. Dykes, Minneapolis, Cazimi Press, 2011.

Ibn Bājja, *Kitāb al-athār al-'ulwīya*. Ed. and trans. Lettinck, in *Aristotle's Meteorology and Its Reception in the Arab World*. Leiden, Brill, 1999.

Isidore, *The* Etymologies *of Isidore of Seville*, Trans. S. Barney, W. Lewis, J. Beach and O. Berghof, Cambridge, Cambridge University Press, 2006.
  On the Nature of Things, Trans. C. Kendall and F. Wallis, Liverpool, Liverpool University Press, 2016.
Jerome, Selected Letters, in W. Fremantle and P. Schaff, Ed. and Trans., *The Principal Works of St Jerome*, New York, Christian Literature Publishing, 1892.
John of Eschenden/Ashenden, Extracts from *Summa iudicialis de accidentibus mundi* are given in Thorndike, Vol. III (qv), pp. 325–346.
John of Saxony, *Canones* in E. Grant, Ed., *A Source Book in Medieval Science*, Cambridge, Harvard University Press, 1974, pp. 465–488.
John of Worcester, *The Chronicle of John of Worcester III: The Annals from 1067 to 1140 with the Gloucester Interpolations and the Continuation to 1141*, Ed. P. McGurk, Oxford, Clarendon Press, 1998.
Leopold of Austria, (French translation of c1320) *Li compilacions de le science des estoiles, Books I–III*, Ed. F.J. Carmody, Berkeley and Los Angeles, University of California Press, 1947.
Manilius, *Astronomica*, Ed and Trans. G. Goold, Loeb Classical Library, Cambridge, Harvard University Press, 3rd edition, 1997.
Murphy, P., *The Anatomy of the Seasons, Weather Guide Book, and Perpetual Companion to the Almanac*, London, Bailliere et al., 1834.
Pliny, *Natural History, Volume V: Books 17–19*, Trans. H. Rackham, Loeb Classical Library 371, Cambridge, Harvard University Press, 1950.
Priscian, *Answers to King Khosroes of Persia*, Trans. P. Huby et al., London, Bloomsbury, 2016.
Ptolemy, *Tetrabiblos*, (standard modern edition of the Greek text) Ed. Boll and Boer, updated by W. Hübner as *Claudii Ptolemaei opera quae exstant omnia, Vol. III, 1, post F. Boll et E. Boer secundi curis*, Stuttgart and Leipzig, Teubner, 1998. See also: Ptolemy, *Tetrabiblos*, Ed. & Trans. F.E. Robbins, Cambridge, Harvard University Press, 1940.
Richard of Wallingford, Ed. J. North in *Richard of Wallingford: An Edition of His Writings with Introductions, English Translation and Commentary*, Vol. 1, Oxford, Clarendon, 1976.
Robert Grosseteste, *De impressionibus aeris*, in L. Baur, Ed., *Die Philosophischen Werke des Robert Grosseteste, Bischofs von Lincoln*, Munster, Aschendorff, 1912, pp. 41–51.
  Hexaemeron, Ed. R. Dales and S. Gieben, Oxford, Oxford University Press for British Academy, 1982. For translation see: *Robert Grosseteste: On the Six Days of Creation*, trans. C. Martin, Oxford, Oxford University Press for British Academy, 1996.
Robert of York (Perscrutator), *De impressionibus aeris*, in Thorndike, *History of Magic and Experimental Science*, Vol. III, New York, Columbia University Press, 1934, pp. 108–117.
Seneca, *Natural Questions*, Trans. H. Hine, Chicago, University of Chicago Press, 2010.
Simon de Phares, *Le Recueil des Plus Celebres Astrologues*, Ed. J-P Boudet, Tome I, Paris, Champion, 1997.

Theophrastus of Eresus, *On Weather Signs*, Eds. D. Sider and C. Brunschön, Leiden, Brill, 2007.

Thomas of Cantimpré, *Thomas Cantimpratensis, Liber de Natura Rerum*, Vol. 1, Text, Ed. H. Boese, Berlin/New York, De Gruyter, 1973.

Virgil, *Georgics*, Book I, in H. Rushton Fairclough, Ed. and Trans., *Virgil: Eclogues, Georgics, Aeneid I-VI*, Loeb Classical Library, Cambridge, Harvard University Press, 3rd edition, 1999, pp. 98–135.

Warntjes, I., *The Munich Computus: Text and Translation. Irish Computistics between Isidore of Seville and Bede, and Its Reception in Carolingian Times*, Stuttgart, Franz Steiner Verlag, 2010.

William of Conches, *Guillelmus de Conchis: Dragmaticon; Summa de philosophia in vulgari*, Eds. I. Ronca, L. Badia, J. Pujol, *Corpus Christianorum Continuatio Medievalia*, 152, Turnhout, Brepols, 1997.

See also: *William of Conches; A Dialogue on Natural Philosophy (Dragmaticon Philosophiae)*, trans. I. Ronca and M. Curr, Notre Dame, University of Notre Dame Press, 1997.

William Merle, Ed. G.J. Symons, *Merle's MS. Consideraciones temperiei pro 7 annis Per Magistrum Willelmum Merle, Socium Domus de Merton: The earliest known journal of the weather: kept by the Rev. William Merle, Rector of Driby, Lincolnshire, 1337-1344*, London, 1891 (printed for Symons by Stanford, London).

William of Moerbeke, *Ptolemy's Tetrabiblos in the Translation of William of Moerbeke*, Eds. G. Vuillemin-Diem and C. Steel, Leuven, Leuven University Press, 2015.

Secondary Works

Adamson, P., *Al-Kindi*, Oxford, Oxford University Press, 2007.

al-Khalili, J., *The House of Wisdom: How Arabic Science Saved Ancient Knowledge and Gave Us the Renaissance*, New York, Penguin, 2011.

Alverny, Marie-Thérèse d '"Les solutions ad Chosroem" de Priscianus Lydus et Jean Scot', in *Jean Scot Erigène et l'Histoire de la Philosophie*, Colloques internationaux du C.N.R.S., 561, Paris, C.N.R.S., 1977, pp. 145–160.

'Translations and Translators' in R.L. Benson and G. Constable, Eds., *Renaissance and Renewal in the Twelfth Century*, Cambridge, Harvard University Press, 1982, pp. 421–462.

Anderson, E., 'The Seasons of the Year in Old English', *Anglo-Saxon England*, 26, 1997, pp. 231–263.

Armstrong, E., *Before Copyright: The French Book-Privilege System 1498–1526*, Cambridge, Cambridge University Press, 1990.

Baker, Peter, 'Byrhtferth's *Enchiridion* and the Computus in Oxford, St John's College 17', *Anglo-Saxon England*, 10, 1981, pp. 123–142.

Bales, K., 'Nicole Oresme and Medieval Social Science', *American Journal of Economics and Social Science*, 42, 1983, pp. 101–111.

Barnes, R., 'Hope and Despair in Sixteenth-Century German Almanacs', in H. Guggisberg and G. Krodel, Eds., *The Reformation in Germany and Europe:*

Interpretations and Issues, a special issue of *Archiv für Reformationsgeschichte*, 1993, pp. 440–461.

Barrow, J., 'Vere, William de (d. 1198)', Oxford Dictionary of National Biography, Oxford, Oxford University Press, Oct 2007, www.oxforddnb.com/view/article/95042 (accessed 25 June 2019).

Bennett, H., *English Books and Readers, 1475 to 1557*, Cambridge, Cambridge University Press, 2nd edition, 1969.

Blades, L., Grimmer, J., and McQueen, A., 'Mirrors for Princes and Sultans: Advice on the Art of Governance in the Medieval Christian and Islamic Worlds', published as a pdf by Stamford University, 2014, on their website: http://stanford.edu/~jgrimmer/BGM_final.pdf (accessed 25 June 2019).

Bourne, E., 'The Messianic Prophecy in Vergil's Fourth Eclogue', *The Classical Journal*, 11, 7, 1916, pp. 390–400.

Bühler, C., 'Sixteenth-Century Prognostications: Libri Impressi cum Notis Manuscriptis – Part II', in *Isis*, 33, 5, 1942, pp. 609–620.

Burnett, C., 'Arabic into Latin in Twelfth Century Spain: The Works of Hermann of Carinthia', *Mittellateinisches Jahrbuch*, 13, 1978, pp. 100–134.

'The Earliest Chiromancy in the West', *Journal of Warburg and Courtauld Institutue*, 50, 1987, pp. 189–195.

Adelard of Bath, London, Warburg Institute, 1988.

'The Eadwine Psalter and the Western Tradition of the Onomancy in Pseudo-Aristotle's Secret of Secrets', *Archives d'Histoire Doctrinale et Littéraire du Moyen Âge*, 55, 1988, pp. 143–167.

'Adelard of Bath and the Arabs' in *Rencontres de la culture dans la philosophie medieval; Traductions et traducteurs de l'antiquite tardive au XIVe siècle*, Louvain-La-Neuve, Cassino, 1990.

'The Introduction of Arabic Learning into British Schools' in Butterworth and Kessel, Eds., *The Introduction of Arabic Philosophy into Europe*, Leiden, Brill, 1994, pp. 40–57.

'Advertising the New Science of the Stars circa 1120–50', in *Le xiiè siècle. Mutations et renouveau en France dans la première moitié du xiiè siècle*, Etudes publiées sous la direction de F. Gasparri, Paris, Le Léopard d'Or, 1994, pp. 147–157.

'King Ptolemy and Alchandreus the Philosopher: The Earliest Texts on the Astrolabe and Arabic Astrology at Fleury, Micy and Chartres', *Annals of Science*, 55, 1998, pp. 329–368.

The Introduction of Arabic Learning into England, London, British Library, 1998.

'The Coherence of the Arabic-Latin Translation Program in Toledo in the Twelfth Century', *Science in Context*, 14 (1/2), 2001, pp. 249–288.

Ed., 'Translations, Scientific, Philosophical and Literary (Arabic)' in E.M. Gerli, Ed., *Medieval Iberia, An Encyclopedia*, New York and London, Routledge, 2003, pp. 801–804.

'Lunar Astrology; the Varieties of Texts Using Lunar Mansions with Emphasis on "Jafar Indus"', *Micrologus* 12, 2004, pp. 43–133.

'Weather Forecasting in the Arabic World', in E. Savage-Smith, Ed., *Magic and Divination in Early Islam*, Aldershot and Burlington, Ashgate, 2004, pp. 201–210.

'Hereford, Roger of (fl. 1179–1198)' *ODNB*, Oxford, Oxford University Press, 2004 www.oxforddnb.com/view/article/23955 (25 June 2019).

'Weather Forecasting, Lunar Mansions and a Disputed Attribution: The *Tractatus pluviarum et aeris mutationis* and *Epitome totius astrologiae* of "Johannes Hispalensis"', in A. Akasoy and W. Raven, Eds., *Islamic Thought in the Middle Ages (Studies in Text Transmission and Translation, in Honour of Hans Daiber)* Leiden, Brill, 2008, pp. 219–266.

'The Translation of Diagrams and Illustrations from Arabic into Latin', in A. Contadini, Ed., *Arab Painting; Text and Image in Illustrated Arabic Manuscripts*, Leiden, Brill, 2010, pp. 161–177.

'al-Kindi, Latin Translations of', in H. Lagerlund, Ed., *Encyclopedia of Medieval Philosophy*, Vol. 1, New York, Springer 2011, pp. 676–678.

'The Arrival of Pagan Philosophers in the North: A Twelfth-Century Florilegium in Edinburgh University Library' in J. Canning, E. King, M. Staub, Eds., *Knowledge, Discipline and Power in the Middle Ages; Essays in Honour of David Luscombe*, Leiden, Brill, 2011, pp. 79–94.

'Al-Qabisi's Introduction to Astrology: From Courtly Entertainment to University Textbook', in R. Fontaine et al., Eds., *Studies in the History of Culture and Science; A tribute to Gad Freudenthal*, Leiden, Brill, 2011, pp. 43–69.

Burnett, C., and D. Juste, 'A New Catalogue of Medieval Translations into Latin of Texts on Astronomy and Astrology', in F. Wallis and R. Wisnovsky, Eds., *Medieval Textual Cultures*, Berlin and Boston, de Gruyter, 2016, pp. 63–76.

Butterfield, D., *The Early Textual History of Lucretius' De rerum natura*. Cambridge, Cambridge University Press, 2013.

Cabaniss, J. Allen, 'Agobard of Lyons', *Speculum*, 26, 1, 1951, pp. 50–76.

Cadden, J., 'Science and Rhetoric in the Middle Ages: The Natural Philosophy of William of Conches', *Journal of the History of Ideas*, 56: 1, 1995, pp. 1–24.

Capp, B., *English Almanacs, 1500-1800: Astrology and the Popular Press*, Cornell University Press, 1979.

'The Potter Almanacs', *eBLJ*, 2004, article 4.

Carey, H., *Courting Disaster: Astrology at the English Court and University in the Later Middle Ages*, New York, St Martin's Press, 1992.

'Judicial Astrology in Theory and Practice in Later Medieval Europe', *Studies in the History and Philosophy of Biological and Medical Sciences*, 41, 2010, pp. 90–98.

'Henry VII's Book of Astrology and the Tudor Renaissance', *Renaissance Quarterly* lxv, 2012, pp. 661–710.

Cesario, M., 'Weather Prognostics in Anglo-Saxon England', *English Studies*, 93, 4, 2012, pp. 391–426.

'An English Source for a Latin Text? Wind Prognostication in Oxford, Bodleian, Hatton 115 and Ashmole 345', *Studies in Philology*, 112, 2, 2015, pp. 213–233.

Chabás, J., and B. Goldstein, *Astronomy in the Iberian Peninsula: Abraham Zacut and the Transition from Manuscript to Print*, Transactions of the American Philosophical Society, Volume 90, Part 2, Philadelphia, A.P.S., 2000.

Chardonnens, L., *Anglo-Saxon Prognostics, 900–1100: Study and Texts*, Leiden/ Boston, Brill, 2007.

'Aelfric and the Authorship of the Old English *De diebus malis*' in C. Giliberto and L. Teresi, Eds., *Limits to Learning; The Transfer of Encyclopaedic Knowledge in the Early Middle Ages*, Leuven/Paris/Walpole, Peeters, 2013, pp. 123–154.

Charles-Edwards, T., *Early Christian Ireland*, Cambridge, Cambridge University Press, 2004.

Charmasson, T., 'L'établissement d'un almanach medical pour l'année 1437', in *Comptes-rendus du 99e Congrès national des sociétés savant, Section des sciences, Fasc. V*, Paris, Bibliotheque Nationale, 1976, pp. 217–234.

Colker, M., 'A Newly Discovered Manuscript of Hermann of Carinthia's *De essentiis*', *Revue d'histoire des textes*, 16, 1988 (1986), 213–228.

Copeland, G., *Nicole Oresme and the Astrologers*, Cambridge, Harvard University Press, 1952.

Copeland and I. Sluiter, 'Martianus Capella, *De Nuptiis Philologiae et Mercurii* CA 420–490', in Copeland and Sluiter, Eds., *Medieval Grammar and Rhetoric: Language Arts and Literary Theory, AD 300–1475*, Oxford, Oxford University Press, 2012, pp. 148–166.

Corning, C., *The Celtic and Roman Traditions: Conflict and Consensus in the Early Medieval Church*, New York and Basingstoke, Palgrave Macmillan, 2006.

Dales, R., *The Scientific Achievement of the Middle Ages*, Philadelphia, University of Pennsylvania Press, 1973.

'The De-animation of the Heavens in the Middle Ages', *Journal of the History of Ideas*, 41, 4, 1980, pp. 531–550.

Declercq, G., *Anno Domini: The Origins of the Christian Era*, Brepols, Turnhout, 2000.

Dekker, E., 'Carolingian Planetary Observations: The Case of the Leiden Planetary Configuration', *Journal for the History of Astronomy*, 39.1, No. 134, 2008, pp. 77–90.

Illustrating the Phaenomena; Celestial Cartography in Antiquity and the Middle Ages, Oxford, Oxford University Press, 2012.

Delisle, L., 'Un Poème adressé à Adèle, fille de Guillaume le Conquérant, par Baudri, abbé de Bourgueil', *Mémoires de la Société des Antiquaires de Normandie*, 28, 1870/71, pp. 187–224.

Dolan, M., *Astronomical Knowledge Transmission through Illustrated Aratea Manuscripts*, New York, Springer 2017.

Dumville, D., *English Caroline Script and Monastic History*, Woodbridge, Boydell Press, 1993.

Dutton, P., 'Thunder and Hail over the Carolingian Countryside' in D. Sweeney, Ed., *Agriculture in the Middle Ages*, Philadelphia, Pennsylvania University Press, 1995, pp. 111–124.

Eamon, W., 'Astrology and Society', in B. Dooley, Ed., *Companion to Astrology in the Renaissance*, Leiden/Boston, Brill, 2014, pp. 141–192.

Eastwood, B., *Ordering the Heavens: Roman Astronomy and Cosmology in the Carolingian Renaissance*, Leiden, Brill, 2007.

The Revival of Planetary Astronomy in Carolingian and Post-Carolingian Europe, 1st ed. Abingdon, Ashgate, 2002; 2nd edition, Abingdon and New York, Routledge, 2018.

Eastwood, B., with G. Graßhoff, *Planetary Diagrams for Roman Astronomy in Medieval Europe, c800–1500: Transactions of the American Philosophical Society*, Vol. 94, Part 3, Philadelphia, A.P.S., 2004.

Edwards, G., 'The Two Redactions of Michael Scot's *Liber Introductorius*', *Traditio*, 41, 1985, pp. 329–340.

Estey, F., 'Charlemagne's Silver Celestial Table', *Speculum*, XVIII, 1943, pp. 112–117.

Febvre, L., and H-J Martin, trans. D. Gerard, *The Coming of the Book*, London, Verso, 1984.

Fitzgerald, J., 'A Middle English Treatise on Comets in Cambridge, Trinity College MS O. 5. 26', *ANQ: A Quarterly Journal of Short Articles, Notes and Reviews*, 21,1, 2008, pp. 11–22.

Fournier, M., 'Boethius and the Consolation of the Quadrivium', *Medievalia et Humanistica*, N.S., 34, 2008, pp. 1–21.

Frederick, R., Landsberg, H., and Lenke, W., 'Climatological Analysis of the Basel Weather Manuscript', *Isis*, 57, 1966, pp. 99–101.

French, R., 'Foretelling the Future: Arabic Astrology and English Medicine in the Late Twelfth Century', *Isis*, Vol. 87, No. 3, 1996, pp. 453–480.

'Teaching Meteorology in Thirteenth Century Oxford. The Arabic Paraphrase', *Physis*, 36, n.s. fasc. I, 1999, pp. 99–129.

Fronska, J., 'The Royal Image and Diplomacy: Henry VII's *Book of Astrology* (British Library, Arundel MS. 66)', *eBLJournal*, 2014, Article 7.

Garrison, M., 'The Library of Alcuin's York', in R. Gameson, Ed, *Cambridge History of the Book in Britain*, Volume 1, Cambridge, Cambridge University Press, 2012, pp. 633–664.

Gee, E., *Aratus and the Astronomical Tradition*, New York, Oxford University Press, 2013.

Gibson,M., Heslop, A., and Pfaff, R., Eds., *The Eadwine Psalter*, Philadelphia, Pennsylvania State University Press, 1992.

Golinski, J., *British Weather and the Climate of Enlightenment*, Chicago and London, University of Chicago Press, 2007.

Grant, E., *Planets, Stars, and Orbs; The Medieval Cosmos, 1200–1687*, Cambridge, Cambridge University Press, 1994.

Green, S., *Disclosure and Discretion in Roman Astrology: Manilius and His Augustan Contemporaries*, New York, Oxford University Press, 2014.

Hamel, J., 'Hermann the Lame' in V. Trimble et al., Eds., *Biographical Encyclopedia of Astronomers*, Vol.1, New York, Springer, 2007, p. 489.

Haskins, C., 'Michael Scot and Frederick II', *Isis*, IV, 1921/22, pp. 250–275.

'Science at the Court of the Emperor Frederick II', *American Historical Review*, XXVII, 4, 1922, pp. 669–694.

'The Translations of Hugo Sanctelliensis', *The Romanic Review*, Vol. II, No.1, 1911, pp. 1–15.

'Adelard of Bath and Henry Plantagenet', *E.H.R.*, XXVIII, CXI, July 1913, pp. 515–516.

Studies in the History of Medieval Science, Cambridge, Harvard University Press, 2nd edition, 1927.

Hasse, D., and A. Büttner, 'Notes on Twelfth-Century Translations of Philosophical Texts from Arabic into Latin on the Iberian Peninsula', 2017, at: www.philosophie.uni-wuerzburg.de/fileadmin/EXT00246/Hasse-Buettner_Menaggio_3_27_Feb_2017.pdf (accessed 25 June 2019).

Healy, J., *Pliny the Elder on Science and Technology*, New York, Oxford University Press, 1999.

Hine, H., 'The Manuscript Tradition of Seneca's *Natural Questions*: Addenda', *Classical Quarterly*, 42, 2, 1992, pp. 558–562.

Hoogendoorn, K., *Bibliography of the Exact Sciences in the Low Countries from ca1470 to the Golden Age (1700)*, Leiden and Boston, Brill, 2018.

Hunt, R., 'English Learning in the Late Twelfth Century', *Transactions of the Royal Historical Society*, 19, 1936, pp. 19–42.

Hunter, R., 'Written in the Stars: Poetry and Philosophy in the *Phaenomena* of Aratus', *Arachnion*, 2, 1995, pp. 1–34.

Innes, M., 'Charlemagne's Will: Piety, Politics and the Imperial Succession', *English Historical Review*, 112, 448, 1997, pp. 833–855.

Ivry, Alfred, *al-Kindi's Metaphysics*, New York, State University of New York Press, 1974.

Jacquart, D., 'Médecine et astrologie à Paris dans la première moitié du XIVe siècle', in G.F. Vescovini and F. Barocelli, Eds., *Filosofia, scienza e astrologia nel Trecento europeo*, Padua, Il Poligrafo, 1992, pp. 121–134.

James, M., *A Descriptive Catalogue of the Western Manuscripts in the Library of Clare College, Cambridge*, Cambridge, Cambridge University Press, 1905.

Jenks, S., 'Astrometeorology in the Middle Ages', *Isis*, 7, 2, 1983, pp. 185–210.

Jermyn, L., 'Weather-Signs in Virgil', *Greece and Rome*, 20, 59, 1951, pp. 49–59.

Johnston, S., 'Digges, Leonard', ODNB, 2004, https://doi.org/10.1093/ref:odnb/7637 (accessed 25 June 2019).

Juste, D., 'Neither Observation nor Astronomical Tables. An Alternative Way of Computing the Planetary Longitudes in the Early Western Middle Ages' in C. Burnett et al., Eds., *Studies in the History of the Exact Sciences in Honour of David Pingree*, Leiden, Brill, 2004, pp. 181–222.

Les 'Alchandreana' Primitifs, Leiden, Brill, 2007.

'Notice on Abu Ma'shar *Flores*', warburg.sas.ac.uk/pdf/fah820b2342376.pdf (accessed 24 June 2019).

Karamanolis, G., 'Early Christian Philosophers on Aristotle' in A. Falcon, Ed., *Brill's Companion to the Reception of Aristotle in Antiquity*, Leiden, Brill, 2016, pp. 460–461.

Kassell, L., 'Almanacs and Prognostications', in J. Raymond, Ed., *The Oxford History of Popular Print Culture*; Volume One: *Cheap Print in Britain and Ireland to 1660*, New York, Oxford University Press, 2011, pp. 432–445.

Kennedy, A., 'A Survey of Islamic Astronomical Tables', *Transactions of the American Philosophical Society*, 46, 2, 1956, pp. 123–177.

Kennedy, A., and W. Ukashal, 'Al-Khwarizmi's Planetary Latitude Tables' *Centaurus*, 14, 1, 1969, pp. 86–96.

King, V., 'An Investigation of Some Astronomical Excerpts from Pliny's *Natural History* found in Manuscripts of the Earlier Middle Ages', unpublished B. Litt. Thesis, Oxford, 1969.

Kurze, D., 'Popular Astrology and Prophecy in the fifteenth and sixteenth Centuries: Johannes Lichtenberger', in P. Zambelli, Ed., *Astrologi hallucinati; Stars and the End of the World in Luther's Time*, Berlin and New York, de Gruyter, 1986, pp. 177–193.

Kusukawa, S., 'Incunables and Sixteenth-Century Books', chapter 4 of A. Hunter, Ed., *Thornton and Tully's Scientific Books, Libraries and Collectors*, 4th edition, Abingdon and New York, Routledge, 2016.

Lacarra, M., Ed., *Estudios sobre Pedro Alfonso de Huesca*, Huesca, Instituto de Estudios Altoaragoneses, 1996.

Lapidge, M., 'Abbot Germanus, Winchcombe, Ramsey and the Cambridge Psalter', in M. Korhammer et al., Eds., *Words, Texts and Manuscripts; Studies in Anglo-Saxon Culture Presented to Helmut Gneuss*, Woodbridge, Brewer, 1992, pp. 99–129.

'The Career of Archbishop Theodore' in Lapidge, Ed., *Archbishop Theodore. Commemorative Studies in His Life and Work*, Cambridge, Cambridge University Press, 1995, pp. 1–29.

'The Career of Aldhelm', *Anglo-Saxon England*, 36, 2007, pp. 15–70.

Lawrence-Mathers, A., 'John of Worcester and the Science of History', *Journal of Medieval History*, 39:3, 2013, pp. 255–274, and references there.

Lawrence-Mathers, A., and Escobar-Vargas, C., *Magic and Medieval Society*, Abingdon and New York, Routledge, 2014.

Leclerq, J., 'Les lettres de Guillaume de Saint-Thierry à Saint Bernard', *Revue Bénédictine*, 79, 1969, pp. 375–391.

Lehoux, D., *Astronomy, Weather and Calendars in the Ancient World: Parapegmata and Related Texts in Classical and Near Eastern Societies*, Cambridge, Cambridge University Press, 2007.

Lemay, R., 'The Teaching of Astronomy in Medieval Universities, Principally at Paris in the Fourteenth Century', *Manuscripta*, 20, 1976, pp. 197–217.

'The Late Medieval Astrological School at Cracow and the Copernican System', *Studia Copernicana*, 19, 1978, pp. 337–354.

'The True Place of Astrology in Medieval Science and Philosophy', in P. Curry, Ed., *Astrology, Science and Society; Historical Essays*, Woodbridge, Boydell, 1987, pp. 57–73.

Lettinck, P., 'Aristotle's *Meteorology* in the Arabic World', in S.M. Razaullah Ansari, Ed., *Science and Technology in the Islamic World: Proceedings of the XXth International Congress of History of Science*, Brepols, Turnhout, 2002, pp. 189–194.

Leyra, I., 'The *Aristotelian Corpus* and the Rhodian Tradition: New Light from Posidonius on the Transmission of Aristotle's Works', *The Classical Quarterly*, 63, 2, 2013, pp. 723–733.

Lippincott, K., 'The textual tradition of the Germanicus *Aratea*' at www.kristenlippincott.com/the-saxl-project/manuscripts/classical-literary-tradition/revised-aratus-latinus/ (accessed 25 June 2019).

Liuzza, R., 'Anglo-Saxon Prognostics in Context: A survey and Handlist of Manuscripts', *Anglo-Saxon England*, 30, 2001, pp. 181–230.

'What the Thunder Said: Anglo-Saxon Brontologies and the Problem of Sources', *Review of English Studies*, 55, no. 218, 2004, pp. 1–23.

Anglo-Saxon Prognostics: An Edition and Translation of Texts from London, British Library, MS Cotton Tiberius A iii, Woodbridge, Brewer, 2010.

Mayer, H., 'Henry II of England and the Holy Land', *English Historical Review*, 97, 1982, pp. 721–739.

McCluskey, S., *Astronomies and Cultures of Early Medieval Europe*, Cambridge, Cambridge University Press, 1998.

'Boethius' Astronomy and Cosmology', in N. Kaylor and P. Phillips, Eds., *A Companion to Boethius in the Middle Ages*, Leiden, Brill, 2012, pp. 47–73.

McCready, W., 'Bede, Isidore and the *Epistola Cuthberti*', *Traditio*, 50, 1995, pp. 75–94.

McKeon, R., 'The Organisations of Sciences and the Relations of Cultures in the Twelfth and Thirteenth Centuries', in Z. McKeon and W. Swenson, Eds., *Culture, Education and the Arts: Selected Writings of Richard McKeon, Vol. 2*, Chicago and London, University of Chicago, 2005, pp. 121–154.

McKitterick, R., 'The Carolingian Renaissance of Culture and Learning', in J. Story, Ed., *Charlemagne: Empire and Society*, Manchester, Manchester University Press, 2005, pp. 151–166.

Mercier, R., 'Astronomical Tables in the Twelfth Century', in C. Burnett, Ed., *Adelard of Bath; An English Scientist and Arabist of the Early Twelfth Century*, London, Warburg Institute, 1987, pp. 87–118.

'The Astronomical Tables of Abraham bar Hiyya', in S. Stern and C. Burnett, Eds., *Time, Astronomy and the Calendar in the Jewish Tradition*, Leiden/ Boston, Brill, 2014, pp. 155–208.

Meyvaert, P., 'Bede, Cassiodorus and the Codex Amiatinus', *Speculum*, 71, 4, 1996, pp. 827–883.

Mimura, T., 'The Arabic original of (ps.) Masha'allah's *Liber de orbe*; its date and authorship', *British Journal for the History of Science*, 48:2, 2015, pp. 321–352.

Morgan Murphy, T., *Pliny the Elder's Natural History: The Empire in the Encyclopedia*, New York, Oxford University Press, 2004.

Mori, J., 'Popular Science in Eighteenth-Century Almanacs: The Career of Henry Andrews of Royston, 1780-1820', *History of Science*, 54,1, 2016, pp. 19–44.

Mostert, M., *The Library of Fleury: A Provisional List of Manuscripts*, Middeleeuwse Studies en Bronnen, 3, Verloren, Hilversum, 1989.

North, J., *Horoscopes and History*, London, Warburg Institute, 1986.

'Some Norman Horoscopes', in Burnett, Ed., *Adelard of Bath*, London, Warburg Institute, 1988, pp. 147–161.

'The Quadrivium', in H. de Ridder-Symoens, Ed., *Universities in the Middle Ages* (Vol. 1 of W. Ruëgg, Ed., *A History of the University in Europe*), Cambridge, Cambridge University Press, 1992, pp. 337–358.

God's Clockmaker: Richard of Wallingford and the Invention of Time, London, Continuum, 2005.

Nothaft, *Walcher of Malvern, De lunationibus and De dracone*, Brepols, Turnhout, 2017.

Scandalous Error: Calendar Reform and Calendrical Astronomy in Medieval Europe, Oxford, Oxford University Press, 2018.

Obrist, B., 'William of Conches, Masha'Allah and Twelfth-Century Cosmology', *Archives d'Histoire Doctrinale et Littéraire du Moyen Age*, 76, 2009, pp. 29–87.

Orchard, A., 'Aldhelm's Library', in R. Gameson, Ed., *The Cambridge History of the Book in Britain*, Vol. 1, Cambridge, Cambridge University Press, 2012, pp. 591–605.

Page, S., 'Richard Trewythian and the Uses of Astrology in Late Medieval England', *Journal of the Warburg and Courtauld Institutes*, 64, 2001, pp. 193–228.

Peters, E., *The Magician, the Witch and the Law*, Harvester Press, Sussex, 1978.

Pfister, C., et al., 'Daily Weather Observations in Sixteenth-Century Europe', *Climatic Change*, 43,1, 1999, pp. 111–150.

Pingree, D., 'The Indian and Pseudo-Indian Passages and Elements in Greek and Latin Astronomical and Astrological Texts' *Viator*, 1976, pp. 141–196.

'The Preceptum Canonis Ptolomei', in J. Hamesse and M. Fattori, Eds., *Rencontres de Cultures dans la Philosophie Medievale: Traductions et Traducteurs de l'Antiquite Tardive au XIVe Siecle*, Louvain-la-Neuve, Publications de l'Institut d'Etudes Medievales-Textes, 1990, pp. 355–375.

Possanza, D., *Translating the Heavens: Aratus, Germanicus, and the Poetics of Latin Translation*, New York, Lang, 2004.

Poulle, E., 'Le traité de l'astrolabe d'Adelard de Bath' in C. Burnett, Ed., *Adelard of Bath. An English Scientist and Arabist of the Early Twelfth Century*, London, Warburg Institute, 1987, pp. 119–132.

'Les astronomes parisiens au XIVe siècle et l'astronomie alphonsine' in *Histoire littéraire de la France publiée par l'Académie des Inscriptions et Belles-Lettres*, Tome 43, Fasc. 1, Paris, 2005, pp. 1–54.

Ramirez-Weaver, E., *A Saving Science: Capturing the Heavens in Carolingian Manuscripts*, Philadelphia, University of Pennsylvania, 2017.

Reichert, M., 'Hermann of Dalmatia and Robert of Ketton: Two Twelfth-Century Translators in the Ebro Valley', in M. Goyens, P. de Leemans, A. Smets, Eds., *Science Translated: Latin and Vernacular Translations of Scientific Treatises in Medieval Europe*, Leuven, Leuven University Press, 2008, pp. 47–69.

Riché, P., *Gerbert d'Aurillac, le pape de l'an Mil*, Paris, Fayard, 1987.

Robinson, M., 'The Heritage of Medieval Errors in the Latin Manuscripts of Johannes Hispalensis (John of Seville)', *Al-Qantara*, XXVIII 1, 2007, pp. 41–71.

Rodriguez Arribas, J., 'Medieval Jews and Medieval Astrolabes: Where, Why, How, and What For?' in S. Stern and C. Burnett, Eds., *Time, Astronomy and Calendars in the Jewish Tradition*, Leiden and Boston, Brill, 2014, pp. 221–272.

Reading Astrolabes in Medieval Hebrew', in MacLeod, Sumillera, Surman and Smirnova, *Language as a Scientific Tool: Shaping Scientific Language Across Time and National Tradition*, New York and London, Routledge, 2016, pp. 89–112.

Ronca, I., 'The Influence of the *Pantegni* on William of Conches's *Dragmaticon*' in C. Burnett and D. Jacquart, Eds., *Constantine the African and Ali Ibn al-Abbas al-Magusi: the Pantegni and Related Texts*, Leiden, Brill, 1994, pp. 266–285.

Rowell, S., 'The Jagiellonians and the Stars: Dynasty-Sponsored Astrology in the Fifteenth Century', *Lithuanian Historical Studies*, 7, 2002, pp. 23–42.

Ryan, W.F. and Schmitt, C., Eds., *Aristotle, The Secret of Secrets: Sources and Influence*, London, Warburg Institute, 1982.

Scharle, M., '"And These Things Follow": Teleology, Necessity and Explanation in Aristotle's *Meteorologica*' in D. Ebrey, Ed., *Theory and Practice in Aristotle's Natural Science*, Cambridge, Cambridge University Press, 2015, pp. 79–99.

Schärlig, A., *Un portrait de Gerbert d'Aurillac: inventeur d'un abaque, utilisateur précoce des chiffres arabes, et pape de l'an mil*, Lausanne, PPUR Presses Polytechniques, 2012.

Schoonheim, P., Ed., *Aristotle's Meteorology in the Arabico-Latin Tradition* Leiden, Brill, 2000.

Scott, T., 'Michael Scot and the Four Rainbows', *Transversal; International Journal for the Historiography of Science*, 2, 2017, pp. 204–225.

Sela, S., *Abraham Ibn Ezra and the Rise of Medieval Hebrew Science*, Leiden/Boston, Brill, 2003.

Shank, M., 'Academic Consulting in Fifteenth-Century Vienna: The Case of Astrology', in E. Sylla and M. McVaugh, Eds., *Texts and Contexts in Ancient and Medieval Science. Studies on the Occasion of John E. Murdoch's Seventieth Birthday*, Leiden, Brill, 1997, pp. 245–270.

Sider, D., and C. Brunschön, 'Survey of Ancient Weather Literature', in Sider and Brunschön, Eds., *Theophrastus of Eresus: On Weather Signs*, Leiden, Brill, 2007, p. 21.

Sidoli and Berggren, 'The Arabic Version of Ptolemy's *Planisphere* or *Flattening the Surface of the Sphere*: Text, Translation, Commentary', *SCIAMUS* 8, 2007, pp. 37–139.

Simmons, R., 'ABCs, Almanacs, Ballads, Chapbooks, Popular Piety and Textbooks', in J. Barnard, D. McKenzie and M. Bell, Eds., *The Cambridge History of the Book in Britain: Volume 4, 1557–1695*, pp. 504–513.

Singer, C., 'Daniel of Morley: An English Philosopher of the XIIth Century' in *Isis*, Vol. 3, No. 2, 1920, pp. 263–269.

Smithuis, R., 'Science in Normandy and England under the Angevins: The Creation of Avraham ibn Ezra's Latin Works on Astronomy and Astrology', in G. Busi, Ed., *Hebrew to Latin, Latin to Hebrew: The Mirroring of Two Cultures in the Age of Humanism*, Berlin, Institut für Judaistik, Freie Universität, and Turin, N. Aragno Editore, 2006, pp. 23–60.

'Abraham Ibn Ezra's Astrological Works in Hebrew and Latin: New Discoveries and Exhaustive Listing', *Aleph, Historical Studies in Science and Judaism*, 6, 2006, pp. 239–338.

Snedegar, K., 'Ashenden, John', *Oxford Dictionary of National Biography*, 2004, https://doi.org/10.1093/ref:odnb/39190 (accessed 25 June 2019).

Soubiran, J., *Aviénus: Les Phénomènes d'Aratos*, Paris, C.U.F., 1981.

Southern, R., *Robert Grosseteste: The Growth of an English Mind in Medieval Europe*, Oxford, Clarendon Press, 1986.

Stalls, C., *Possessing the Land: Aragon's Expansion into Islam's Ebro Frontier under Alfonso the Battler, 1104-1134*, Leiden, Brill, 1995.

Taub, L., *Ancient Meteorology*, London and New York, Routledge, 2003.

Science Writing in Greco-Roman Antiquity, Cambridge, Cambridge University Press, 2017.

Tester, J., *A History of Western Astrology*, Woodbridge, Boydell, 1990.

Thomson, R., *A Descriptive Catalogue of the Medieval Manuscripts of Merton College, Oxford*, Cambridge, Brewer, 2009.

Thorndike, L., 'Daniel of Morley', *The English Historical Review*, 37, 148, 1922

History of Magic and Experimental Science: Vol. II, 2nd Edition, New York, Columbia University Press, 1929; *Vols. III and IV*, New York, Columbia University Press, 1934.

'A Weather Record for 1399–1406 AD', *Isis*, 32, 1940, pp. 304–323.

'Robertus Anglicus', *Isis*, 34, 1943, pp. 467–469.

'The Latin Translations of the Astrological Tracts of Abraham Avenezra', *Isis*, 35, 4, 1944, pp. 293–302.

'More Manuscripts of the *Dragmaticon* and *Philosophia* of William of Conches', *Speculum*, 20, 1, 1945, pp. 84–87.

'The Latin Translations of Astrological Works by Messehalla', *Osiris*, 12, 1956, pp. 49–72.

'A daily Weather Record from the Years 1399 to 1401', *Isis*, 57, 1966, pp. 90–99.

Tolan, J., *Petrus Alfonsi and His Medieval Readers*, Gainesville, University of Florida Press, 1993.

Töyrylä, H., *Abraham Bar Hiyya on Time, History, Exile and Redemption*, Leiden/Boston, Brill, 2014.

van der Vyver, A., 'Les plus anciennes Traductions latines médiévales (Xe –Xie siècles) de Traités d'Astronomie et d'Astrologie', *Osiris*, 1936, 1, pp. 658-691.

Vanden Broecke, S., *The Limits of Influence: Pico, Louvain and the Crisis of Renaissance Astrology*, Leiden, Brill, 2003.

Vincent, N., 'The Court of Henry II', in C. Harper-Bill and N. Vincent, Eds., *Henry II: New Interpretations*, Woodbridge, Boydell, 2007, pp. 278–334.

Volk, K., *Manilius and His Intellectual Background*, New York, Oxford University Press, 2009.

'The World of the Latin *Aratea*' in T. Fuhrer and M. Erler, eds., *Cosmologies et cosmogonies dans la litterature antique*, Vandoeuvres, Fondation Hardt, 2015, pp. 253–287.

Volckmann, E., *Alte Gewerbe und Gewerbegassen*, Wurzburg, Gebrüder Memminger, 1921.

Westgard, J., 'Bede and the Continent in the Carolingian Age and Beyond'; in S. DeGregorio, Ed., *The Cambridge Companion to Bede*, Cambridge, Cambridge University Press, 2010, pp. 201–215.

White, L., Jr., *Medieval Technology and Social Change*, New York, Oxford University Press, 1962.

Whyte, N., 'Roger of Hereford's *Liber de Astronomice iudicandi*: A Twelfth-Century Astrologer's Manual', M.Phil Dissertation, Cambridge, 1991, published online as a pdf at: http://nicholaswhyte.info/roger.htm (accessed July 19, 2019).

Willetts, P., 'A Reconstructed Astronomical Manuscript from Christ Church Library, Canterbury', *British Museum Quarterly*, 30, 1965–1966, pp. 22–30.

Williams, Steven, *The Secret of Secrets: The Scholarly Career of a Pseudo-Aristotelian Text in the Latin Middle Ages*, Ann Arbor, Michigan, University of Michigan Press, 2003.

Wilson, M., *Structure and Method in Aristotle's Meteorologica: A More Disorderly Nature*, Cambridge, Cambridge University Press, 2013.

Wright, R., 'Abbo of Fleury in Ramsey (985-987), in E. Taylor, Ed., *Conceptualising Multilingualism in England, c800-c1250*, Brepols, Turnhout, 2011.

Zambelli, P., Ed., *The Speculum Astronomiae and Its Enigma*, Dordrecht and Boston and London, Kluwer, 1992.

Index